D1458691

I Never Knew That

About

THE RIVER THAMES

Christopher Winn

I Never Knew That

About

THE RIVER THAMES

ILLUSTRATIONS
BY
Mai Osawa

EBURY
PRESS

5 7 9 10 8 6 4

Published in 2010 by Ebury Press, an imprint of Ebury Publishing

A Random House Group Company

Text © Christopher Winn 2010
Illustrations © Mai Osawa 2010

The Random House Group Limited Reg. No. 954009
Addresses for companies within the Random House Group can be found at
www.randomhouse.co.uk

A CIP catalogue record for this book is available from the British Library

The Random House Group Limited supports The Forest Stewardship Council (FSC),
the leading international forest certification organisation. All our titles that are printed on
Greenpeace approved FSC certified paper carry the FSC logo. Our paper procurement
policy can be found at www.rbooks.co.uk/environment

Mixed Sources
Product group from well-managed
forests and other controlled sources
FSC   www.fsc.org Cert no. TT-COC-2139
© 1996 Forest Stewardship Council

To buy books by your favourite authors and register for offers visit www.rbooks.co.uk
Series designed by Peter Ward
Typeset by Palimpsest Book Production Limited, Falkirk, Stirlingshire
Printed and bound by CPI Mackays, Chatham ME5 8TD

ISBN 9780091933579

For Rupert, a true Man of the Thames, and
for Emma, Loelia and Eden. Thank you
for all your friendship and support over the years.

Contents

Henley-on-Thames, home of the Royal Regatta

Preface

'Serene yet strong, majestic yet sedate,
Swift without violence, without terror great'
Matthew Prior (1664 – 1721),
English poet and diplomat,
describing the River Thames

The River Thames weaves its way through England and England's history like a shining silver strand. Some of the country's great events have taken place upon its banks, from the conversion of Saxon kings to Christianity at Dorchester, the crowning of the first English kings at Kingston, and the very first English parliament at Shifford, to the sealing of the Magna Carta at Runnymede and the plotting for the Glorious Revolution at Hurley.

Kings and Queens of England have been born, have lived and died beside the Thames, using the river as a regal highway between royal palaces from Hampton Court to Greenwich.

The Thames is not the broadest or the longest of rivers, it has no spectacular waterfalls or ravines or rapids, but it affords us sights that are unforgettable: cathedrals, cities, quintessential English villages, the Henley Royal Regatta, the Boat Race, the first English university at Oxford, the world's widest and flattest brick arch at Maidenhead, the biggest inhabited castle in the world at Windsor, the most famous botanic gardens in the world at Kew, the Mother of Parliaments at Westminster, the Tower of London and Tower Bridge, the docks that once formed the biggest and busiest port in the world from Roman Billingsgate to modern Tilbury, the world's biggest dome and the Prime Meridian at Greenwich – the Thames flows from west to east not just across England but across the hemispheres.

Indeed, a journey down the River Thames is a journey not just through the heart of the English countryside, but through the heart of the English people and the English way of life.

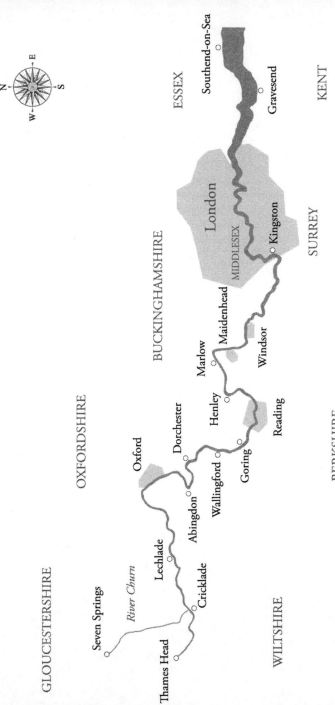

The River Thames

I Never Knew That About The River Thames is a journey down England's greatest river from source to sea, calling in on people and places along the way.

Measured from Thames Head, the River Thames is 215 miles (346 km) in length, the longest river that flows wholly within England. It runs from the west of England to the east through 9 counties, for much of the way forming the county boundaries and separating Middle England from Southern England in much the same way as it divided the Saxon kingdoms of Wessex and Mercia.

There are 45 locks on the Thames between Lechlade and Teddington, bringing the river down from a height of 361 ft (110m) at Thames Head to near sea level at Teddington, where it becomes tidal. The river is navigable from the estuary as far as Lechlade, while for small un-powered craft the Rights of Navigation extend to Cricklade. Between the source and Teddington the Thames is administered by the Environment Agency, while from Teddington to the sea it is run by the Port of London Authority.

Despite the presence of considerable heavy industry to the east of London, the Thames is today recognised as one of the cleanest urban rivers in the world.

Along with common practice, and to avoid confusion as the river twists and turns, where places of interest are described as being located 'on the left bank' or 'on the right bank' this means while facing downstream.

I have included the River Churn as an alternative source to Thames Head because I spent some of my formative years living beside the Churn and was brought up to believe it was the true source of the Thames.

Thames Head
to Cricklade

Thames Head – official source of the River Thames

Thames Head

There's a little cup in the
Cotswold Hills
Which a spring in a
meadow bubbles and fills
Spanned by a heron's wing,
crossed by a stride,
Calm and untroubled by
dreams of pride,
Guiltless of fame and
ambition's aims

That is the source
of the lordly Thames!
BRET HARTE

THE OFFICIAL SOURCE OF THE RIVER
THAMES lies in Gloucestershire, 356 ft
(105.8 m) above sea level, in a pretty
buttercup-strewn Cotswold meadow
called TREWSBURY MEAD, 3 miles (4.8
km) south-west of Cirencester. Beneath
the shade of an old ash tree on the edge
of a copse sits a simple stone inscribed
with the words:

The Conservators of the River Thames
1857–1974
This Stone was Placed Here to Mark
the Source of the River Thames

The spot can be reached across the field by footpath, but it's a good thing that the actual spring, the first of four that combine to make up the source, is clearly marked with a pile of pebbles, because for most of the year there is no water to be seen here at all; there is just a shallow, dry river bed and a pleasant rural scene, occasionally enhanced by a lowing herd of cows supremely uninterested in the fact that they are chewing such significant cud.

However, there is water not far below the surface, and indeed, after heavy rain, the whole field can become a lake.

Thames and Severn Canal

Rising up behind the source of the Thames is a steep embankment which marks the course of the disused THAMES AND SEVERN CANAL, opened in 1789 as part of a series of waterways linking London and Bristol. The route of the canal, last used commercially in 1911, runs for 30 miles (48 km) from Lechlade, where the Thames ceases to be navigable for boats of any size, to Wallbridge near Stroud, where the Stroudwater Navigation continues on to the Severn Estuary south-west of Gloucester.

The canal was what was known as a 'broad canal' capable of taking boats with a beam (width) of up to 14 ft (4.3 m) and with a draw of up to 4 ft (1.2 m). Because

of the porous Cotswold limestone the canal leaked badly and water supply was a constant problem, so a pumping station was built at Thames Head to replenish the canal from the springs – water that should have flowed east to London found itself flowing west to Bristol instead – and this extraction could be one of the reasons why the Thames Head springs are now largely dry.

Sapperton Tunnel

A short walk northwards along the route of the canal from Thames Head, under a railway, past a derelict round-house and along a deep cutting, brings you to the magnificent neo-classical COATES PORTAL, entrance to the extraordinary 2.1-mile (3.4 km) long SAPPERTON TUNNEL. At 3,817 yards (3,490 m), it WAS THE LONGEST TUNNEL IN BRITAIN when it opened in 1789, and remained so until 1811, when it was overtaken by a tunnel on the Huddersfield Canal. There is no towpath through the tunnel, so boats had to be 'legged' through by two people lying on a plank across the bow of the boat and 'walking' along the tunnel walls – dangerous and gruelling work. From the gaping mouth of the tunnel the dank, dripping brickwork recedes into an inky, echoing blackness and it must have taken some courage to enter in, even for hardened watermen.

The tunnel fell into disuse around 1910 and the Coates Portal was restored in 1977 by the Cotswold Canal Trust, who are in the process of restoring sections of the Thames and Severn Canal. Because the roof has collapsed in a couple of places, it is not at present possible to go all the way through the Sapperton Tunnel, but the Trust is making repairs and it is hoped the tunnel will be open for its full length before too long.

Thames Path

Not only does the Thames River begin at Thames Head but so too does the THAMES PATH, THE LONGEST RIVERSIDE WALK IN EUROPE which accompanies the river for 184 miles (296 km) as far as the Thames Barrier in Greenwich. And the only way to follow the infant Thames for the first 20 miles (32 km) or so is along the footpath – the river is too shallow for any kind of boat until Cricklade at the earliest.

Fosse Way

From the Thames Head, the course of the river leads off to the south-east and the Thames is crossed for the first time by the Fosse Way, the Roman road leading south from Cirencester towards Devon. 'Fosse' means 'ditch' and when originally

built in the 1st century the Fosse Way was little more than a defensive ditch on the western frontier of Roman Britain, on a line from Exeter to Lincoln.

A short distance beyond the Fosse Way water finally appears as the river springs permanently into life from a small walled enclosure known as LYD WELL, and then heads off towards Kemble, whose slim church spire rises out of the trees in the near distance.

Kemble

KEMBLE is built on the site of a 7th-century pagan Anglo-Saxon cemetery, ONE OF THE MOST WESTERLY EVER FOUND IN ENGLAND. The present village church has a good Norman doorway and a tower from 1250, to which the spire was added in 1450. In 1872 the whole church was restored, and it also gained a new south transept when the chapel of ease at nearby Ewen was dismantled and rebuilt at Kemble brick by brick.

Kemble Airfield

One mile (1.6 km) beyond the village, on the far side from the river, is KEMBLE AIRFIELD, now known as COTSWOLD AIRPORT, which makes its presence felt in the village when the wind is in the right direction. It was built by the RAF just before the Second World War and became a sort of aeroplane garage where aircraft were sent for servicing and a lick of paint – the QUEEN'S FLIGHT were spruced up there.

For 16 years Kemble was home to the RED ARROWS, the RAF's aerobatic team, who would practise in the skies above several times a day, drawing crowds from miles around.

Kemble has since passed through many hands including, for a while, the US Air Force, but is now privately owned and provides a range of services such as aircraft restoration, maintenance, salvage and break-up – it is said to be THE BUSIEST AIRCRAFT SCRAPYARD IN THE WORLD. Kemble remains a working airfield, hosting flying weekends and air shows, and is also home to the BRISTOL AERO COLLECTION, displaying THE ONLY COMPLETE BRISTOL BRITANNIA LEFT IN THE WORLD.

Ewen

As the river approaches the village of EWEN it becomes steadily more prominent, a rippling stream of crystal clear water on a bed of stones, but today it is too weak to power Ewen Mill, once THE FIRST MILL ON THE RIVER THAMES, now called Mill Farm. Ewen is fortunate for having the 16th-century Wild Duck Inn, aptly named since this is THE FIRST PLACE ON THE RIVER DOWN FROM THE SOURCE WHERE DUCKS ARE FOUND. Also in Ewen is THE FIRST OF THE MANY BEAUTIFUL RIVERSIDE MANSIONS for which the Thames is justly famous, in this case an attractive Georgian house set back beyond a green lawn, with a white gazebo by the water.

Somerford Keynes

This was the Saxons' 'summer ford' and St Adhelm, Abbot of nearby Malmesbury, built a church here at the end of the 7th century – there is still a SAXON DOORWAY from this building blocked up in the north wall of the present-day church of All Saints, which itself dates from the early 13th century. In a recess nearby are the remains of a carved headstone, thought to be Viking, showing two creatures, possibly dragons, fighting.

Beside the church, and formerly approached by an avenue of elm trees, is a charming, gabled stone manor-house from Tudor days. In the garden there is a matching stone dovecote with mullioned windows and a smart new gazebo.

Sitting astride the river below the manor-house is KEMBLE MILL, the third mill from the source. It is overlooked by POOLE KEYNES, built on the site of a palaeolithic village, possibly 10,000 years old, THE OLDEST SETTLEMENT ON THE UPPER REACHES OF THE THAMES.

The fourth mill from the source is LOWER MILL, which has been turned into a luxury housing development and has apparently attracted interest from the likes of BRAD PITT and ANGELINA JOLIE. In the summer of 2008, THE FIRST BEAVERS TO BE BORN IN BRITAIN FOR 400 YEARS were born at Lower Mill.

Cotswold Water Park

For the next few miles, the river runs through the heart of THE LARGEST MAN-MADE INLAND WATER FEATURE IN EUROPE, the COTSWOLD WATER PARK, which acts as a kind of overflow for the some 140 lakes, created out of abandoned gravel quarries. Most of the lakes are used for recreational purposes, some have beaches, and some serve as landscape features for luxury housing schemes such as the Lower Mill Estate.

Ashton Keynes

As the river arrives in ASHTON KEYNES, THE FIRST VILLAGE ACTUALLY ON THE RIVER THAMES, it flows past a 17th-century manor-house on the north bank and then divides in front of the delightful Long House. The main channel then flows south alongside picturesque High Road, which is lined on one side with

houses accessed by individual bridges across the water – Ashton Keynes boasts some 20 bridges in total. ASHTON HOUSE, near the south end of the street, lurks behind a high yew hedge but throws out one wing to the river's edge, with a gazebo oriel window that projects over the river at the end of a high garden wall, giving the effect of a castle rising from a moat.

Scattered throughout the village at significant junctions are the stumps of four 14th-century preaching crosses, all of them damaged by Oliver Cromwell's Roundheads.

On the northern edge of the village a network of mounds and ditches identifies the site of ASHTON KEYNES CASTLE, a ringwork and bailey castle built in the early 12th century by the Keynes family. The Keynes came over with William the Conqueror and their status as favoured local squires is reflected in the assortment of villages in the area that bear their name.

Waterhay

After leaving Ashton Keynes, the Thames receives a good boost from SWILL BROOK, which joins it just above Waterhay Bridge. Once considered a mere dribble, Swill Brook is now much bigger than the parent Thames at this point, owing to the water park which has diverted water from the Thames and greatly reduced its flow.

WATERHAY, on the south bank, is now just a couple of farms and cottages, but it used to be a village of some size, with a 13th-century church to match. By the end of the 19th century the village had diminished to such an extent that the church was dismantled and rebuilt up the road in Leigh, leaving just the chancel standing forlornly in the middle of a field.

North Meadow

The river now passes through a landscape of water meadows, rich in wild flowers, and winds its way around the conical-shaped landmark of Hailstone Hill to reach NORTH MEADOW, just before Cricklade, a Site of Special Scientific Interest that lies on the flood plain between the Churn and Thames rivers. Since the development of mechanised farming in the 18th century, most meadows of this kind have been drained and put to arable farming, but North Meadow was preserved in perpetuity as common land by the Saxon court-leet of Cricklade and provides a precious

habitat for THE LARGEST COLLECTION OF RARE SNAKE'S-HEAD FRITILLARIES IN BRITAIN, some 80 per cent of all these flowers in the country.

Cricklade

The river laps the northern edge of the Saxon burgh of CRICKLADE, which is THE FIRST TOWN ON THE RIVER THAMES and THE ONLY WILTSHIRE TOWN ON THE RIVER THAMES. Originally a small settlement beside the Roman Ermine Street where it crossed the Thames flood plain on a raised wooden causeway, Cricklade was fortified against the Danes by Alfred the Great in about 890, and the layout of the Saxon town and ramparts can still be traced.

In 979 a mint was established in the town, operating until 1100, and Cricklade coins occasionally come to light – there are some examples in the town museum. The Royal Collection in Copenhagen has a fine example of a Cricklade coin sporting the head of King Canute. An old coaching inn, the Red Lion, now stands on the site of the CRICKLADE MINT.

St Sampson's

Cricklade's most prominent landmark from the river is the imposing tower of the parish church, ONE OF ONLY FIVE CHURCHES IN BRITAIN DEDICATED TO ST SAMPSON, THE CELTIC SAINT. The church itself was built in the 12th century on the site of a Saxon chapel, but the tower was added in 1552 by John Dudley, the Duke of Northumberland, father-in-law of Lady Jane Grey. He was executed not long afterwards.

St Sampson's Cricklade

Cricklade in Legend

Over the years various romantic legends have attached themselves to
Cricklade, fostered and enhanced by numerous writers and commentators.
Some believe that Cricklade is where St Augustine converted the Anglo-
Saxons of Wessex to Christianity in 597, before moving on to Aust on the
River Severn to meet the Welsh bishops. Others claim that the name Cricklade is a corruption of Greeklade, the home of learned monks who
established ENGLAND'S FIRST UNIVERSITY here in the days of the Mercian
King Penda, pre-dating Oxford by 600 years. And William Morris reck-
oned that the tower of St Sampson's was paid for by the proceeds of a
gambling win, as suggested by carvings of the four playing card symbols
on the ceiling.

Whatever the truth, Cricklade, once described by William Cobbett as
'that villainous hole ... a more rascally place I never set my eyes on ...' is a
very pleasant place today and is set, as the town motto tells us, 'in lovely
surroundings'.

Oldest Roman Catholic Church

The Rights of Navigation

Near the river is the church of ST MARY'S, which stands on an earth bank above the High Street that was once part of the Saxon ramparts. Of Saxon origins, it was rebuilt by the Normans and retains a fine NORMAN CHANCEL ARCH. In 1981 the Church of England made St Mary's redundant, and it was later taken back into the Roman Catholic Church, making it THE OLDEST ROMAN CATHOLIC CHURCH IN BRITAIN.

Cricklade's Town Bridge, a single arch built in 1852, is the limit of navigational rights on the River Thames, which up to here acts as a public highway across private land. Between Cricklade and Lechlade, however, the river is too shallow for any kind of substantial cargo boat, and once the Thames and Severn Canal had been completed in 1789 the Thames above Lechlade was rather abandoned as a viable thoroughfare. There are plans to restore the section to navigation and occasionally a light cargo is carried up to Cricklade in order to ensure that the navigational rights are not lost.

Well, I never *knew this* *about*
THE RIVER THAMES

HORATIO HORNBLOWER, C.S Forester's naval hero, travels along the Thames and Severn Canal in a horse-drawn narrow boat on his way from Gloucester to London in *Hornblower and the Atropos* – and has to help 'leg' it through the Sapperton Tunnel when one of the boatmen gets sick.

Between 1936 and 1940 Ashton Keynes was the site of the COTSWOLD

BRUDERHOF (house of brothers), a pacifist religious community founded in Germany in the 1920s. Persecuted by the Nazis because of their refusal to serve in the armed forces, the Bruderhof fled to England, where they set up a thriving farm business, along with crafts and publishing ventures. They attracted a substantial number of English followers, but with the outbreak of the Second World War anti-German sentiment forced the Bruderhof to flee once more, this time to Paraguay in South America. The Bruderhof buildings, just north of the village, are now occupied by the Cotswold Community School.

The checkered red-brown and white pattern of the snake's-head fritillary is the inspiration for the coat-of-arms and flag of CROATIA, recognisable from the shirts worn by the Croatian national football team.

River Churn

Seven Springs – alternative source of the River Thames

Just downstream from the Town Bridge at Cricklade, the Thames is joined by the River Churn, regarded by many as the true source of the River Thames. Arguments for the River Churn as the source of the Thames are:

a) Seven Springs, where the Churn rises, is the furthest direct source from the mouth of the Thames, adding about 4 miles (6.4 km) to the length of the river.

b) Seven Springs sits at 700 ft (213 m) above sea level, nearly twice the height of the source at Thames Head.

c) Unlike Thames Head, Seven Springs never dries up.

Seven Springs

The SEVEN SPRINGS of the RIVER CHURN rise in Gloucestershire, just short of the steep Cotswold escarpment that looks north-west across the Golden Valley. A couple of miles further north and the waters would tumble west to feed the River Severn, but at Seven Springs the Cotswolds tilt towards the south and east, and that way runs the River Churn.

The countryside is Cotswold charm at its most heavenly with wide fields of blowing barley, clumps of trees and honey-coloured dry-stone walls. The actual springs, cool and clear, bubble up through Cotswold stones in a deep wooded dell beside the main road from Andoversford to Gloucester, and join together to form a stream that flows under the road and into a pond in the grounds of the Seven Springs pub.

Where the stream emerges from under the road there is a plaque in the wall above it that reads:

HIC TUUS
O TAMESINE PATER
SEPTEMGEMINUS FONS

The inscription means 'Here, O Father Thames, is your sevenfold source'. Having gathered itself in the pond, the Churn begins its journey to London and runs off south through trees towards . . .

Coberley

COBERLEY (Cuthbert's Ley) is mentioned in the Domesday Book as the property of Roger de Berkeley. There are long barrows in the fields around, and just to the north of the village are the remains of a Roman villa where some notably fine mosaics have been found, along with coins, brooches and other arte-facts. In 2007 some excavations were made there for Channel 4's *Time Team* programme.

The parish church of St Giles stands a little apart from the village, close to the river, and is approached through a small door next to a huge arched gateway leading into the private garden of Coberley Court.

Coberley Hall

The high wall next to the churchyard once guarded COBERLEY HALL, sadly demolished after the owner had lost his all in the South Sea Bubble. CHARLES I stayed at Coberley Hall during his retreat from the siege of Gloucester in 1643; and later his son Prince Charles, fleeing after the Battle of Worcester in 1651 and disguised as a groom, took shelter for the night of 10 September in the old rectory that preceded the pres-ent Georgian one.

Coberley Church

St Giles's Church, much restored by a Victorian rector, was rebuilt in the 14th century by SIR THOMAS DE BERKELEY, whose splendid tomb can be seen inside the church. Clad in the armour he wore at the Battle of Crecy in 1346, his tall figure rests on top of the tomb, his hands clasped in prayer, his head supported by angels, a lion at his feet.

Lying beside Sir Thomas is his wife, the Lady Joan. After Sir Thomas died, Lady Joan married SIR WILLIAM WHIT-TINGTON of Pauntley in Gloucestershire, by whom she had a son, Richard. Sir William was outlawed for marrying a de Berkeley widow without the permission of the King and died in penury not long afterwards, so young Richard was forced to make his way to London to earn a living. He became apprenticed to a mercer and grew up to be a hero of legend and pantomime, beloved of children the world over, four times Mayor of London DICK WHITTINGTON.

The tomb of Dick Whittington's mother is a thrilling treasure to come across in this quiet country church, the first church on the stripling River Churn – or Thames?

In the south wall of the sanctuary IS THE ONLY HEART MEMORIAL TO BE FOUND IN THE COTSWOLDS, indicating the burial place of the heart of Sir Giles de Berkeley, Sir Thomas's father. His body rests in Little Malvern, where he had gone to take the waters.

A plaque beneath the heart memorial informs us that Sir Giles's charger, LOMBARD, is buried outside in the churchyard, and we can see Lombard's headstone up against the outside of the sanctuary wall in line with his master's heart.

Half a mile (0.8 km) further south the river widens into a series of ornamental lakes in the gardens of . . .

Cowley Manor

COWLEY MANOR is an Italianate mansion of 1855 which sits above the River Churn in grounds of 50 acres (20 ha) with terraces, a rock garden and a grand Victorian cascade.

Local sentiment has it that the REVD CHARLES DODGSON (aka Lewis Carroll) first met ALICE LIDDELL (who became his Alice in Wonderland) in the gardens at Cowley Manor – Alice's uncle was the rector of Cowley and she frequently came to stay with him at the Rectory, now the Old Rectory, an elegant Georgian house set back down a long drive from the main village street, while Dodgson is known to have visited his fellow clergyman there on more than one occasion.

Around the turn of the 20th century Cowley Manor was the home of SIR JAMES HORLICK (1844–1921), the 'J' of J. & W. Horlicks, the malted milk drink company. Sir James remodelled the

house and is now reputed to revisit it from time to time by climbing in through the large window that overlooks the adjacent churchyard where he is buried. He has been spotted frequently over the years, walking along the first-floor corridor, and is always, apparently, impeccably civil.

The small church at Cowley is 12th century and unbelievably beautiful with, inside, a rare 15th-century stone pulpit and a good Norman font.

Cowley Manor went on to become a conference centre, then an old people's home, and is now a luxury hotel and spa belonging to Jessica Sainsbury. The hotel literature does not mention whether Sir James Horlick has availed himself of the new spa facilities.

Colesbourne

The next village to receive the Churn is COLESBOURNE. Here the river runs by the foot of Colesbourne Park, home of the ELWES family. The present house was built in 1958 to replace the crumbling Victorian pile which had been erected on the site of the original – a medieval manor-house with a Queen Anne façade.

Henry Elwes

The grounds of Colesbourne Park are graced with a profusion of rare and exotic trees from all over the world, planted by the naturalist HENRY ELWES (1846–1922), who in 1897 became THE FIRST PERSON TO RECEIVE THE ROYAL HORTICULTURAL SOCIETY'S HIGHEST HONOUR, THE VICTORIA MEDAL. His greatest work was *THE TREES OF GREAT BRITAIN AND IRELAND*, produced in partnership with the botanist Augustine Henry in 1906, which documents and describes the finest specimens of every species of tree grown in Britain and Ireland, and is still today regarded as the definitive study of British trees. Elwes visited every tree recorded in the book himself, a task that took him nearly 15 years.

Colesbourne Park is famous today for its magnificent display of snowdrops, made up of some 200 varieties developed by the present Lady Elwes from the original collection of Henry Elwes. Open days are held on weekends during January and February.

Rendcomb

The river continues south to flow through a wild and deep valley past the playing fields of RENDCOMB COLLEGE, where UN SECRETARY-GENERAL KOFI ANNAN'S SON KOJO excelled at rugby. The college, perched on a noble terrace high above the river, has been a progressive independent school since 1920, and is also the alma mater of

three-time champion jockey RICHARD DUNWOODY.

The college is housed in another Victorian Italianate mansion, this time built in 1867 for a member of the Goldsmid banking family, SIR FRANCIS HENRY GOLDSMID (1808–78), who in 1833 was THE FIRST JEW TO BECOME AN ENGLISH BARRISTER.

Lying in the shadow of the great house is the Tudor church of St Peter, dedicated in 1517 and ONE OF THE LAST ENGLISH CHURCHES TO BE BUILT BEFORE THE REFORMATION. Its greatest treasure is a 12TH-CENTURY NORMAN FONT with magnificent carvings around the bowl of 11 of the Disciples – and a shapeless figure representing Judas.

medieval. There is a scratch dial on one of the tower buttresses, by which the villagers have been telling the time for 800 years; and nearby, carved into the stonework, is a MANTICORE, a grotesque creature with the head of a man and the body of an animal. Another similar carving can be found on the south transept. No one is quite sure what they signify.

The church is entered through a noble 14th-century wooden door with delicate ironwork, which swings beneath a five-tier zigzag Norman arch. The interior is most unexpected, and was restored in the 1920s by local conservation architect WILLIAM CROOME. There is Jacobean panelling, a restored Norman chancel arch flanked by round pillars with richly carved capitals, a modern rood loft constructed by Croome himself, a beautiful wooden pulpit from 1480, and an altar frontal from Chartres Cathedral. Remarkable.

Through the trees there are glimpses of the lovely Queen Anne rectory, while further up the hill is the manor-house, also Queen Anne. From here the Churn winds on through the trees towards the distant towers of . . .

North Cerney

Followed closely by the A435, the river now glides past the garden of the Bathurst Arms in NORTH CERNEY and looks across the road at the saddle-backed Norman tower of All Saints, the most unusual church of an impressive collection in the Churn valley. From the outside the church is a curious jumble of 12th-century Norman and early

Cirencester

On reaching CIRENCESTER, CAPITAL OF THE COTSWOLDS, the river veers off to the left and skirts the eastern edge of town, passing through the grounds of Cirencester Abbey, at one point swelling into a lake graced with swans and ducks. There is little left of the abbey, which was destroyed in the Dissolution of the Monasteries, save for an impressive 12th-century gateway at the west end of the lake. At the other end is a short stretch of wall from a much earlier Cirencester – the Roman Corinium.

Corinium

The full name of the Roman town was CORINIUM DOBUNNORUM, and it was founded in AD 75 on the site of a Roman fort set up just after the Roman invasion as an administrative centre for the local British tribe, the Dobunni, who had welcomed the Roman invaders and whose capital until then had been at Bagendon, further up the Churn valley.

Corinium lay on the path of numerous ancient tracks such as the ICKNIELD WAY and the WHITE WAY and soon became an important hub in the Roman road network, with ERMINE WAY from Silchester, AKEMAN STREET from St Albans and THE FOSSE WAY from Lincoln to Exeter all passing through the town. By the 2nd century it had become THE SECOND LARGEST TOWN IN ROMAN BRITAIN, only a shade smaller than London. By the 4th century it was BRITAIN'S LARGEST AGRICULTURAL

CENTRE and lay at the heart of THE BIGGEST NETWORK OF ROMAN VILLAS IN THE NORTH OF EUROPE. It was also THE LARGEST PRODUCER OF MOSAICS IN BRITANNIA.

All that remains in situ from those glory days is the amphitheatre, whose grass-covered walls lie at the centre of a park on the south-west edge of the modern town.

Corinium suffered under the Saxons, who won the town from the British at the Battle of Dyrham in 577 and went on to squabble over it amongst themselves, with the Mercian King Penda finally wresting control from the Saxons of Wessex at the BATTLE OF CIRENCESTER in 628.

Cathedral of the Cotswolds

In 1117 Henry I founded Cirencester Abbey and the town eventually re-established itself as the centre for the prosperous Cotswold wool trade, becoming THE LARGEST WOOL MARKET IN ENGLAND during the Middle Ages.

St John the Baptist

In the 15th century, long before the destruction of the abbey, the wool merchants of Cirencester used some of their wealth to transform the small Norman church of St John the Baptist into the finest 'wool' church in Britain and THE LARGEST PARISH CHURCH IN GLOUCESTERSHIRE. The view from Dyer Street of the church and its magnificent porch soaring over the pretty market square is one of the most sublime town centre views in England.

Treasures inside the church include a rare, pre-Reformation, 15th-century 'wine glass' stone pulpit, glowing in red and gold, which somehow escaped destruction by Henry VIII's 'reformers', a silver goblet given by Anne Boleyn to the doctor who looked after her daughter, the future Elizabeth I, and the 15th-century stained glass of the west window. In St John's Chapel a 13th-century arch rests on a base stone retrieved from Roman Corinium – 1,000 years of history separates the bottom of the arch from the top.

The superb tower, a landmark for

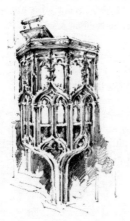

miles around, dates from the early 15th century and houses THE OLDEST PEAL OF 12 BELLS IN ENGLAND. It is 162 ft (49.3 m) high, and from the top there is the best view of 18th-century CIRENCES-TER PARK, the home of Lord Bathurst, which lurks on the western edge of the town behind ONE OF THE LARGEST YEW HEDGES IN THE WORLD, horseshoe shaped and over 40 ft (12 m) high.

After leaving Cirencester the River Churn bypasses SIDDINGTON, where the doorway of the Norman church sports a superbly carved tympanum showing Jesus blessing the kneeling figures of his disciples Peter and Mark. It then crosses over the path of the Thames and Severn Canal and bubbles under a dismantled railway bridge to . . .

South Cerney

The delightful village of SOUTH CERNEY, which gets its name from the river – Churn – clearly attracts the quality, for it boasts not one but four manor-houses. The church is largely Norman with a solid four-square tower that leans slightly to the west and sports a bright blue clock, successor to the three old scratch dials on the tower by which early villagers told the time.

In a glass case inside the church are two fragments that must be amongst THE EARLIEST WOODCARVINGS TO BE FOUND IN ENGLAND, the exquisitely carved head and foot of Christ taken from a 12th-century crucifix in Compostela. In the central light of the west window can be seen the figure of Mrs Anne Edwards, the widow of a local clergyman, who in 1834 founded an imposing college at the north end of the village to house less fortunate widows of local clergymen.

The river now runs on sweetly between a lane called Bow Wow and the walled garden of the Old Vicarage, past a charming stone gazebo, then gets muddled up for a while in the Cotswold Water Park before squeezing through a narrow gap between Cerney Wick, with its pretty chapel of ease, and a disused lock on the Thames and Severn Canal. On the far side of the lock is a round-house, nicely restored as someone's home.

From here, it's a fairly straight dash beside the Ermine Way to join (or continue) the Thames just downstream from the Town Bridge at Cricklade.

Well, I never   *knew this*
about
THE RIVER CHURN

Buried in the churchyard at COWLEY is ROBERT BROWNING, who once kept an inn in Dorset, and was an ancestor of the poet Robert Browning.

After the Romans left, CIRENCESTER, or Corinium, continued for a time as a Romano-British fortress, and the Welsh monk Nennius, in his *Historia Brittonum*, claims that the British King Arthur was crowned there.

Cirencester's unique architectural jewel, the three-storey south porch of ST JOHN'S CHURCH, dates from 1490 and was built as ecclesiastical offices for the abbey. It is renowned for its exquisite fan-vaulted ceiling.

Cirencester Park is home to THE CIRENCESTER POLO CLUB, THE OLDEST POLO CLUB IN BRITAIN.

Cirencester is home to THE FIRST AND OLDEST AGRICULTURAL COLLEGE IN THE ENGLISH-SPEAKING WORLD, founded in 1840 by the 4th Earl of Bathurst.

CRICKLADE TO LECHLADE

Inglesham Roundhouse – lock-keeper's cottage at the start of the Thames and Severn Canal

Castle Eaton

So farwell Cricklad, come off yt ground
We'el sail in Boats, towards London Town
Ffor this now is, the highest station,
By famous Tems for Navigation.

From Cricklade to just beyond Lech-lade, the River Thames, allowing for the odd kink, forms the boundary between Gloucestershire on the north bank and Wiltshire on the south bank.

The road bridge at the Wiltshire village of CASTLE EATON, 4 miles (6.4 km) downriver, is made of iron girders and must be one of the ugliest on the Thames. Just beyond is the more gracious sight of THE RED LION, FIRST PUB ACTUALLY ON THE BANKS OF THE RIVER THAMES, a charming 18th-century red-brick building, with gardens running down to the water.

A little further on, right beside the river, is the 12th-century church of St Mary the Virgin, sporting a natty little spire in the middle, which looks modern but was probably put there in the 13th century. It was redesigned by William Butterfield in the 1860s and houses the sanctus bell. Inside the church is a ravishing, richly carved wooden pulpit from the days of Elizabeth I.

Across the fields can be seen the mighty, square tower of the church in the next village, Kempsford, which sits on the north bank in Gloucestershire.

Kempsford

A garden saw I, ful of blosmy bowes
Upon a river, in a grene mede
GEOFFREY CHAUCER, on Kempsford

The Saxons fortified this important 'ford of the great marsh', named possibly after a Saxon hero called Kynemere, and the earthwork they built on the north bank can still be seen. The Thames here formed the frontier between the Saxon kingdoms of Mercia (north bank) and Wessex (south bank). Across the river in present-day Wiltshire, once part of Wessex, there is a 100-acre (40 ha) meadow named BATTLEFIELD where forces from the two kingdoms met in bloody confrontation on 16 January 800.

After the Norman invasion William II gave the manor of KEMPSFORD to his friend Patrick Chaworth, and a church and castle arose where four kings would be entertained – Edward I, Edward II, Edward III and Henry IV. The estate eventually passed down to Maud Chaworth, who in 1298 married HENRY PLANTAGENET, 3RD EARL OF LANCASTER. He retired to Kempsford in his dotage and in 1336 replaced the Norman chancel of the church at Kempsford with the decorated one we see today.

Henry Plantagenet's son, Henry of Grosmont, 4th Earl of Lancaster, settled at Kempsford but was driven away by tragedy. His young son, another Henry, drowned in the river and the father, overcome with misery, left the village never to return. As he rode away his horse lost a shoe, which was retrieved by the villagers and nailed to the door of the church – THE HORSESHOE IS STILL THERE TO THIS DAY.

The 4th Earl distinguished himself fighting for Edward III on the battlefields of France and was a founding member of the Order of the Garter. In 1351 he was made 1st DUKE OF LANCASTER, becoming THE SECOND ENGLISH DUKE after the Black Prince, Duke of Cornwall.

John of Gaunt

Kempsford eventually passed to the Duke's eldest daughter Maud, but she died of the plague in 1362 and everything went to her younger sister BLANCHE. In 1359 Edward III's third son JOHN OF GAUNT married Blanche and so procured Kempsford along with the title Duke of Lancaster.

In 1385 John of Gaunt built the great perpendicular church tower that so distinguishes Kempsford from afar, as a memorial to his wife. The vaulted ceiling of the tower is painted in glorious colour and displays the 16 red roses of Lancaster.

In the early 17th century the castle was pulled down and a grand Jacobean house built in its place, but this was demolished 150 years later by the new owner, LORD COLERAINE, to pay off his debts. Some of the materials from the house were used to build the manor farm, but the bulk was loaded on to barges and taken 5 miles (8 km) downstream to build Buscot Park (see p. 28).

Today all that is left to remind us of Kempsford's former status is the noble church tower and Lady Maud's Walk.

RAF Fairford

While floating through the duck-filled reeds and bulrushes that abound on this stretch of the River Thames, the observant traveller cannot have failed to notice the steady stream of enormous aircraft passing low overhead, or have been unaware of the background rumble of aero engines against the gentle lapping of the water.

All this noise and activity emanates from the mighty NATO airbase of RAF Fairford, which occupies the countryside north of Kempsford.

RAF FAIRFORD was constructed in 1944 as a base for British and American troop-carrying aircraft involved in the D-Day Normandy landings. In 1950 a 10,000 ft (3,000 m) runway was laid down and Fairford was used by the US Air Force as a prominent forward air base for B47 bombers during the Cold War.

In 1969 Fairford became THE TEST BASE FOR CONCORDE, and in 1971 THE VERY FIRST CONCORDE EVER MADE LANDED AT FAIRFORD after its flight from the production centre at Filton near Bristol. Concorde continued to use Fairford until 1978.

The US Air Force returned in 1979, and in 1986 American KC 135 STRATOTANKERS FLEW FROM FAIRFORD TO SUPPORT THE BOMBING RAIDS ON LIBYA. American B52 bombers were based at Fairford for the Gulf War of 1991, the Kosovan War in 1999 and the Iraq war in 2003.

RAF Fairford is today considered THE LEADING NATO FORWARD AIR BASE IN EUROPE and receives occasional visits from futuristic B-2 SPIRIT STEALTH BOMBERS.

On leaving Kempsford, the Thames passes by the gorgeous Yew Tree Farm, seen across a meadow on the Wiltshire side, continues under Hannington Bridge, built in 1841 with three skewed brick arches, and then turns north toward Inglesham, where the Thames and Severn Canal begins its journey to Thames Head, the Sapperton Tunnel and Stroud.

Yew Tree Farm

Inglesham

'This church was repaired in 1888–9 through the energy and with the help of William Morris who loved it.'

The tiny, rustic church of ST JOHN THE BAPTIST AT INGLESHAM stands on a pagan mound between the river, which here encompasses an islet, and Inglesham House, which is pretty much all that is left of the old village of Inglesham. The church comes down to us from Saxon days, although most of the building we see today is early 12th century. There are the steps and shaft of a Saxon cross in the churchyard, and inside, brought in from the wind and rain and placed in the south aisle, is a very special treasure – a weather-worn sculptured relief of the MADONNA AND

CHILD, executed by a Saxon craftsman, and still redolent of ancient faith.

The Norman nave is packed with furniture from every age and style. There are bare wood Georgian box pews, a font from 1468, a Jacobean squire's pew and pulpit with canopy, 15th-century screens, and fragments of old stained glass in some of the windows. On the east wall of the 13th-century chancel is a 14th-century stone reredos.

The sloping walls of the church are chequered red and ochre, with faded paintings and texts from the Bible such as the Ten Commandments.

We owe this authentic, unspoiled interior, with its layers of English history, to William Morris, who would row up here from Kelmscott (see p. 30) and direct repairs to the church, saving it from the worst excesses of the Victorian restorers. St John the Baptist Church at Inglesham WAS ONE OF THE FIRST TO BE SAVED BY THE SOCIETY FOR THE PROTECTION OF ANCIENT BUILDINGS, founded by Morris and others in 1877.

Inglesham Roundhouse

A little further downstream, on the opposite bank, creating a supremely beautiful scene, is a quaint little cottage draped in willows, which sits beside THE FIRST LOCK ON THE THAMES AND SEVERN CANAL, just where the Thames turns for Lechlade and the River Cole joins from Fairford.

Behind the cottage is the ROUND-HOUSE, which was where the lock-keeper lived. There are several

examples of this unusual design dotted along the canal, notably at Marston Meysey, Cerney Wick and at Coates, near Thames Head.

The Thames and Severn Canal, opened in 1789, was a bold and ambitious attempt to link two of England's great ports, London and Bristol, but it leaked badly and never had the time to become commercially successful before facing competition from the emerging railways. Sections of the canal continued in use until the 1930s when the whole route was abandoned, but the new enthusiasm for spending leisure time on England's waterways has boosted attempts to restore such canals for purposes undreamed of by the great canal builders of the 18th century.

The Inglesham lock and roundhouse are due to be restored by the Cotswold Canal Trust when funding becomes available.

Head of Navigation

This point marks the head of navigation for the River Thames, although the rights of navigation continue as far as Cricklade.

In the past, when there was more water in the river and boats were smaller, some craft could carry on to Cricklade, but today only punts or rowing boats can progress further than here, and even then only when the water is running high. Above here the river is left to its own devices, without locks and weirs, with unprotected banks, weeds and rushes and sudden shallows and eddies.

The footbridge across the river here, which replaced the donkey tow-bridge, acts as a warning marker for those with powered boats who are advised to turn around here.

Next stop is Lechlade, which has already been beckoning for some time, thanks to the majestic spire of the 15th-century St Lawrence Church, which soars above the trees and draws the eye from miles around.

Before the church is reached there is a bustling marina, a turning circle where the banks have been scooped out so that narrowboats can turn around, and the first road bridge across the Thames of any real age or character.

Halfpenny Bridge

The opening of the Thames and Severn Canal hugely increased both the volume of river traffic at Lechlade, with barges arriving from both east and west, and also trade in general. It quickly became necessary to replace the small pedestrian ferry that had sufficed until then with something more substantial that could bear heavy road traffic, and in 1792 the handsome, bow-backed HALFPENNY BRIDGE was opened, taking its name from the ½d

toll levied on walkers using the bridge –
except for churchgoers. The arch had to
be made good and high to allow the new,
bigger barges to pass underneath.

The pedestrian toll was done away
with in 1839 by popular demand, and all
tolls had ceased by 1875, but the stone
tollhouse remains at the east end of the
bridge.

Lechlade

*'A praty old village with a
stone spire to the church'*
JOHN LELAND

The mellow, honey-coloured market
town of LECHLADE is situated near to
where the Thames is joined by the River

Leach, from which the town gets its
name. Four counties meet at the river
here, Gloucestershire and Oxfordshire
on the north bank, Wiltshire and Berkshire on the south bank.

This is THE FIRST PLACE ON THE
THAMES WHERE THE RIVER IS DEEP
ENOUGH FOR COMMERCIAL TRAFFIC, and
it was consequently a busy river port
with a wharf where barges were loaded
with all kinds of products destined for
Oxford and London, from local cheeses
to the stone used for the dome of St
Paul's Cathedral.

Lechlade is still a bustling place, but
the trade now is in commuter traffic and
tourists, the latter of whom are either
exploring the Cotswolds or have come
up the river on cabin cruisers and
narrowboats.

Sheer Poetry

In September 1815 the poet PERCY
BYSSHE SHELLEY, his girlfriend MARY
(later his wife), her stepbrother CHARLES
CLAIRMONT and fellow poet THOMAS
LOVE PEACOCK arrived in Lechlade

exhausted, having rowed up the river from Windsor. They stayed the night at the New Inn, with Shelley feasting on 'three mutton chops, well peppered', and next day all felt so refreshed that they determined to row the length and breadth of England's waterways, and set off upriver to do just that. However, when they reached the entrance to the Thames and Severn Canal and were told that it would cost them £20 to use the canal, they abandoned the idea, and instead rowed on to look at the little church at Inglesham before returning to Lechlade for another night at the New Inn. That evening Shelley took a stroll through the churchyard and was inspired to compose 'A Summer Evening Churchyard, Lechlade'. The path he used is now called Shelley's Walk, and there is a plaque on the wall commemorating the occasion, which includes some lines from the poem:

Here could I hope
That death did hide from human sight
Sweet secrets

The stunningly beautiful 18th-century Church House beside the graveyard was built by a Lechlade wharf owner, John Aing. Mounted on the garden wall is a delightful gazebo, possibly the finest of the many gazebos to be seen on the journey down the River Thames.

The New Inn, where Shelley and his party stayed, still provides hospitality for 'rowers' and other visitors, as does Lechlade's oldest hostelry, the Swan Inn, across the pretty market-place.

Well, I never knew this about
THE RIVER THAMES

Past the MILLENNIUM WOOD, planted by the people of Cricklade to celebrate the new Millennium, and just after the Ermine Way, the Thames is joined by the DOWN AMPNEY BROOK, which reaches here after flowing past the rectory at Down Ampney, 1 mile (1.6km) upstream, where composer RALPH VAUGHAN WILLIAMS was born in 1872. The tune Vaughan Williams composed for the hymn 'Come Down, O Love Divine' was named 'Down Ampney' in honour of his birthplace.

The RED LION at CASTLE EATON boasts a thriving 'PÉTANQUE CLUB'. Pétanque is a type of boules, and is the version of bowls that Sir Francis Drake was playing on Plymouth Hoe when the Spanish Armada was sighted.

John of Gaunt's wife Blanche was patron of the poet GEOFFREY CHAUCER, who came to stay at KEMPSFORD and was often seen pacing deep in thought along a path on top of the Saxon fortifications known as LADY MAUD'S WALK.

Here he wrote a poem, 'Chaucer's Dream', to celebrate Blanche's marriage and ten years later wrote another, 'The Book of the Duchess', to mourn her death.

The George in KEMPSFORD is named after George IV, friend of Lord Coleraine of Kempsford Manor – at least until Coleraine became 'too free and coarse for the royal taste' and fled to Paris to escape his debtors.

Because of the length of its runway

RAF FAIRFORD IS THE ONLY ABORT LANDING SITE FOR THE SPACE SHUTTLE IN THE UK, and has NASA-trained medical and fire crews available at all times for emergencies.

Every year RAF FAIRFORD hosts THE BIGGEST MILITARY AIR SHOW IN THE WORLD, THE ROYAL INTERNATIONAL AIR TATTOO – according to The Guinness Book of Records the 2003 Air Tattoo was THE BIGGEST MILITARY AIR SHOW EVER STAGED, with a cast list of 535 aircraft.

LECHLADE TO RADCOT

Old Father Thames, watching over St John's Lock

Halfpenny Bridge at Lechlade is the traditional starting point for a cruise down the river to London, a journey known as a THAMES MEANDER – certainly from here until at least Oxford the river itself can most accurately be described as meandering. Once you leave Lechlade there are no more towns on the river until Oxford.

St John's Lock

A pleasant 1-mile meander downstream is ST JOHN'S LOCK, THE FIRST AND HIGHEST LOCK ON THE THAMES, 250 ft (76 m) above sea level. The view back from here of the blue river threading its way through lush green meadows towards Shelley's 'dim and distant spire' at Lechlade is ravishing.

It was the opening of the Thames and Severn Canal that made it necessary to build a lock here, and St John's was completed one year after the canal in 1790.

St John's Lock is watched over by OLD FATHER THAMES, brought to rest here in 1974 from Thames Head, where he was being vandalised. Carved from

Portland cement by Italian sculptor Rafaelle Monti for the Great Exhibition of 1851, Old Father Thames was rescued from the Crystal Palace when it burned down in 1936 and was later placed at the source, where he suffered all sorts of indignities. He is safe now under the lock-keeper's watchful eye, but still looks a bit bemused.

St John's Bridge

Just down from the lock, at THE OLDEST BRIDGING POINT ON THE THAMES OUTSIDE LONDON, is ST JOHN'S BRIDGE. Like the lock, it was named after the Priory of St John the Baptist, founded here by King John's Queen Isabella early in the 13th century. The first crossing consisted of a series of wooden structures, destroyed by floods in 1206, and the first stone bridge was begun here in 1229 and maintained by the monks. The present single-arch bridge was built in 1886.

There is little left of the priory, which was dissolved by Edward IV in 1475, except for a few fragments in the gardens of the TROUT INN which stands at the north end of the bridge. The Trout Inn was originally an almshouse for the priory and until 1704 was known as 'Ye Sygne of St John Baptist Head'.

Bloomer's Hole

The elegant arch of BLOOMER'S HOLE footbridge marks the beginning of a series of sharp bends in the river where the spire at Lechlade sometimes appears ahead and then disappears, only to reappear behind.

Bloomer's Hole Bridge is THE NEWEST FOOTBRIDGE ON THE THAMES and was the final link that completed the Thames Path. It is made of steel but clad in wood so that it looks like a more rustic timber structure. It was lowered into place by a Chinook helicopter in 2000.

Buscot

Peeping through the trees on the south bank at the final U-bend of this section of the river is a delightful pairing of a 13th-century church and an Old Parsonage belonging to the village of BUSCOT, which is now largely owned by the National Trust.

The church boasts a late Norman zigzag chancel arch and some superb windows by Edward Burne-Jones. The lovely OLD PARSONAGE, set back from the river behind a walled garden, was built in 1703. When it was no longer needed for the rector the house was sold by the Church Commissioners to an American author called PETER STUCKLEY, who lived there with his companion Mr Mussett, a designer of statues – some of his work can be seen in the garden. On his death Peter Stuckley left the house to the National Trust with the condition that any tenant should have American literary connections. The present tenant is indeed an American author and the house can be visited by application to said tenant.

Buscot Lock

Church and Parsonage overlook BUSCOT LOCK, which at 110 ft (33 m) long is THE SMALLEST LOCK ON THE RIVER THAMES and was opened in 1790 to serve the barges heading for the Thames and Severn Canal. It was built by the owner of Buscot Park, EDWARD LOVEDEN LOVEDEN (1749–1822), who would become known locally as 'Old Father Thames' for his work as president of the parliamentary committee set up in 1793 to oversee the improvement of navigation on the Thames. He was responsible for many of the cuts and canals that straighten the course of the river and shorten distances, and was a prime mover behind the building of the Thames and Severn Canal. His motives were not entirely altruistic, as he made a fortune out of toll fees from Buscot Lock.

Buscot Park

BUSCOT PARK, which sits in beautiful grounds on a hill about 1 mile (1.6 km) south-east of the village of Buscot, was built in 1779 for Edward Loveden Loveden, on the estate he had inherited as a boy from his great-uncle. The neo-

classical house was designed by JAMES DARLEY and largely constructed from materials carried down the river by barge from Kempsford Manor, which was in the process of being demolished by Lord Coleraine (see Kempsford).

Despite the fees from Buscot Lock, a noble inheritance from his father and three financially shrewd marriages, Loveden Loveden was mortgaged to the hilt when he died, and his great-grandson Sir Pryse Pryse was forced to sell Buscot Park in 1859 to ROBERT TERTIUS CAMPBELL (1811–87), whose fortune came from the goldfields of Australia.

Brandy Island

Campbell was an innovative agriculturalist who set about transforming the Buscot estate. He dredged the river below the lock and set up two waterwheels at Hart's Weir to pump water up to reservoirs by the house (see opposite). The water was then used to irrigate the fields via a system of brick-lined drainage channels. His main crop was sugar beet, and this was used both to fatten up his cattle and to make brandy, which he exported to France. He even laid down a narrow-gauge railway to transport the beet from his fields to the distillery he had erected down by the river near Buscot Lock. What little is left of the distillery is now a water works, but the enterprise is remembered in the name of the site, Brandy Island.

The brandy was not a great commercial success, and Buscot ended up bankrupting Campbell as it had his predecessor, with the result that the estate had to be sold after his death.

Barons Faringdon

In 1889 the house was bought by Alexander Henderson, a successful financier, created 1ST BARON FARING-DON in 1916, who filled the house with pictures from his dazzling art collection. Among them was a series of four paintings by Edward Burne-Jones called The Legend of Briar Rose. Henderson acquired the original four pictures in 1890 and when Burne-Jones visited Buscot and saw his paintings in their new surroundings he decided to add a number of scenes linking the pictures together to form a frieze, which can still be seen in the Saloon at Buscot.

Buscot is renowned for its remarkable water gardens, which were laid out in the early 20th century by HAROLD PETO, with fountains, waterfalls and long vistas from the house to the lakes. One vista culminates at a monumental urn containing the relics of the 2nd Baron Faringdon, who was one of the 'bright young things' of the 1920s.

Today Buscot Park is owned by the National Trust and open to the public, but is leased back to the Faringdons who remain in residence.

Pillboxes

The next stretch of river is relatively straight and moseys past a number of overgrown concrete pillboxes, placed here in 1940 to reinforce the river as a line of defence against a German invasion, as a thousand years before it had been a fortified boundary for the Saxons, both against each other (Wessex versus Mercia) and against the Danes.

As the river reaches the pretty wooden footbridge at Eaton and its attendant cottage, the scene today is tranquil, but it wasn't always so.

Hart's Weir

This was formerly where the river plunged over HART'S WEIR, which had THE GREATEST FALL OF ANY WEIR ON THE UPPER THAMES, some 4 ft (1.2 m) in low water. It was also the site of THE LAST FLASH LOCK ON THE THAMES.

Hart's Weir, the low bridge across it and the flash lock were all removed in 1936 and replaced by Eaton Footbridge, while the popular Anchor Inn, which stood next to the keeper's cottage, was burned down in 1980. The weir keeper was also the publican for the ANCHOR, a hostelry which was established to serve the river traffic and the men who operated the two water-wheels set up here by Robert Tertius Campbell to pump water to the Buscot Park estate.

The National Trust, which owns the

Flash Locks

Flash locks were the earliest kind of lock in use on the Thames. A set of boards or paddles was placed across a section of the weir to act as a gate, held against the current by upright beams called rymers. When a boat was ready to pass through, a number of the paddles were removed and the build-up of water would rush or 'flash' through, with the boat surfing on top of the surge. Afterwards the paddles were lowered back into place to raise the water level once more.

The manoeuvre was exhilarating and extremely hazardous, requiring great skill and timing, both from the boatman and the fellow operating the gate. A good description of shooting a Thames flash lock can be found in C.S. Forester's *Hornblower and the Atropos*, in which Hornblower takes the helm of the barge on which he is travelling as a passenger from Gloucester to London via the river and the Thames and Severn Canal.

land today, decided not to rebuild the Anchor, and all that is left of this once bustling place are the keeper's cottage and the mooring cuts for the barges that delivered goods to Buscot Park, now used by pleasure boats.

Kelmscott Manor

Just peeping over the top of the screen of trees on the left bank ahead is the gabled roof of KELMSCOTT MANOR, a mellow stone farmhouse built in 1570,

which 300 years later became the country house of the great Victorian writer and reformer WILLIAM MORRIS.

Morris had for some time been 'looking about for a house for the wife and kids', a retreat from their busy life in London, and in 1871, while exploring with his wife Jane and their friend the pre-Raphaelite artist DANTE GABRIEL ROSSETTI, he came across 'Kelmscott, a little village about two miles above Radcot bridge – a heaven on earth; an old stone Elizabethan house . . . and such a garden! Close down on the river, a boat house and all things handy'.

Kelmscot and Radcot are actually spelt with just one 't', but Morris seemed to prefer two – hence Kelmscott Manor is now always spelt with two 't's while its parent village (and Radcot) make do with one.

Morris took out a joint lease on Kelmscott Manor with Rossetti, and for the first four or five years was unable to really enjoy it because Rossetti was obsessed with Morris's wife Jane, painting numerous pictures of her and writing her endless love poems. Morris decided to let them get on with it in the hope that Rossetti would tire of the affair, which in the end he did. Rossetti was a man of the city, hated the damp cold of the old house, disliked the village, which he described as 'the doziest clump of old beehives', and found country life dull and monotonous.

Kelmscot didn't like Rossetti very much either. Addicted to laudanum, he insulted the villagers and swore at the fishermen as they walked past the house on their way to the river. Eventually he was more or less forced to leave and Morris was able to enjoy Kelmscott, and Jane, in peace. The newly reconciled couple received many distinguished guests at Kelmscott, such as George Bernard Shaw and W.B. Yeats, with whom they took long walks by the river and played draughts in the evening.

Morris and his family were amongst the first to use the River Thames purely for pleasure, and on one famous occasion they travelled up the river from their London home at Hammersmith to Kelmscott in a large punt that Morris called a houseboat, and his daughter May described as 'a sort of insane gondola'.

Morris was at his happiest at Kelmscott and it inspired much of his work. He loved the way the manor looked so natural in its setting, as though it had 'grown up out of the soil', and Kelmscott more than any other building inspired his belief that buildings embodied the past, and were imbued

with the spirits of those who had lived there before. The aim of the Society for the Protection of Ancient Buildings, which Morris founded in 1877, and which led indirectly to the National Trust, was to protect old buildings such as Kelmscott from insensitive modernisation or restoration that ignored their atmosphere and history.

He loved the views from the house, writing '. . . through its south window you . . . catch a glimpse of the Thames clover meadows and the pretty little elm crowned hill over in Berkshire . . .', and his designs were taken from the natural world he saw around him at Kelmscott.

He named his London house and his KELMSCOTT PRESS after his country home, and in his novel *News from Nowhere* Kelmscott Manor illustrates the frontispiece and becomes 'the old house by the Thames', the centre of his Socialist paradise after the revolution.

Morris died in London in 1896 and his body was brought to Lechlade by train (the station was closed by the Beeching cuts in 1962) and then carried to the church at Kelmscott on a simple red and yellow farm wagon covered in bulrushes, flowers and willow. He was buried beneath a long, roofed tomb designed by his friend the architect Philip Webb. His wife Jane and their daughters Jenny and May are buried alongside.

Kelmscott Manor is now owned by the Society of Antiquaries and is open to the public at certain times during the summer months. It has been kept as near as possible to how it was when William Morris and Jane lived there, furnished throughout with original furniture, decorations and paintings. The garden is also laid out as Morris had it. It is still subject to frequent floods, as it was in Morris's day, when the whole family would row in a boat across the lawn and straight on to the river. The house and indeed the entire village are almost unchanged since William Morris lived there, and a visit to this hidden and timeless place is pure relaxation.

Eaton Hastings

On the south bank, just after an acute 'S' bend, trees and a barn conceal the small church of St Michael and All Angels, set on a small eminence behind the former rectory at Eaton Hastings, one of old Berkshire's deserted villages. The church is part Norman and has a 13th-century chancel, a west window designed by William Morris and two windows by Burne-Jones. The 1st Baron Faringdon of Buscot Park is buried here beneath an angel in a flowing gown carved by George Frampton. The village was diminished, probably by the plague, and now consists just of the church and a few scattered farms and cottages.

Radcot

At RADCOT, the river splits in two, with the original course flowing under OLD RADCOT BRIDGE, THE OLDEST BRIDGE OVER THE THAMES. Most of the present structure of three ribbed Gothic arches dates from 1200, and there are Saxon records that place a bridge here in AD 958 or before – this was a main route between the Saxon kingdoms of Wessex and Mercia.

The central arch of Radcot Bridge was rebuilt in 1393 after being destroyed at the BATTLE OF RADCOT BRIDGE in 1387. A niche on the downstream side of the central arch is thought to have held a memorial cross for those who died in the battle.

The Battle of Radcot Bridge

In 1387 Richard II's favourite, Robert de Vere, Earl of Oxford, marching south with reinforcements for the King in London, arrived at Radcot to find that the Earl of Derby, later Henry IV, had smashed the central arch of the bridge and was waiting with his soldiers on the other side. De Vere and his army were now trapped between the Earl of Derby and more enemy soldiers coming down from the north. His men fled and were either captured or drowned, and de Vere was forced to jump into the river with his horse and swim upstream to safety and exile in France.

This victory led to the Merciless Parliament of 1388, when the powerful barons known as the Lords Appellant, who opposed Richard II's desire to make peace with France, ruled that all King Richard's advisors and supporters should be executed for treason.

New Radcot Bridge

There were formerly three channels here, each crossed by a bridge, but today there are only two in use; the original river course under Old Radcot Bridge

and a new channel to the north, cut in 1787 for boats heading for the Thames and Severn Canal. The new cut is crossed by New Radcot Bridge, built in 1787, which has a very narrow single arch and is on a slight bend, making navigation extremely difficult – as Fred Thacker, author of *The Stripling Thames*, put it in 1920, 'many a steersman has here in mere seconds lost the sedulously acquired reputation of a lifetime'. Sitting in the pleasant gardens of the 19th-century Swan Hotel next to the bridge on a fine day, sipping from a flagon of best ale, and watching red-faced helmsmen gesticulating and swearing as they careen into the side of the bridge one after another, must be one of life's supreme pleasures.

After Radcot Lock the river now wiggles through a very narrow, winding, overgrown stretch between willow trees and wild meadows to Rushey Lock.

Well, I never *knew this* *about*
THE RIVER THAMES

The word 'MEANDER' comes from the historical name for the BUYUK MENDERES RIVER in southwestern Turkey, famous for its slow, winding course.

An unusual entertainment for which the Trout Inn at St John's Bridge is renowned is AUNT SALLY, a pub game popular with the Victorians which involves throwing things at a wooden skittle known as an

Aunt Sally, which is dressed up in an old woman's clothes. While mainly confined to pubs in and around Oxfordshire, Aunt Sally is taken very seriously by those who play it regularly and there are some highly competitive leagues here of long standing.

There are two stories as to the origin of the name BLOOMER'S HOLE. One tells of a waggoner called Bloomer who was drowned here while trying to cross the river with his horse and cart. A more cheerful tale suggests that a local rector called the Revd Bloomer was caught bathing here in the nude. Both men could be said to have committed a bit of a bloomer – could this be where the term comes from?

William Morris's most famous wallpaper design, THE WILLOW BOUGH PATTERN, was inspired by the willows down on the banks of the River Thames at Kelmscott.

RADCOT TO OXFORD

Tadpole Bridge – giving access to a Trout that once belonged to a Herring

Rushey Lock

RUSHEY LOCK can boast of one of the more unusual landmarks to be found on the Thames, a large, smiling topiary frog squatting in the gardens of the keeper's cottage. The cottage itself once served as a guesthouse and, because of its isolated position, attracted celebrities who wished to relax away from prying eyes. ERROL FLYNN stayed here, as did the ASTORS and DOUGLAS FAIRBANKS.

The river now flows under the graceful TADPOLE BRIDGE, a smaller version of Halfpenny Bridge at Lechlade. On the right bank is the Trout Inn, which at one time sported over the door the legend: 'The Trout, kept by A. Herring'.

Buckland House

Looking down from the crest of the hills about 1 mile (1.6 km) to the south of Tadpole Bridge is BUCKLAND HOUSE, described by Pevsner as 'the most splendid Georgian house in the country'. It was built in Palladian style by JOHN WOOD THE YOUNGER (architect of the

Royal Crescent in Bath) for SIR ROBERT THROCKMORTON in 1757. The gardens were laid out by a Catholic contemporary of Capability Brown, RICHARD WOODS, and include lakes, a temple and THE BEST-PRESERVED ICE HOUSE IN BRITAIN. Queen Mary, wife of George V, had many of her precious objets d'art stored in the basement of Buckland House during the Second World War.

Shifford

On the Oxfordshire bank, close to the 1,000-acre (400 ha) Chimney Meadows nature reserve, is SHIFFORD, the Saxons' 'sheep ford', now consisting of a farm, a cottage and a church in a field by the river. Here in this field, in AD 890, KING ALFRED held THE FIRST RECORDED ENGLISH PARLIAMENT. In the words of an Anglo-Saxon poem, 'There sat at Shifford many thanes, many bishops and many learned men, wise earls and awful knights; there was Earl Elfrick, very learned in the law; and Alfred, England's herdsman, England's darling; he was King of England; he taught them that could hear how they should live.'

Longworth

Up on a ridge overlooking the Thames is the charming village of LONGWORTH, with an ancient church and manorhouse. The house was the home of the prominent regicide SIR HENRY MARTEN (1602–80), one of the commissioners who signed the death warrant of Charles I. Longworth was also home to another unpopular figure.

> I do not love thee Dr Fell,
> The reason why I cannot tell;
> But this I know, and know full well,
> I do not love thee, Dr Fell.

The Old Rectory at Longworth was the birthplace of the aforementioned DR JOHN FELL (1625–86), Dean of Christ Church and Bishop of Oxford. In his position as Dean, Dr Fell had occasion to chastise a student, the future satirist Tom Brown, but offered to withdraw the threat of expulsion if Brown apologised and composed on the spot a translation of Martial's epigram on Sabadius: 'I do not love thee, Sabidius, nor can I say why: I can only say this, I do not love thee.'

While best remembered as the subject of Tom Brown's witty epigram, Dr Fell greatly expanded the Oxford University Press (see p. 41), and was a founder of the Sheldonian Theatre, in which he installed the university's first printing presses. He was also responsible for the building of Christ Church's famous gatehouse Tom Tower, and for transferring to it from the cathedral the Great Tom bell from which the tower takes its name.

Buried in the churchyard of St Mary's Longworth is former UN Weapons Inspector DR DAVID KELLY (1944–2003), who lived in Southmoor, near Longworth, and died in controversial circumstances at HARROWDOWN HILL,

a woodland beauty spot between Longworth and the Thames.

> On Harrowdown the golden
> gorse now flames
> While in rich meadows set
> with many flowers
> The cattle graze beside
> the silver Thames
> Or seek its shallows cool
> in sunny hours.
> WILFRED HOWE-NURSE
> (poet who formerly lived in
> Dr David Kelly's house)

Newbridge

NEWBRIDGE, which carries the main road between Abingdon and Witney, is THE SECOND OLDEST BRIDGE OVER THE THAMES, and is so called by virtue of being newer than Old Radcot Bridge upstream. Newbridge was built in 1250 and, like Radcot, was constructed by monks to connect the

Cotswold wool towns with the south.

The River Windrush joins just upstream of Newbridge, having flowed from the Cotswolds through Bourton-on-the-Water, Burford and Witney, where its waters helped in the making of Witney's famous blankets.

Two Inns

Newbridge is a popular place for gathering, being blessed with two fine pubs, one on either side of the river. On the right bank, just upstream of the bridge, is the MAYBUSH, built on the site of a 15th-century hermitage lived in by the bridge-keeper, a hermit called Thomas Brigges or Thomas of the Bridge. The Maybush is thought to be 16th century and witness to skirmishes here during the Civil War when the bridge was broken in the middle to prevent Royalist soldiers from Oxford using it to march south.

On the Oxfordshire bank, just downstream from the bridge, is the romantically named ROSE REVIVED, tucked away behind weeping willows and bulrushes. The story goes that a passing Oliver Cromwell dropped in for refreshment (presumably before smashing up the bridge) and ordered two flagons of ale, one for himself and one for the rose he was wearing, which was drooping. He placed the rose in the flagon and, sure enough, it revived.

In the good old days, when the Maybush was in Berkshire and the Rose Revived in Oxfordshire, the two hostelries had different closing times, and when one closed there would be a stampede across the bridge to the other,

where customers could enjoy another half-hour of drinking.

Northmoor

NORTHMOOR, beside Northmoor Lock, is a very pretty marshland village gathered around the small 13th-century church of St Denys. Here, in 1766, ignoring the pursed lips of the gentry, WILLIAM FLOWER, 2ND VISCOUNT ASHBROOK, married beautiful BETTY RUDGE, daughter of the local ferryman, whom he had fallen in love with while fishing on the Thames. Proving that there was far more social mobility in previous centuries than now, the ferryman's daughter's granddaughter became DUCHESS OF MARLBOROUGH when she married Winston Churchill's great-grandfather, George Spencer-Churchill, 6th Duke of Marlborough, in 1846.

Bablock Hythe

Crossing the stripling
Thames at Bablockhythe
Trailing in the cool stream
thy fingers wet,
As the slow punt swings round.
From 'The Scholar Gypsy'
by MATTHEW ARNOLD

There has been a ferry for over 1,000 years at BABLOCK HYTHE, and it has been known as an important crossing point since the time of the Romans. Although in the middle of nowhere, Bablock Hythe was always well patronised as it lies on a direct route from Oxford to the West.

In the Scholar Gypsy's day the ferry consisted of a wide, flat-bottomed punt hauled across by means of a rope suspended above the river – which constituted as fine a booby trap to passing traffic as you could wish for. The rope was eventually replaced by a chain that lay on the river bed and could be raised by a winch when needed. For 30 or 40 years until the 1960s a slightly precarious vehicle ferry that could hold two or three cars or a small lorry plied back and forth.

Today the ferry service is rather intermittent, although someone from the pub might take you across in a small outboard motor boat if asked.

There has been an inn at Bablock Hythe for almost as long as the ferry. Up until about 20 years ago it was called the Chequers, but when the pub was completely rebuilt in the early 1990s the name was changed to the Ferry Inn and later to the Ferryman.

The design of the modern pub firmly eschews the chocolate-box beauty of its predecessor, instead opting to chime with the more indeterminate delights of the sprawling caravan site next door.

Stanton Harcourt

Travelling downstream from Bablock Hythe it is sometimes possible to glimpse the tower of STANTON HARCOURT church across the flat Oxfordshire fields to the west.

The Harcourt family has owned the manor here since the 12th century and the church is full of Harcourt

tombs. Sir Robert Harcourt, died 1470, lies beside his wife Margaret who, like her husband, is wearing THE ORDER OF THE GARTER – ONE OF TWO WOMEN TO SPORT THIS RARE HONOUR IN OXFORDSHIRE, the other being Chaucer's granddaughter the Duchess of Suffolk, who rests in the church at Ewelme. ROBERT HARCOURT, STANDARD BEARER TO HENRY VII, lies beneath a fragment of the flag he bore at Bosworth Field in 1485 and waved in triumph over the corpse of Richard III to usher in the era of the Tudors. A slightly less heroic note is struck by the gilded figure of SIR WILLIAM HARCOURT, Liberal Chancellor of the Exchequer who brought in Death Duties in 1894.

When the main branch of the Harcourts moved to Nuneham Courtenay in 1757, they dismantled much of their old manor-house at Stanton Harcourt for use in the stately new home. What they left behind is hugely attractive, a stone and half-timbered farmhouse with, at one end, an enormous four-square, battlemented, medieval Great Kitchen, with an octagonal roof that acted as a funnel or chimney for the smoke from the kitchen's open fires.

Behind the kitchen is the 15th-century POPE'S TOWER, built above a domestic chapel. At the top, reached by a winding stairway, is a small panelled room where the poet ALEXANDER POPE worked for two

summers on his translation of Homer's *Iliad*, as a guest of Viscount Harcourt. On a pane of glass in one of the windows he wrote, 'In the year 1718 Alexander Pope finished here the fifth volume of Homer.'

Wytham Great Wood

At this point Oxford is only about 4 miles (6.4 km) to the east as the crow flies, but the distance by river is some 11 miles (18 km) as the Thames does a sweeping loop north around the hanging WYTHAM GREAT WOOD before turning back south and into Oxford. After winding past the great earthen bank that contains Farmoor reservoir, completed in 1976, the river passes through PINKHILL LOCK and then under the rather gorgeous classical arches of ...

Swinford Bridge

Balustraded SWINFORD (swine ford) BRIDGE, many people's choice as the most beautiful bridge over the Thames, is ONE OF ONLY THREE TOLLBRIDGES ON THE RIVER THAMES (the others are at Whitchurch and Dartford). It was built for £5,000 by the Earl of Abingdon in 1767, at the request of George III who had fallen into the water while using the ferry. In gratitude, the King passed an act of parliament granting the earl and his 'heirs and assigns' the income from the tolls and – this is the nub – TAX FREE for ever. Indeed, along with the added bonus that the act prohibited the build-

ing of another bridge within 3 miles, the earl's public-spiritedness has ever since 'been amply repaid by the revenue derived from this undertaking'.

In 2009 the bridge was sold at auction for just over £1 million, and with cars being charged 5p and lorries 50p it is expected to raise a tax-free £100,000 annually. The risk is that the owner of the bridge has to maintain and repair it, but it still looks like a pretty sound investment.

Eynsham

Swinford Bridge carries a B-road from Oxford into EYNSHAM, one of the oldest villages in England, mentioned in the Anglo-Saxon Chronicle. Eynsham Abbey was founded in 1005, and the first Abbot of Eynsham was AELFRIC, THE MOST PROLIFIC WRITER IN OLD ENGLISH that we know of. His works include an introduction to Bible studies, the lives of the saints, a Latin grammar in English and a translation of the venerable Bede's *De Temporibus*.

The RIVER EVENLODE enters the Thames near Eynsham, the last of the tributaries from the Cotswolds.

King's Lock

KING'S LOCK by Wolvercote marks THE NORTHERNMOST POINT ON THE RIVER THAMES. Just above the lock is the start of the DUKE'S CUT, connecting the Thames with the Oxford Canal to Coventry and the Midlands, and a small back stream which served the OXFORD

UNIVERSITY PAPER MILLS, whose tall red-brick chimney could once be seen across the fields at Wolvercote. There was a mill at WOLVERCOTE as far back as the 14th century, when it was used for fulling cloth. In about 1680 the mill was converted to making paper for the expanding Oxford University Press. It was demolished in 2004.

Isis

At Thames Bridge, where the river flows under the Oxford ring road, the Thames becomes known as the ISIS, and it continues to be referred to by that name while it flows through Oxford and as far as Iffley Lock.

Historically, the Thames was known by many as the Isis right from the source as far as its junction with the River Thame at Dorchester, where it became Thame-isis or Thames. On Ordnance Survey maps the river is still marked as the 'River Thames or Isis'.

Trout Inn

After Thames Bridge comes the slightly skew GODSTOW BRIDGE, in two parts, with the older, 17th-century section to the north following the original course of the river and the newer section of 1892 traversing a lock cut. Tucked in just past the older bridge is the celebrated TROUT INN, with its riverside terrace and peacocks.

Owing to its favoured location by the river and its proximity to the centre of Oxford, the Trout Inn has been popular with undergraduates since it was built in the late 17th century. Evelyn Waugh mentions the Trout in *Brideshead Revisited* and it has become known to a more modern audience as a favourite haunt of INSPECTOR MORSE. Colin Dexter, author of the Morse books, was a regular, and the Trout appeared in a number of episodes of the TV adaptation starring John Thaw as Morse. In 2001 the Trout was honoured by a visit from former US PRESIDENT BILL CLINTON and his daughter CHELSEA, who was on a post-graduate course at University College.

The Trout is built on the site of the former hospice to GODSTOW NUNNERY, the stark remains of which stand on the other side of the river, the subject of a much-admired painting by the Victorian watercolour artist George Price Boyce.

Fair Rosamund

The Benedictine nunnery at Godstow was consecrated in the presence of King Stephen in 1139 and provided an education for the daughters of noble families. One of the first to be educated there was ROSAMUND CLIFFORD, who was famed for her beauty and came to be known as the FAIR ROSAMUND.

It was while walking along the banks of the Thames near Godstow that Rosamund first met Henry II, who instantly fell in love with her and carried her off to his palace at nearby Woodstock. Here, according to legend, he built her a bower hidden from the world by an impenetrable maze. Henry's jealous Queen Eleanor found her way through the maze by following a silken thread from Rosamund's dress and demanded of her rival that she drink poison or 'get thee to a nunnery!' Rosamund chose the nunnery at Godstow, where she died not long afterwards in 1176. She was buried before the high altar and her magnificent tomb was every day strewn with flowers sent by the king. In 1191 Bishop Hugh of Lincoln visited and ordered 'that Harlot's body' to be removed to a smaller chapel so that 'other women, warned by her example, may refrain from unlawful love'. The chapel where she was buried is roofless now, and is just about all that is left of the nunnery. Fair Rosamund is said to haunt the Trout, appearing as a 'White Lady' and smelling of the heather which lined her tomb.

Alice in Wonderland

'Duckworth and I made an expedition up the river to Godstow with the three Liddells: we had tea on the bank there ... On which occasion I told them the fairytale of Alice's Adventures Under Ground, which I undertook to write out for Alice ...'

It was while sitting in a meadow beside the nunnery at Godstow, one July afternoon in 1862, that the REVD CHARLES DODGSON first told the story of Alice's

Alice in Wonderland

'Alice was beginning to get very tired of sitting by her sister on the bank and of having nothing to do; once or twice she had peeped into the book her sister was reading, but it had no pictures or conversation in it, "and what is the use of a book," thought Alice, "without pictures or conversations?" So she was considering in her own mind (as well as she could, for the hot day made her very sleepy and stupid) whether the pleasure of making a daisy chain would be worth the trouble of getting up and picking the daisies, when suddenly a white rabbit with pink eyes ran close by her ...'

Adventures Underground to ALICE
LIDDELL. Dodgson, a mathematics tutor
at Christ Church College, had invited the
daughters of the Dean, ten-year-old
Alice and her sisters Edith and Lorina,
for a picnic, along with his university
friend the Revd Robinson Duckworth.
The five of them made regular outings
to Godstow, rowing up the river from
Folly Bridge with a 'large basket full of
cakes' while Dodgson made up stories to
entertain them. Alice asked Dodgson to
write the stories down for her, and in
1865 Alice's Adventures Underground
was published as *Alice's Adventures in
Wonderland*. Dodgson wrote under the
name Lewis Carroll to avoid publicity.

Godstow Lock

GODSTOW LOCK IS THE FIRST ELECTRI-
CALLY OPERATED LOCK ON THE RIVER
THAMES, travelling downstream.
Below Godstow Lock, for the first
time the dreaming spires of Oxford
come into view across the wide open
spaces of . . .

Port Meadow

And that sweet city with
her dreaming spires
She needs not June for
beauty's heightening
MATTHEW ARNOLD

PORT MEADOW is 350 acres (142 ha) of
lush flood meadow that for over 1,000
years has been used as common grazing
land. It was given in perpetuity to the
people of Oxford by King Alfred, in
return for their help in defending the
area against the Danes. Today the
meadow provides a wonderful recreation area where people can walk their
dogs, children can gambol and fly kites,
families can picnic, and horses, cattle,
geese and swans can graze.

During the Civil War, Oxford was a
Royalist stronghold and Charles I's army
set up camp on Port Meadow. In the
17th and 18th centuries the fields were
used for horse races and, in the Second
World War, evacuees from Dunkirk
were rested here. The meadows are

often subject to flooding, and in a cold winter the water can freeze over and be used for skating.

The river is very shallow at its banks here and the cattle and horses can wander down and drink in safety with their front feet planted in the water, while the passing pleasure boats are unable to moor up and frighten the animals or spoil the view. The whole scene, with its misty backdrop of Oxford spires, is redolent of Olde England and is utterly charming.

Binsey

On the opposite bank from Port Meadow is the tiny hamlet of BINSEY, with its little Norman church whose first recorded incumbent was NICHOLAS BREAKSPEAR, THE ONLY ENGLISHMAN TO BECOME POPE (Adrian IV). Binsey's pretty 17th-century thatched pub, THE PERCH, is said to be haunted by an indebted sailor who drowned himself in the river.

GERARD MANLEY HOPKINS wrote a poem about the avenue of poplars at Binsey when he visited in 1879 and found the trees being felled:

My aspens dear whose
airy cages quelled
Quelled or quenched in
leaves the leaping sun
All felled, felled, all are felled.

The poplars were replaced and the new trees survived until 2004, when they too reached the end of their natural lives and were felled – new saplings were planted and are doing well.

Medley Weir

The River Thames as it flows between Port Meadow and Binsey is a romantic spot and some 400 years ago the poet GEORGE WITHER came to MEDLEY WEIR, a little way downstream, to lament his lost love:

In summertime to Medley
My love and I would go
But now, alas, she's left me,
Falero lero loo.

Medley Weir, alas, is no more, but close to where it used to bubble is an important place for boat-building. There are signs that boats were made at this spot

Punting

Surprisingly, Bossoms of Oxford make the poles for Cambridge punts – Cambridge poles are wooden while Oxford punt poles are made of aluminium. In Oxford the punts are operated with the smooth raised platform, called the till or box, at the front and the punter standing inside the boat on the shallow decking. In Cambridge the punter actually stands on the till, which is at the back of the boat.

in prehistoric times, while today it is the home of BOSSOMS OF OXFORD, one of the oldest and most famous boatyards on the Thames. Founded in 1830, it remained in the Bossom family until 1944 and is one of few surviving boatyards in England that exhibited at the first London Boat Show in 1954.

Well, I never knew this about
THE RIVER THAMES

To the north of Rushey Lock can be seen the impressive 170 ft (52 m) high, 13th-century spire of St Mary the Virgin in BAMPTON. The spire is unique in Oxfordshire for having four dormer windows at its base. Bampton is home TO THE OLDEST TROUPES OF MORRIS DANCERS IN BRITAIN, three family troupes that carry on a tradition going back more than 600 years.

The Old Rectory at LONGWORTH was also the birthplace of R.D. BLACKMORE (1825–1900), author of Lorna Doone, whose father was briefly curate at Longworth.

The presence of the village of APPLETON, in the Vale of the White Horse on the right bank near Northmoor Lock, is indicated by the unusual capped tower of St Lawrence Church peeking above the trees about a ½ mile (800 m) away across the fields. Right next to the church, tucked behind half a moat is APPLETON MANOR, which dates from 1190 and is ONE OF THE OLDEST HOUSES IN ENGLAND. Appleton Manor could claim to be THE BIRTHPLACE OF THE ENGLISH MERINGUE – the earliest

known recipe for what we now call meringue, or as she put it 'bisket bread', was written down by LADY ELINOR FETTIPLACE of Appleton Manor in 1603.

WYTHAM GREAT WOOD is owned by the University of Oxford and is used for zoology studies and climate change research.

EYNSHAM LOCK was the PENULTIMATE LOCK TO BE BUILT ON THE THAMES, beginning operation in 1928.

Buried in the cemetery at WOLVERCOTE are SIR THOMAS CHAPMAN (1846–1919), father of Lawrence of Arabia, and J.R.R. TOLKIEN, author of the *Lord of the Rings* trilogy.

Revd Charles Dodgson was familiar with BINSEY, and he turned the healing well at Binsey into the treacle well in *Alice in Wonderland*. Binsey was also the home of Alice Liddell's governess, MISS PRICKETT, on whom Dodgson modelled the Red Queen.

OXFORD

Oxford Castle – Saxon fort, royal home, prison and hotel

Oxford Castle

At the site of Medley Weir, at the south end of Port Meadow, the river splits around Fiddler's Island and then heads into the centre of Oxford along several different courses. Castle Mill Stream follows the original course of the Thames and runs right past the walls of OXFORD CASTLE, which was built as a motte and bailey castle in 1071 on the western edge of the Saxon fortified town. The castle, amazingly undiscovered by most visitors to Oxford, incorporates part of a stone Saxon tower, which survives in almost all its lofty magnificence, as does the Motte or Mound.

The castle became the home of Henry I's only daughter EMPRESS MATILDA and in the winter of 1142 was besieged by Matilda's cousin King Stephen. Matilda was lowered from the castle walls dressed all in white, so as to be camouflaged against the snow, and escaped across the frozen river to Wallingford (see p. 70). For most of its existence the castle has been used as a prison. In 1996 the prison was closed, and the castle has since been converted into a shopping centre and hotel – Oxford Castle is THE FIRST PRISON IN BRITAIN TO BE TURNED INTO A HOTEL.

Osney Bridge

What now forms the main channel for boats was cut by the monks of Osney Abbey to power their mill, and enters modern Oxford under OSNEY BRIDGE. This was built in 1889 on the site of a stone bridge constructed by the monks, the central arch of which collapsed in 1885 sending several pedestrians into the water and causing the death of 11-year-old Rhoda Miles.

With headroom of only 7½ ft (2.28 m) Osney Bridge has THE LOWEST CLEAR-ANCE OF ANY BRIDGE ON THE RIVER THAMES. Large boats cannot pass under it, which is rather fortuitous since it means that the ubiquitous 'gin palaces' are forced to turn back here and leave the beauties of the upper Thames to more sedate narrowboats, small cabin cruisers, canoes, punts and rowing boats.

Osney Abbey

A few hundred yards further down-stream is OSNEY LOCK, built by prisoners from Oxford Castle Prison in 1790. Next to the lock is a barn, the only surviving structure from OSNEY ABBEY, founded in 1129 by Robert D'Oyly, Governor of Oxford. In 1222 ENGLAND'S FIRST JEWISH MARTYRDOM took place at Osney when a deacon of the Christian church called Robert was put to death for marrying a Jewish woman and renouncing Jesus.

After Osney the main boating chan-nel winds its way through the rather unexciting back streets of Oxford west of the city centre, with not much to see until Folly Bridge hoves into view.

Folly Bridge

FOLLY BRIDGE brings the main road from Abingdon and the south into Oxford. In Saxon days there was a timber construc-tion here, and the first stone bridge, or Grand Pont, was built in 1085 by Robert D'Oyly as part of a long causeway along the line of the Abingdon road. The Norman bridge survived until the 19th century, when it was replaced by the pres-ent structure built by Ebenezer Perry, which was completed in 1827.

The bridge has been known by several different names, Grand Pont, South Bridge and, in the 13th century, Friar's Bridge – in honour of Friar Roger Bacon, who had an observatory and laboratory on the top floor of a tower at the north end of the bridge. In

Great Tom

Between 1541 and 1545 Osney Abbey served as Oxford's cathedral. GREAT TOM, OXFORD'S LOUDEST BELL, originally hung in the bell tower at Osney before it was moved to the new Oxford Cathedral in 1545. It now hangs in TOM TOWER over the entrance to Christ Church.

Each evening Great Tom strikes 101 times at 9pm Oxford local time (which is 9.05 Greenwich Time). Before the coming of the railways led to time being standardised across the country every town had its own local time, which can be calculated by how far east or west that town lies from the Prime Meridian at Greenwich. Christ Church originally had 100 students and Great Tom strikes 101 times for each student plus one, summoning them back to the college before the gates are locked for the night. The bell resumes at 8am and then chimes for every hour, Greenwich Time, until 9.05pm.

the 17th century the tower was taken over by a Mr Welcome, who added another storey, giving the building a top-heavy appearance as if it was about to topple over. It became known as 'Welcome's Folly', and although the folly was demolished in 1779 the name stuck to the bridge.

Roger Bacon

(c.1214–92)

ROGER BACON was born of a wealthy family in Ilchester, in Somerset, and trained at Oxford in logic and natural philosophy.

Blessed with an enquiring mind, he was way ahead of his time. He studied optics and refraction, making observations that led to the development of spectacles and telescopes; he foresaw aeroplanes, steamships and cars; and he practised alchemy, or what we now call chemistry, inventing a form of gunpowder. From his observatory on Folly Bridge he watched

the heavens, using maths to calculate the positions of the planets and the stars and how they affected life on earth. Later in life he became a Franciscan Friar, but he continued to write books and pamphlets about his experiments and was eventually condemned by the Franciscan brotherhood and imprisoned because of 'certain suspected novelties' – meaning his interest in alchemy and astrology.

Bacon's lasting legacy was his *OPUS MAJUS*, which he wrote in medieval Latin for Pope Clement IV. The book describes his studies, experiments, discoveries and conclusions, and his writings influenced scholars and scientists for hundreds of years afterwards. As one of the first scientists, long before the term was invented, he is often referred to today in the continuing debate between Science and Religion, as his firm assertion in *Opus Majus* is that theology and the Bible are the foundation of all the sciences.

Modern Follies

Folly Bridge is in two parts, separated by a small island on which there was once a mill. The most interesting building there today is No. 5 FOLLY BRIDGE, a redbrick castellated house festooned with iron balconies and niches filled with statues, allegedly of the fallen women who worked there when the place was a brothel. In 1911 it became rather more respectable as the home of science historian ROBERT GUNTHER, founder of Oxford's Museum of the History of Science.

Close to Folly Bridge are two Oxford landmarks. SALTERS STEAMERS were founded in 1858 as Salters Bros and built the colourful college barges that were moored by Christ Church meadows to act as floating clubhouses for the university rowing clubs. Today Salters provide anything from steamboat trips on the Thames, as far as Staines, to narrowboats, cabin cruisers, punts and rowing boats for pottering around Oxford. They have also built several boats that have been rowed to victory in the Boat Race.

The HEAD OF THE RIVER pub occupies a former warehouse and gets its name from the winner of the Summer Eights rowing races which take place in May downstream from Folly Bridge.

It is by Folly Bridge that academic Oxford comes down to the Thames to go boating, which is appropriate, because this is where Oxford started.

Oxford

'That sweet city with her dreaming spires'
MATTHEW ARNOLD
(viewing from Boars Hill)

Oxford began as a place where Saxon farmers could ford the River Thames with their cattle or oxen. The original ford is thought to be near Folly Bridge.

Sometime early in the 8th century, a king's daughter named FRIDESWIDE, exiled from court for refusing to marry, founded a small priory where Oxford Cathedral now stands. The priory offered hospitality to those using the ford, and in 872 King Alfred stopped here for refreshment while on his way

Radcliffe Camera –
first round library in England

up the river. He fell into conversation with the monks and there followed a spirited debate that lasted for several days. Oxford's reputation for learned discussion was born.

A fortified Saxon town developed, with its own mint established by King Athelstan in 925; King Canute held a Council of Saxons and Danes; and the Normans built a castle beside the Thames (see p. 46).

The Oxford of today sprang from the petulant decision of Henry II in 1167 to order English students home from France, simply because his rebellious Archbishop Thomas à Becket had taken

refuge there. The returning scholars made their way to Oxford, renowned as a place of learning since Alfred's day, and set up halls of learning similar to those they had known on the Continent.

UNIVERSITY COLLEGE, THE OLDEST OF THE 38 OXFORD COLLEGES, was founded in 1249 by William of Durham, who left money in his will to support ten students of the arts. Oxford is therefore THE OLDEST UNIVERSITY IN THE ENGLISH-SPEAKING WORLD and second only to the Sorbonne in Europe.

Provisions of Oxford

Nine years after University College opened, Oxford experienced the first faint stirrings of English democracy when Simon de Montfort and a group of disgruntled nobles, upset by Henry III's expensive foreign commitments, met in Oxford and drew up the PROVISIONS OF OXFORD. These reaffirmed and refined the principles of Magna Carta (see p. 129) and formally stripped the King of his absolute power, by setting up committees and councils to oversee Church matters and taxation. A 'Council of Fifteen' was formed, which Henry had to consult about the handling of 'the common business of the realm and of the king'. These bodies would meet several times a year at a Great Council or parliament.

Henry's subsequent disregard for the Provisions led to war between the King and the barons, and in 1265 Simon de Montfort looked to widen his support by summoning the barons, the knights of the shires, and some burgesses or 'commoners', to meet downriver at Westminster for England's, and the modern world's, first truly representative parliament – the Mother of Parliaments.

The Provisions of Oxford was THE FIRST DOCUMENT OF ITS KIND TO BE WRITTEN IN ENGLISH, AS WELL AS FRENCH AND LATIN, so that it could be understood by everyone.

Oxford Cathedral

OXFORD CATHEDRAL is THE SMALLEST ANGLICAN CATHEDRAL IN ENGLAND. It was begun by the Normans in the 12th century on the site of the Saxon convent church built over the shrine of St Frideswide. In 1524, a few years before the Dissolution of the Monasteries, Cardinal Wolsey took over what

had become the priory church and demolished the west end to make room for Tom Quad, the courtyard of his new 'Cardinal College'. He intended to knock down the rest of the church too, and replace it with a new college chapel, but fell from power and died before this could happen. In 1546 Henry VIII refounded Cardinal College as Christ Church, with St Frideswide's established as both the college chapel and the cathedral church of Oxford – hence Oxford Cathedral is THE ONLY CHURCH IN THE WORLD THAT IS BOTH A CATHEDRAL AND A COLLEGE CHAPEL, and Christ Church is THE ONLY COLLEGE IN THE WORLD THAT IS ALSO A CATHEDRAL. Only Oxford academics can really understand it. Tom Quad and the dining hall of Christ Church were used as locations for the Harry Potter films.

Some Oxford Colleges

BALLIOL COLLEGE was founded in 1263 by JOHN BALLIOL, father of King John of Scotland, and THE ORIGINAL SWEETHEART. When he died in 1268 Balliol's wife Devorgilla had her husband's 'sweet heart' embalmed in an ivory casket banded with silver, which she carried around with her until her own death in 1290. She was buried at New Abbey in Kirkcudbrightshire in Scotland with the casket on her breast – and the abbey became known as Sweetheart Abbey. Master of Balliol in the mid-14th century was JOHN WYCLIFFE, who later translated the New Testament of the Bible into

English. Hanging in an interior passageway is a pair of oak gates, 700 years old and amongst the OLDEST WOODEN GATES IN ENGLAND. They used to stand at the entrance to the college and still bear scorch marks from the flames that consumed the Oxford Martyrs, Latimer and Ridley, as they were burned at the stake in the road outside.

BRASENOSE (founded 1509) takes its name from an old bronze knocker shaped like a nose that hung on the door of the original Brasenose Hall lodging house from which the college emerged. The knocker now hangs over the high table in Hall, having been retrieved in 1890 from a house in Stamford, Lincolnshire, where it was taken by students who moved there in the 14th century to get away from unrest between students and townsfolk in Oxford.

MAGDALEN COLLEGE (founded 1458) is identified by its fine Perpendicular

Great Tower of 1492, which in 1505 became THE FIRST BUILDING IN ENGLAND TO HAVE A CLOCK FIXED ON TO ITS EXTERIOR. At 6am on May Day morning the college choir sings from the roof of the tower, a tradition much enjoyed by OSCAR WILDE, who graduated from Magdalen in 1878 with a double first in Literae Humaniores. The poet JOHN BETJEMAN also attended Magdalen, accompanied by his teddy bear Archibald, which gave Evelyn Waugh the idea for Sebastian Flyte's teddy bear Aloysius in *Brideshead Revisited*. Betjeman, however, failed to get a degree, partly because he didn't get along with his tutor C.S. LEWIS, author of the Narnia novels, who taught at Oxford from 1925 until 1954. Comedian DUDLEY MOORE (1935–2002) also attended Magdalen.

MERTON COLLEGE (founded 1264) was OXFORD'S FIRST SELF-GOVERNING COLLEGE and boasts OXFORD'S OLDEST QUAD, MOB QUAD. MOB LIBRARY, founded in 1373 and THE OLDEST CONTINUOUSLY FUNCTIONING UNIVERSITY LIBRARY IN THE WORLD, houses THE FIRST PRINTED WELSH BIBLE. J.R.R. Tolkien invented the Elven language between giving lectures at Merton.

Boat-houses

Downstream from Folly Bridge the dreaming spires reveal themselves again, the Cathedral and the towers of Christ Church providing an elegant backdrop to the greensward of Christ Church meadows. The Summer Eights

Some Oxford Firsts

The UNIVERSITY OF OXFORD BOTANIC GARDEN, opened in 1621, was THE FIRST BOTANIC GARDEN IN BRITAIN.

The ASHMOLEAN MUSEUM, opened in 1683, was THE FIRST OFFICIAL PUBLIC MUSEUM IN THE WORLD – indeed, the word 'museum' was coined to describe it. The original contents came from the private collection of plants and curiosities gathered from around the world by royal gardeners JOHN TRADESCANT ELDER AND YOUNGER, which they willed to antiquarian ELIAS ASHMOLE, who in turn donated them to Oxford.

The RADCLIFFE CAMERA, designed by JAMES GIBBS and completed in 1749, was paid for with money from the royal physician DR JOHN RADCLIFFE and was THE FIRST ROUND LIBRARY IN ENGLAND. It boasts THE THIRD LARGEST UNSUPPORTED DOME IN ENGLAND and today functions as the main reading room for the BODLEIAN LIBRARY.

The WORLD'S FIRST LOLLIPOP LADY was unwrapped in Oxford in 1933.

In 1954 Oxford was the location for THE FIRST SUCCESSFUL ATTEMPT TO RUN ONE MILE IN UNDER FOUR MINUTES. The feat, which had been considered impossible, was achieved at the Iffley Road sports ground by 25-year-old ROGER BANNISTER, who as a consequence in January 1955 became THE FIRST RECIPIENT OF THE *SPORTS ILLUSTRATED* SPORTSMAN OF THE YEAR AWARD.

rowing races take place here in May, over a distance of 1½ miles between Iffley Lock and Folly Bridge. Along the left bank are the college boat-houses that store the racing boats, most of them modern but some remaining from the 1930s when they were built to replace the college barges. It is from the rowing clubs here that the Oxford Boat Race crew is chosen.

River Cherwell

Flowing into the Thames on either side of the boat-houses is the RIVER CHERWELL, fresh from its journey past Magdalen Tower. There were times past when the Cherwell poured out here so strongly that it backed up the Thames and caused a considerable tidal bore that travelled for up to 1 mile (1.6 km) through the city.

*Well, I never knew this
about*
THE RIVER THAMES

C.S. LEWIS died on 22 November 1963 – the same day that President Kennedy was assassinated.

MAGDALEN COLLEGE GARDENS are famous for their collection of rare SNAKE'S-HEAD FRITILLARIES, which flower in April (see p. 6).

'To the beautiful memory of Kenneth Grahame, husband of Elspeth and father of Alastair, who passed the river on July 6, 1932, leaving childhood and literature the more blessed because of him'
Epitaph to Kenneth Grahame written by his cousin Anthony Hope, author of *The Prisoner of Zenda.*

Behind Magdalen College Deer Park, in the churchyard of ST CROSS, lies the author of *The Wind in the Willows*, KENNETH GRAHAME (1859–1932). He is buried in the same grave as his son, ALASTAIR. The tales of riverbank folk that became *The Wind in the Willows* were originally told as bedtime stories for Alastair, who is thought to have possessed some of the excessive characteristics found in Mr Toad. Alastair was born blind in one eye and suffered from chronic bad health; and two days before his 20th birthday in May 1920, while an undergraduate at Oxford, he committed suicide by lying down on a railway track.

His father never really recovered from the tragedy.

The first batch of FRANK COOPER'S OXFORD MARMALADE was made in 1874 in Frank Cooper's Oxford shop, and was based on a recipe handed down to Cooper's wife, Sarah Jane, from her mother. It became very popular with the Oxford dons, and in 1910 a jar was taken to the Antarctic by Captain Scott – it was found buried in the snow years later, empty.

The first motor car made by MORRIS, BRITAIN'S FIRST MASS-PRODUCTION CAR COMPANY, was the MORRIS OXFORD, named after the city where it was produced in 1913. The MORRIS MINOR, also made in Cowley on the southern fringes of Oxford, was introduced in 1948 and went on to become THE FIRST MILLION-SELLING BRITISH CAR.

IFFLEY TO CLIFTON HAMPDEN

St Mary the Virgin, Iffley — one of England's finest Norman churches

Iffley Lock

The river now flows past Iffley Meadow, home to another colony of snake's-head fritillaries, to IFFLEY LOCK, where there was once a picturesque mill which burned down in 1908. The lock was built in 1631 and was THE FIRST POUND LOCK ON THE THAMES.

Iffley Lock is the starting point for the Eights and Torpids rowing races, which are given the off by the starting cannons that stand outside the Isis Tavern, a 19th-century island hostelry on the right bank that can only be reached by foot along the towpath. Until 1979 beer supplies were delivered by punt, but they now arrive in an electric hand cart. Peter de Wint painted the scene from the towpath, with Iffley Church in the background.

> Pound Locks are the type of lock used almost exclusively on rivers and canals today. They consist of a pound or chamber with a gate at each end which opens or closes to allow water to fill or empty the pound.

St Mary's, Iffley

ST MARY THE VIRGIN, IFFLEY, one of
the jewels of the Thames, sits on a hill
overlooking the river. It was built in
1170 and is one of the finest, most
unspoiled Norman churches in the
whole of England. Particularly fine is
the west end, with its glorious deep
doorway, three Norman windows and
a round window restored in 1858. Also
the south doorway, which boasts stone
carvings of flowers similar to those
found in the cathedral porch at Santi-
ago di Compostela in Spain. More
modern is a beautiful stained-glass
Nativity window by John Piper, given
to the church by his widow Myfanwy
in 1995.

Iffley has somehow kept its peaceful
village atmosphere despite being
subsumed into Oxford and squeezed
against the river by the encroaching
industrial suburbs of Cowley.

Downstream from Iffley Lock the
Isis becomes the Thames once more.

Sandford Lock

SANDFORD LOCK IS THE DEEPEST LOCK
ON THE NON-TIDAL THAMES, with a fall
of 8ft 10ins (2.68 m). Built in 1630, it
WAS ONE OF THE FIRST THREE POUND
LOCKS TO BE BUILT ON THE THAMES,
along with Iffley and Swift Ditch near
Abingdon. There was a famous mill
here owned by the Knights Templar
which in its latter days was converted
from grinding corn to making coloured
paper. It closed in 1982 and has been
converted into modern housing.
Beside the lock is the King's Arms,
where there has been an inn since the
15th century.

Just up from the lock is the infamous
SANDFORD 'LASHER', a devilishly fast-
flowing weir above a deep pool with
treacherous undercurrents, described by
Jerome K. Jerome as 'a very good place
to drown yourself in'. A stone obelisk
beside the weir commemorates those
who did indeed drown in the pool, and
in 1921 two more names were added,
one of them being MICHAEL
LLEWELLYN-DAVIES, adopted son of
J.M. Barrie and inspiration for the boy
with the top hat in *Peter Pan*.

The river now begins to flow west
towards Abingdon, and on the right
(formerly Berkshire) bank is the boat-
house for Radley College, a rowing
school to rival Eton.

Radley

RADLEY COLLEGE was founded in 1847
and structured along the lines of a
university college. The original school
building was RADLEY HALL, built in the
1720s for SIR JOHN STONHOUSE, with
grounds later landscaped by Capability
Brown. Down by the lake in front of the
main house is COLLEGE OAK, an ancient
oak tree with a girth of 28 ft (8.5 m). It is
thought to be over 400 years old and it
was apparently rejected by the Royal
Navy in Nelson's day as too diseased to
be any good for shipbuilding, and yet
here it still stands, defiant if a bit
forlorn.

Old Radleians include Oscar Wilde's

son CYRIL HOLLAND, actor DESMOND LLEWELLYN (Q from the James Bond films), actor DENNIS PRICE (the suave murderer in *Kind Hearts and Coronets* and Jeeves in BBC Television's *The World of Wooster*), cricketer TED DEXTER (Lord Ted), comedian PETER COOK and former Poet Laureate SIR ANDREW MOTION.

Nuneham House

Flat pastureland now begins to give way to woods, and across the Thames from Radley, high on a green knoll overlooking a great sweeping bend in the river, is NUNEHAM HOUSE, set in gardens by Capability Brown that tumble down to the river's edge, where ornamental trees dangle their branches in the water.

> O'er Nuneham Courtnay's flowery glades
> Soft breezes wave their fragrant wings
> THOMAS LOVE PEACOCK

Nuneham House was built in 1756 for the 1st Earl of Harcourt, who moved here from Stanton Harcourt. The old village of Nuneham Courtenay rather spoilt the view from the new house and so it was demolished and rebuilt away

to the east. George III described Nuneham as 'the most enjoyable place I know', and his granddaughter Queen Victoria agreed, commenting 'this is a most lovely place'. It became a favourite picnic place for Victorians rowing the 5 miles (8 km) down from Oxford, and was one of the places where Charles Dodgson would bring Alice Liddell and her sisters, as Alice herself tells us: 'One of our favourite whole-day excursions was to row down to Nuneham and picnic in the woods there . . . sometimes we were told stories after luncheon that transported us into Fairyland.'

> The man of wealth and pride
> Takes up a space that
> many poor supplied;
> His seat, where solitary
> sports are seen,
> Indignant spurns the
> cottage from the green.

There is a tradition that Nuneham Courtenay was Oliver Goldsmith's 'Deserted Village' of Auburn. In 1761 Goldsmith actually witnessed a village some 50 miles (80 km) from London being removed to make way for a new 'seat of pleasure' for a wealthy landowner – the description seems to fit.

Nuneham House is now owned by Oxford University and leased to the Brahma Kumaris World Spiritual University. It is unfortunately not open to the public, so we can only try to imagine the splendours that the Victorians were able to so enjoy.

Swift Ditch

The river now flows due west towards Abingdon. Just before Abingdon Lock a stream breaks off to the left along SWIFT DITCH (meaning short cut), the original course of the Thames. What forms the main channel today was cut in the 10th century by the monks of Abingdon Abbey, who altered the course of the river so that it would wash their abbey walls and provide them with power and supplies right on the doorstep. The approach to Abingdon along this new route is very similar to the approach to Lechlade, with a graceful spire and an ancient bridge beckoning the weary traveller in.

Abingdon

ABINGDON is one of BRITAIN'S OLDEST CONTINUOUSLY OCCUPIED TOWNS, on a site first settled in the Iron Age. Abingdon Abbey was founded for Benedictine monks in 676. Sacked by the Danes, the abbey grew rich in Saxon times, covering 300 acres (121 ha) and possessed of a huge church – by the time of the Dissolution of the Monasteries it was the sixth richest abbey in England. Not much remains today except the rebuilt gatehouse and one of the loveliest rooms in England, a timbered long gallery that runs the length of the first floor of the old abbey guesthouse. The same building has a remarkable example of an ingenious early type of chimney, where smoke escapes through numerous small lancets grouped around a gable at the top of a massive stone stack.

Abingdon's picturesque stone bridge is called BURFORD BRIDGE, a corruption of 'Borough-Ford', and was built in 1416 by Abingdon merchants to compete with Wallingford, whose own bridge was taking Abingdon's trade.

County Hall

'Of the free standing town halls
of England with open ground floors
this is the grandest'
NIKOLAUS PEVSNER

A winding road lined with Georgian
houses leads into a small market-place
that is completely overwhelmed by the
enormous, monumental COUNTY HALL,
hunched above high pillars and seeming
to draw everything towards it as a
Hoover inhales a rug. Built in 1678–82 by
stonemason Christopher Kempster, a
student of Wren, it recalls the days when
Abingdon was the county town of Berkshire. Bypassed by the Victorian railway
boom, Abingdon had that noble status
wrested away by Reading in 1867 – and,
to rub salt in the wound, Abingdon was
cast into Oxfordshire in 1974. County
Hall now houses a museum, and a small
daily market shelters in the open space
beneath the tall pillars. At the coronation
of George III, free buns were dropped
from the balcony of County Hall so that
the peasantry below could celebrate – a
tradition that is still observed in Abingdon on important royal occasions.

St Helen's

The 13th-century church of ST HELEN'S,
with its landmark 150 ft (46 m) spire, has
five aisles, making it wider than it is long
– a width of 108 ft (33 m) makes it the
SECOND WIDEST CHURCH IN ENGLAND,
after Holy Trinity, Kendal. Inside, over
the north aisle, is a glorious medieval
wooden roof painted with subjects
from the Tree of Jesse.

The churchyard is surrounded by
delightful many-chimneyed almshouses,
the most venerable being Long Alley,
which backs on to the river and was
built in 1446.

MG

For over 50 years Abingdon was the
home of MG cars – MG standing for
Morris Garages, who were the Oxford
distributors of Morris cars. The first
MGs, which went on sale in 1925, were
modified sporting versions of standard
Morris Cowleys and Oxfords, and they
proved so popular that MG moved to its
own factory on the outskirts of Abingdon in 1929. Morris was gradually
subsumed into the disastrous monolith
British Leyland, and despite their cars
having built up a cult following, the MG
factory closed in 1980. The MG marque
is now owned by the Chinese.

Culham Cut

On leaving Abingdon the Thames
flows south for a while and meets up

again with the Swift Ditch by the lovely old arches of medieval Culham Bridge. It then gets back on course to head east between an abundance of institutions on the left or Oxfordshire bank and delightful villages on the right bank, the latter only slightly spoilt by having the cooling towers of Didcot Power station in the background. Culham Cut was created in 1809 to bypass a difficult and twisting section of the river.

Culham

At the end of the Culham Cut on the Oxfordshire bank is CULHAM itself, a very old village with a pretty green, a medieval manor-house and a church at the riverside. The church is a Victorian replacement for a 9th-century chapel belonging to Abingdon Abbey, while the 15th-century manor-house originated as an abbey grange and has a huge and picturesque dovecote from 1685.

Just west of Culham is BRITAIN'S ONLY EUROPEAN SCHOOL, founded in 1978, which provides an education for 800 students, who can choose to be taught in any two official European Union languages. It is housed in the former Culham College, which was established in 1832 as a Church of England teacher training college by Samuel Wilberforce, Bishop of Oxford, son of anti-slavery campaigner William Wilberforce.

Further west is the CULHAM SCIENCE CENTRE, which occupies the site of a wartime Fleet Air Arm airfield, and is operated by the UK Atomic Energy Authority. It is the home of Britain's fusion research programme and is THE LARGEST FUSION EXPERIMENTAL FACILITY IN THE WORLD.

Sutton Courtenay

On the opposite bank is one of the loveliest villages on the Thames, SUTTON COURTENAY, which is blessed with three exceptional historic houses. The village began life as a collection of Saxon huts in the 6th century, and the manor of Sutton was given to the newly founded Abingdon Abbey by Ine, King of Wessex, in 688. The village takes its second name from the Norman family of Courtenay, who were given the manor in the 12th century, but later moved to Powderham Castle in Devon when they inherited the title Earl of Devon.

Manor House

SUTTON COURTENAY MANOR HOUSE was a long-standing royal home for Saxon and Norman kings, and Henry I's daughter MATILDA was born there in 1101. Matilda was the only one of Henry's legitimate children to survive him and as Empress Maud she disputed the throne with her cousin Stephen – although acclaimed Queen, she was never actually crowned. In 1177 Matilda's own son Henry II gave the manor where his mother was born to his friend REGINALD COURTENAY, and so began the Courtenay connection.

The east wing of the manor house in which Matilda was born still stands.

In 1192 Reginald's son Robert built a sturdy Norman Hall next to the manor. This survives today as the centrepiece for a private residence and is noted for its finely carved Norman doorway.

Sutton Courtenay Abbey

The 'Abbey' at Sutton Courtenay was built in the early 13th century to serve as a grange for Abingdon Abbey, and from it the abbey estates were administered. In about 1285 the house was expanded by the Courtenays, who added a high Great Hall with timbered roof that survives to this day, and from then on it was used as the village rectory. In 1958 the Abbey became the property of DAVID ASTOR, publisher and editor of the *Observer*, who lived in the Manor House. He rented it out for a small fee as a refugee children's home, during which time the Abbey was visited by the Dalai Lama, who welcomed fellow Tibetan refugees in the Great Hall.

The Abbey was sold to a Christian charity in 1980 and is run today as a retreat and conference centre.

Buried at Sutton Courtenay

Resting in the churchyard of the mainly 14th-century All Saints Church at Sutton Courtenay are Herbert Henry Asquith, the last Liberal prime minister, David Astor and author George Orwell, buried under his real name of Eric Arthur Blair.

HENRY HERBERT ASQUITH (1852–1928) was Prime Minister from 1908 to 1916 and used the Wharf, his home down by the river at Sutton Pools, as his country retreat from the strains of office. During his term as PM, Asquith's administration was confronted with the Suffragettes, Irish Home Rule and the First World War – it was at the Wharf that he signed the document that took Britain to war. In 1925 Asquith acquired the title Earl of Oxford and Asquith, a grand-sounding moniker that provoked the stately Lady Salisbury to declare, 'It's rather like a suburban villa calling itself Versailles.'

DAVID ASTOR (1912–2001) was the third child of the 2nd Viscount Astor and Nancy Astor from Cliveden (see p. 114). For 27 years he was editor of the *Observer* newspaper, his greatest coup being to uncover Anthony Eden's dishonesty over the Suez crisis in 1957. He was a friend and admirer of George Orwell, whom he employed on the *Observer*, and it was at his suggestion that Orwell is buried at Sutton Courtenay, where David Astor lived for much of his life in the manor-house.

GEORGE ORWELL (1903–50) wrote two of the most profound and influential novels of the 20th century, *Animal Farm*, an allegorical account of how a popular revolution becomes corrupted, based on Stalin's Russia, and *1984*, which depicts life under a totalitarian society. The latter introduced into the English language the phrases 'Big Brother', 'Thought Police' and 'Doublespeak'; its title was a reversal of the year in which he wrote it, 1948. Orwell's pen-name was taken from the River Orwell in Suffolk, where his parents lived, and such is his influence on popular and political culture that the term Orwellian is now widely used to describe authoritarian or repressive measures, attitudes or social conditions that threaten a free society.

Long Wittenham

LONG WITTENHAM, like Sutton Courtenay, is bypassed by a new channel, the Clifton Cut, which opened in 1822, leaving the straggling village street to follow the old winding river course alone. This was West Saxon territory, and the village cross sits on a base from where St Birinius preached to the converted Saxons in 634, while the church stands on a 6th-century pagan Saxon burial site.

Inside the 12th-century church is a rare Norman lead font, carved with a ring of 30 arches each containing a bishop with his hand raised in blessing. It is one of only 38 such fonts in England – and this one may be rarer still as it is possibly the only one in England to retain its original base. Most lead fonts were melted down by the Roundheads in the Civil War to make bullets, but at Long Wittenham the parishioners craftily disguised their font by encasing it in wood.

In the south chapel, at the base of a piscina, is a tiny sculpture of a cross-legged knight, thought to be Gilbert de Clare, Earl of Gloucester, one of the leading Barons behind the Provisions of Oxford (see p. 50). He was Lord of Wittenham and stayed here while attending the King in Oxford. The sculpture, perhaps THE SMALLEST SCULPTED EFFIGY IN ENGLAND, is thought to signify that de Clare's heart was buried here in his favourite church, most probably by his wife Princess Joan, daughter of Edward I. The rest of him lies in Tewkesbury Abbey.

Well, I never knew this about

THE RIVER THAMES

On Whit Sunday 1862, the REVD CHARLES DODGSON (Lewis Carroll) walked down from Christ Church and preached HIS FIRST EVER SERMON in the early Norman church at SANDFORD. The occasion is commemorated by the annual 'Alice' sermon, based on a theme from *Alice in Wonderland*.

Abingdon's original lock, now acting as a weir, dates from 1624 and is THE OLDEST SURVIVING LOCK CHAMBER IN EUROPE.

In 1927 MG built a one-off prototype saloon with a fabric body of gold and stippled black which was used as a runaround when the company moved to Abingdon. The local people nick-named the car the 'OLD SPECKLED UN', and when the Abingdon-based brewery Morlands was asked to produce a special beer to celebrate the Golden Jubilee of the MG factory in 1979, by popular demand the new brew was called 'Old Speckled Hen'.

JOHN FAULKNER, THE WORLD'S OLDEST JOCKEY, lies near a big elm tree in the riverside churchyard at APPLEFORD. He rode his first winner at the age of eight in 1837, the year that Queen Victoria came to the throne, and rode in his last race in 1903, two years after she had died and when he was 74. He lived in Appleford all his life, fathered 32 children and passed away in 1933 at the age of 104.

Tucked away on the south bank, just before the bridge at Clifton Hampden, is the BARLEY MOW, visited by the 'Three Men in a Boat' and described by Jerome K. Jerome as 'the quaintest old world inn up the river'. It is possible he wrote some of *Three Men in a Boat* while staying here. The pub, with its 'low pitched gables and thatched roof and latticed windows', was burned down in 1975 but has been restored.

CLIFTON HAMPDEN TO WALLINGFORD

Clifton Hampden – a classically beautiful Thames-side village

Clifton Hampden

CLIFTON means 'tun on a cliff', in this case a high sandstone cliff, such as is found nowhere else on the Thames, while the HAMPDEN comes from JOHN HAMPDEN, parliamentarian and cousin of Oliver Cromwell, whose family once owned the manor. The river is relatively shallow here, as the river bed is composed of a very hard sandstone which is impossible to dredge. Heavily laden barges had to unload at Burcot, a little way downstream, their cargoes then proceeding to Oxford by road.

The approach to Clifton Hampden from upstream is sublime. A tiny-spired church, embowered in trees and perched on a sandstone 'cliff', beckons from beyond a supremely handsome red-brick bridge of six beautiful Tudor arches. The bridge is the work of SIR GEORGE GILBERT SCOTT, who apparently sketched out the design on his shirt cuff at dinner with the village squire HENRY HUCKS GIBBS in 1857. The bridge replaced a ferry and until 1946 was a tollbridge.

Jerome K. Jerome thought Clifton Hampden 'a wonderfully pretty village, old fashioned, peaceful and dainty with flowers'. It is still almost film-set pretty, full of 17th-century thatched cottages swathed in flowers, and is still peaceful, despite the presence of a Radiohead recording studio on the main road.

Steep steps climb up to give a magnificent view of the village from the churchyard. On the south side, in a grave marked by a small stone cross, lies SERGEANT WILLIAM DYKES, a soldier in Wellington's army who fired THE FIRST SHOT AT THE BATTLE OF WATERLOO in 1815, when his gun went off accidentally.

The church is 12th century with later additions. Its great treasure, now built into the north wall but once forming a lintel over an earlier door, is a crude but remarkably lively depiction of a boar hunt, carved in stone by a Norman craftsman. In 1844 the church was largely rebuilt by Sir George Gilbert Scott at the request of Henry Hucks Gibbs, owner of most of the village. At the same time Gibbs, a financier and Governor of the Bank of England, commissioned Scott to build a parsonage on the cliff top above the church for the incumbent, his uncle the Revd Joseph Gibbs.

Henry Hucks Gibbs was created 1st Lord Aldenham in 1896. He was a colourful character, 'an awesome polymath who rode to hounds, blew off his right hand in a shooting accident and finished off the manuscripts which he was illuminating with his left hand'.

The parsonage was later converted into the Manor House, by Lord Aldenham's third son Vicary, co-author of THE COMPLETE PEERAGE of 1911.

Burcot

Downstream from Cilfton Hampden is BURCOT, a hamlet mostly hidden from the river. A small boat-house indicates BURCOTE BROOK, where Poet Laureate JOHN MASEFIELD (1878–1967) lived from 1932 until his death. Burcote Brook burned down not long afterwards and was replaced by a Cheshire Home.

As the river turns south, the smart, capped tower of Dorchester Abbey comes into view across the fields.

Dorchester

DORCHESTER, officially Dorchester-on-Thames, is really Dorchester-on-Thame, sitting as it does on the banks of the River Thame, a ½ mile (800 m) up from its junction with the Thames. Just to the south of the village are the Dyke Hills, the remains of an Iron Age fort, indicating that this was a strategic position long before the Romans settled here and built the walled town of Dorocina.

Dorchester (not to be confused with Dorchester, the county town of Dorset) was the first city of Wessex, before Winchester, and in 634 BISHOP BIRINIUS

arrived here, sent by Pope Honorius I to convert the Saxons of the Thames valley to Christianity. Standing knee-deep in the Thames, in the presence of the Christian KING OSWALD OF NORTHUMBRIA, Birinius baptised CYNEGILS OF WESSEX, uniting the two great kingdoms against the last pagan king, Penda of Mercia, and effectively establishing England as a Christian country.

A cathedral was built on the spot, at the heart of what was then THE LARGEST DIOCESE IN BRITAIN, covering most of Wessex and Mercia, and Birinius became the first Bishop of Dorchester. Two hundred years later King Alfred transferred the Wessex part of the see to Winchester, and not long after that the Mercian portion went to Lincoln.

Birinius's cathedral was replaced by a Norman monastery church, which was given to the villagers at the Reformation to use as a parish church. It is a wonderful building to find in such a quiet backwater, over 100 ft (30 m) long and filled with treasures that include the shrine of St Birinius, a magnificent east window and the finest Jesse window in England, with the Tree of Jesse illustrated not only in the stained glass but also in the stone mullions. The family tree of Christ burgeons upwards from a reclining Jesse, the delicate boughs exquisitely carved with biblical figures mirrored in the window lights and complemented by the scant hint of faded wall paintings.

There is also a rare lead font and a vigorous alabaster effigy of a knight, possibly Sir John Holcombe, drawing his sword, sculpted with such flowing

grace that it is said to have inspired the sculptures of Henry Moore.

The winding main street of Dorchester is lined with attractive old buildings of every description, including a number of coaching inns from the days when Dorchester sat astride the London to Oxford road.

Day's Lock

DAY'S LOCK, where the Thames begins to curve around Dorchester, is THE MAIN GAUGING STATION FOR MEASURING THE FLOW OF WATER IN THE THAMES. The name is taken from a family of Catholic yeomen who lived in the area in the 17th century.

Wittenham Clumps

Overlooking Day's Lock from its own riverside pasture is the church of LITTLE WITTENHAM, burial place of LADY DUNCH, Oliver Cromwell's aunt, and the much reviled lady of the now vanished manor. Her name lives on with the twin hills that rise beyond the church, which are known locally as Mother Dunch's Buttocks, and indeed, from certain angles they do present a rump-like silhouette, although maybe their other colloquial name, Berkshire Bubs, is more accurate. Their official name is the SINODUN HILLS, Sinodun being Celtic for 'old fort', and on top of Castle Hill, the tallest 'bub', are the remains of an Iron Age hill fort. Each is crowned with a clump of trees, much diminished by storms over the years, and hence the hills are most usually known as the Wittenham Clumps. Rising in isolation from the Thames plain, they are a landmark for miles around and the views from the top are far reaching, all across the Vale of the White Horse, north across the Thames to Dorchester and beyond, and east along the Thames valley to the Chilterns.

Shillingford

The hamlet of SHILLINGFORD, as seen from the river, consists of a many-splendoured stone mansion with substantial boathouse located on the approaching bend, and a fine hotel with gardens sweeping down to the water beside the elegant balustraded bridge of 1827. SHILLINGFORD BRIDGE is exactly half-way between Windsor and Lechlade and between Reading and Oxford.

Benson

Buried in St Helen's churchyard in BENSON is meteorologist WILLIAM HENRY DINES (1855–1927), who made THE FIRST REGULAR STUDIES OF WIND FORCES IN THE UPPER AIR, carrying out numerous experiments with balloons and kites from his home at nearby Pyrton Hall in the first years of the 20th century. His work as THE FIRST SCIENTIST TO 'MAP THE AIR' has proved invaluable in weather forecasting and also the understanding of air pockets and their effect on aeroplane flight.

The clock on the Georgian tower of St Helen's Church in Benson has two elevens because the nine was painted on upside down as XI. During the Second World War 'Lord Haw Haw', the traitorous Nazi broadcaster, promised an air raid on 'an airfield near the village

whose clock has two elevens' and shortly afterwards RAF Benson was bombed.

During the Second World War RAF Benson was headquarters of the RAF's photographic reconnaissance missions, and it was Spitfires and Mosquitoes from Benson that brought back damage assessment pictures from the Dambuster raids, which went for analysis to Mongewell Park down the river.

Until 1995 RAF Benson was the home of the Queen's Flight. Today it serves mainly as the home of the RAF's support helicopters as well as those of the Thames Valley police.

Howbery Park

On the left bank just after Benson is HOWBERY PARK, a business park centred around a red-brick Victorian mansion built in 1850 for William Blackstone MP, grandson of Sir William Blackstone of Wallingford (see p. 72). The house bankrupted him and Blackstone ended up in debtors' prison in Oxford. After the war Howbery Park became the home of the government's HYDRAULIC RESEARCH STATION, to study flood protection and coastal erosion. It was privatised in 1982 and is now known as HR Wallingford.

Jethro Tull

(1674–1741)

At the end of the 17th century Howbery was farmland belonging to the Tull family and it was here, in 1701, in fields now concreted over, that JETHRO TULL INVENTED THE SEED DRILL.

Jethro Tull trained as a lawyer but was forced to come and help out on his father's farm at Howbery because the family was experiencing financial difficulties. Crops were sown by hand in those days, and Jethro disliked the hard work involved. He also objected to paying wages that the family could ill afford, and so he set about devising a machine that could do the work much more quickly and efficiently – and cheaply.

In 1701, using pieces of an old pipe organ that he had dismantled, Jethro Tull built THE WORLD'S FIRST KNOWN SEED DRILL, a rotating cylinder with grooves cut into it to allow seed to fall from the hopper into a funnel. This in turn directed the seed into a furrow cut by a plough in front of the machine. The furrow was then covered over with soil by a harrow fixed to the back of the machine. The whole contraption was pulled along by a horse and could sow up to three rows at once.

Well, I never knew this
about
THE RIVER THAMES

CYNEGLIS OF WESSEX, baptised at Dorchester, was THE FIRST CHRISTIAN ANCESTOR OF OUR PRESENT ROYAL LINE.

Since 1984 DAY'S LOCK has been the venue for THE WORLD POOHSTICKS CHAMPIONSHIPS, which are held from the bridge below the lock. The championships are based on the game described in A.A. Milne's *Winnie-the-Pooh* books, where competitors throw a stick into the river upstream from a bridge and then dash to the other side to see which stick appears on the current first. The event, which is held annually in spring, was the idea of a former lock-keeper at Day's Lock, Lynn David, and the money raised is donated to the Royal National Lifeboat Institution. The championships attract thousands of people every year from all over the world, and while the individual competition is usually won by a skilled local child, the team event has been won by teams from as far away as Australia and Japan.

On the eastern slope of Castle Hill, one of the Wittenham Clumps, is the POEM TREE, a beech tree upon which JOSEPH TUB, a local maltster and frustrated poet, carved a poem in 1845.

SHILLINGFORD was the birthplace of VIVIAN STANSHALL (1943–95), founder member of the Bonzo Dog Doo-Dah Band, and voice of the narrator on Mike Oldfield's classic album *Tubular Bells*.

RAF Benson often records ENGLAND'S COLDEST TEMPERATURE.

WALLINGFORD TO GORING

Wallingford – second town in England to receive a Royal Charter

Wallingford

The approach to WALLINGFORD is regal, with the river passing by the handsome trees and green mounds of the old castle gardens and towards Wallingford Bridge, one of the most venerable and picturesque bridges on the Thames, with behind it the distinctive hollow stone spire of St Peter's Church rising from its octagonal lantern.

Wallingford, in Saxon, means 'ford owned by the Welsh', which could indicate it was a ford on the road from London to Wales, or that it was a ford guarded by a tribe of Welshmen or indigenous Britons – or Wallingford could just mean 'wooded ford'. Much simpler.

Whichever it is, there has been a vital ford here since Roman times. The Saxons guarded it with an earthwork, from which some fine examples of 'burgh walls' survive, and Wallingford even became the capital town of Saxon Berkshire, with its own mint.

Wallingford Castle

In 1069 William the Conqueror ordered Robert D'Oyly, who would later build the castle at Oxford, to erect a castle at Wallingford, and this castle was destined to become one of the most important in England.

In 1142 the EMPRESS MATILDA fled to Wallingford Castle after her escape through the snow from King Stephen at Oxford (see p. 46). This episode eventually led to negotiations resulting in the Treaty of Wallingford, in which it was agreed that when Stephen died, Matilda's son Henry of Anjou would become king, rather than Stephen's heir. In 1154 Henry succeeded to the throne as HENRY II, THE FIRST PLANTAGENET KING, and the following year he held his first Great Council at Wallingford. He also granted the town its ROYAL CHARTER, making it only THE SECOND TOWN IN ENGLAND TO RECEIVE ONE.

PRINCESS JOAN, THE 'FAIR MAID OF KENT', mother of Richard II and wife of the Black Prince, died in Wallingford Castle in 1385.

Some years later Richard II's child wife ISABELLA was sent to Wallingford for safe keeping while her husband was in Ireland. Richard died shortly afterwards and Isabella went on to marry Charles, Duke of Orleans, sender of the first Valentine card. Isabella's younger sister CATHERINE DE VALOIS married Henry V, and some years after Henry died in 1422 Catherine met OWEN TUDOR at Wallingford; it was within the walls of Wallingford Castle that the love affair began which was to lead to the Tudor dynasty – their grandchild was Henry VII.

In the Civil War Wallingford Castle was THE LAST ROYALIST STRONGHOLD IN ENGLAND TO SURRENDER TO OLIVER CROMWELL. It was not captured until 1646, after a 16-week siege. The castle was then demolished and the stone used for other buildings in the town, including the tower of St Mary-le-More Church in the market-place. In 1837 a Gothic house was built on the ruins, but this was in turn knocked down in the 1970s and the site has been made into a park.

Wallingford Bridge

WALLINGFORD BRIDGE is 900 ft (274 m) long and has 17 arches. It is thought that the first stone bridge here was built in 1250 by Richard, Duke of Cornwall, brother of Henry III, and there is some work remaining from this period. During the siege of the castle by Oliver Cromwell in the Civil War the central arches of the bridge were removed and replaced by a drawbridge. The present three central arches with their balustrades were built in 1809 and at the same time the road was widened, which is why the arches on the upstream side are rounded while those on the downstream side are pointed.

The unusual hollow stone spire seen from the bridge belongs to St Peter's, originally a Saxon church built to guard or welcome visitors at the entrance to the town. The spire, the look of which has drawn much unwarranted criticism over the years, was put up in 1777 and may have been designed by Sir William Blackstone, who is buried inside the church.

Wallingford Town

Wallingford is today a most attractive town with a fine market-place where a market has been held every Friday since Henry II's charter of 1155. The actual charter is kept in the handsome Jacobean pillared town hall, now an art gallery. Behind the hall is the tower of St Mary-le-More, from where a curfew has been sounded at 9pm every night since the time of William the Conqueror. St

Leonard's Church retains Saxon herringbone brickwork in the north wall and two splendidly carved Norman arches.

The river leaves Wallingford past the tiny Norman church at CROWMARSH GIFFORD on the left bank.

Sir William Blackstone

(1723–80)

'Better that ten guilty persons escape than that one innocent suffer.'
BLACKSTONE'S FORMULATION

SIR WILLIAM BLACKSTONE WAS THE FIRST PROFESSOR OF ENGLISH LAW AT OXFORD UNIVERSITY and his greatest work was Commentaries on the Laws of England, THE FIRST COMPREHENSIVE SURVEY OF ENGLAND'S COMMON LAWS THAT COULD BE UNDERSTOOD BY THE LAYMAN. The book was influential in the development of the American legal system and is still quoted as an authority by the US Supreme Court, as well as being considered required reading for British lawyers. There is a statue of Sir William standing outside the US Courthouse in Washington DC and another in the Great Hall of the Law Courts in London.

Blackstone built himself a fine house beside St Peter's Church called Castle Priory, now a hotel, with gardens sloping down to the river.

Winterbrook House

A little further downriver on the right bank, just before Winterbrook Bridge, is WINTERBROOK HOUSE, a beautiful Queen Anne house owned by crime writer AGATHA CHRISTIE and her second husband Max Malloran from 1934 until her death in 1976. The house was the inspiration for Danemead, Miss Marple's home in the village of St Mary Mead, while Wallingford was the model for Market Basing, which appears in many of her mysteries. She is thought to have written a number of her Miss Marple mysteries while at Winterbrook as well as her radio play *Three Blind Mice*, later adapted for the stage as *The Mousetrap*, which opened in 1952 and is still playing – THE LONGEST-RUNNING PLAY IN THE WORLD. Agatha Christie died at Winterbrook House in 1976 and is buried in the country churchyard at CHOLSEY, 1 mile (1.6 km) to the west.

Just past Winterbrook Bridge on the left bank there is a wide lawn, a glimpse of a red-brick mansion behind a wall, and a large run-down boat-house beside an inlet that leads to a tiny disused Norman church. This is . . .

Mongewell Park

MONGEWELL PARK was the final home of SHUTE BARRINGTON (1734–1826), Bishop of Durham, who married the heiress to the estate as his second wife. Barrington's Georgian house was knocked down and replaced in 1890 in William and Mary style by Alexander Frazer. At the end of the First World War, during which it served as a hospital, the house was sold to HENRY GOULD, an American millionaire and atheist who had the pathway to the church sunk out of sight so that he didn't have to watch the villagers walking to church from his study window.

In the Second World War Mongewell Park was taken over by RAF Bomber Command, and it was here that the damage caused by the Dambusters raid was analysed.

Between 1948 and 1997 Mongewell housed CARMEL COLLEGE, THE ONLY JEWISH BOARDING SCHOOL IN EUROPE. During this time various school buildings were erected in the grounds including a synagogue and an amphitheatre. The boat-house was designed by Sir Basil Spence, the architect of Coventry Cathedral.

Alumni of Carmel College include Oscar-nominated film director ROLAND JOFFE (*The Killing Fields*, *The Mission*) and one of Britain's richest top ten, SIR PHILIP GREEN, owner of the Arcadia Group, which has amongst its portfolio Debenhams, Selfridges and Topshop.

Mongewell Park was abandoned when the school left in 1997 and became a rather spooky area of dereliction but is now being redeveloped for housing. The little church of St John the Baptist by the river is now in the care of the Churches Conservation Trust and is worth a visit. There are two Norman arches and a Norman doorway, and some splendid memorials inside, including one to Shute Barrington who is buried here.

Across the river from Mongewell on the right bank is the new Oxford Brookes University boat-house. Wallingford provides the longest straight stretch of water on the Thames above Henley and serves as an excellent practice course for the Oxford Eights Week crews as well as Oxford's Boat Race crews and Olympic rowers.

North Stoke

Next up, just visible through trees on the left bank, is the early 13th-century church of ST MARY, NORTH STOKE, famous for its fabulous collection of medieval wall paintings dating back to 1300. The subject of the martyrdom of St Stephen is UNIQUE IN WALL PAINTINGS OF THIS AGE IN ENGLAND.

Buried in the church is the singer DAME CLARA BUTT (1872–1936), who lived nearby at Brook Lodge in South Stoke. With her powerful and distinctive contralto, Dame Clara was renowned for her range and 'cavernous' lower register and was said to possess 'the most glorious voice ever heard'. Her recording of 'Land of Hope and Glory' was THE BEST-SELLING RECORD OF THE DAY, and Sir Thomas Beecham declared that 'on a clear day you could

have heard her across the English Channel'. She was buried to the strains of her own celebrated rendition of 'Abide with Me'.

Film actor MICHAEL CAINE lived near the church at the Rectory Farmhouse until 2001.

THE SPRINGS HOTEL in North Stoke was formerly owned by Deep Purple's vocalist IAN GILLAN, who built the guitar-shaped swimming pool in the grounds.

Moulsford

The masterpiece that is MOULSFORD RAILWAY BRIDGE was built in 1839 by Isambard Kingdom Brunel and carries the main London to Bristol railway across the Thames on four superb elliptical skew arches that, when seen from the north side, create an amazing visual effect.

The river arrives in MOULSFORD ('mules ford'), on the right bank, past a small church designed by Sir George Gilbert Scott on the site of a 13th-century chapel, and the fine gently sloping terraced gardens of the gorgeous Elizabethan MOULSFORD MANOR, home from 1994 to 2004 to the late Robert Maxwell's son Kevin and his wife Pandora. Moulsford Manor is a favourite location for the ITV series *Midsomer Murders*.

Beetle and Wedge

Moulsford is best known for the BEETLE AND WEDGE, a stylish restaurant and hotel converted from an old boat-house. H.G. WELLS stayed here while writing *The History of Mr Polly*, and turned the *Beetle and Wedge* into the Potwell Inn. 'It was about two o'clock in the afternoon one hot day in high May when Mr Polly, unhurrying and serene, came to that broad bend of the river to which the little lawn and garden of the Potwell Inn run down.'

The Beetle and Wedge featured in Jerome K. Jerome's *Three Men in a Boat*, and George Bernard Shaw was a frequent visitor in the days when the inn ran a ferry taking the towpath across the river.

The name refers to the 'beetle' or mallet that was used to hammer in the wedge for splitting logs before they were floated down the river.

The Thames now enters its most spectacular reach as it begins to weave its way between steep wooded banks through the Goring Gap where the Berkshire Downs come down to the Thames to meet the Chiltern Hills. Past the Leatherne Bottel, once a delightful riverside pub, now an upmarket restaurant, lie the twin villages of Goring and Streatley.

Well, I never knew this about
THE RIVER THAMES

Actress SHEILA HANCOCK remembers being taught to swim in the Thames at WALLINGFORD when she was evacuated there during the Second World War.

Wallingford regularly stars as the town of CAUSTON in the television series *Midsomer Murders*.

Commenting on her second marriage, to archeologist Max Malloran, AGATHA CHRISTIE said, 'An archaeologist is the best husband a woman can have. The older she gets, the more interested he is in her.'

Agatha Christie used MONGEWELL PARK, across the river from where she lived, as inspiration for the mansion in *The Mousetrap*.

Just downstream from the Beetle and Wedge at Moulsford, the Thames for a moment becomes the Nile as it glides past the exotic and colourful Egyptian House, designed by architect John Outram and completed in 2000.

The island beside the weir at CLEEVE LOCK is owned by rock musician PETE TOWNSHEND of The Who.

GORING TO WHITCHURCH

Goring – home to one of the oldest bells in England still in use

Goring

The quaint and somewhat flimsy-looking Goring and Streatley Bridge of 1923 carries the Ridgeway and the Icknield Way safely across the river. At the same spot there was originally a ford – the most important prehistoric crossing of the Thames. Later a ferry plied between the two villages, but this enterprise was not without its hazards – in 1674 the ferry got drawn into the weir pool and overturned with the loss of 60 lives.

Tucked up against the bridge are

Goring's old mill and church. The church is largely Norman and retains the original Norman turret beside the tower. Inside the tower hangs ONE OF THE OLDEST BELLS IN ENGLAND STILL IN USE, dating from 1290. The rood screen is carved out of wood from HMS *Thunderer*, one of Nelson's ships at the Battle of Trafalgar. On the north wall of the sanctuary is a brass memorial to HUGH WHISTLER (d.1615), whose family for several generations owned Gatehampton Manor, a mile or so downstream. There are more memorials to the Whistlers at Whitchurch (see

p. 81), ancestors of the painter James McNeill Whistler (see p. 181).

In the summer of 1893 OSCAR WILDE and LORD ALFRED DOUGLAS rented FERRY COTTAGE in Goring, and here Wilde began his play *An Ideal Husband*, giving three of the characters local names – Lord Goring, Sir Robert Chiltern and the Countess of Basildon. Ferry Cottage was later expanded for the wartime leader of Bomber Command, SIR ARTHUR 'BOMBER' HARRIS (1892–1964), who lived there from his retirement in 1953 until his death.

PETE TOWNSHEND of The Who had a studio in his home in Goring and recorded many of the band's most popular albums there, including *Quadrophenia*.

Pop singer GEORGE MICHAEL lives in MILL COTTAGE, beside the church. His house appears in an unfinished painting by Turner, which hangs in the Tate Britain.

Streatley

The 'street' of STREATLEY is the RIDGE-WAY, one of our most ancient thoroughfares, which comes down off the Berkshire Downs here and meets the ICKNIELD WAY, another pre-Roman road, before crossing the Thames to Goring and continuing eastwards along the crest of the Chilterns. From the summit of Streatley Hill, which rises steeply behind the village, the view of the Goring Gap is superb and well worth the arduous climb, although *Punch* contributor JOSEPH ASHBY-

STERRY didn't seem to think so when he visited in the 1890s – 'I'd much rather sit here and laze, than scale the hill at Streatley!'

In fact he did sit and laze, probably at the luxurious SWAN, which still boasts an idyllic riverside terrace overlooking the weir. Moored alongside is the MAGDALEN COLLEGE BARGE, THE LAST SURVIVING COLLEGE BARGE, now used as a venue for receptions and conferences.

The Saunders, proprietors of the Swan in the 19th century, also provided the ferry service across to Goring before the wooden tollbridge was built in 1837. THE LAST FERRYMAN was MOSES SAUNDERS, who founded a boat-building firm at Streatley in 1830. One hundred years later the firm was bought by Alliot Verdon Roe of AVRO, the first Englishman to achieve powered flight, and became SAUNDERS-ROE, makers of flying-boats and hovercraft.

STREATLEY HOUSE, easily the most imposing house in the High Street, was built in 1765 and until 1938 belonged to the MORRELL brewing family, who also owned much of the village.

The Three Men in a Boat and their dog Montmorency lunched at THE BULL, on the main road through Streatley, 'much to Montmorency's satisfaction'. Buried in the garden, beneath two yew trees, are a monk and a nun of the 1440s who used to have secret assignations at The Bull, and were caught, put to death and buried in unconsecrated ground as punishment for their forbidden love.

'They shall grow not old,
as we that are left grow old ...'
LAURENCE BINYON

LAURENCE BINYON (1869–1943), author
of those famous words, grew old at
STREATLEY. In 1933 he retired from the
British Museum, where he had worked as
an expert on Oriental art, and moved to
Westridge Green, just up the road from
Streatley. After his death in 1943 his ashes
were scattered in the churchyard at
ALDWORTH, ¼ mile (400 m) away.

The Grotto

On leaving Goring the river passes by a
modern glass summerhouse jutting out
over the water, which belongs to THE
GROTTO, a splendid cream-painted
mansion built on the site of a grotto and
summerhouse, created for VISCOUNT-
ESS FANE of Basildon Park in 1720. The
grotto consisted of a rock chamber
filled with shells and a rock pool
described by the amateur landscape
gardener and poet William Shenstone as
'a very beautiful disposition of the
finest collection of shells I ever saw'.
The Viscountess is said to have
drowned in a well and apparently haunts
the grotto to this day.

The grotto was destroyed by Sir Francis Sykes when he acquired Basildon
Park, but the Viscountess's summerhouse was extended at the beginning of
the 19th century by local MP Arthur
Smith into the house we see from the
river today.

From 1953 until 2006 the house was
the headquarters of the Institute of

Leisure and Amenity Management
(ILAM). ILAM has since become ISPAL,
the Institute for Sport, Parks and Leisure.

On the left bank, after another Brunel
railway bridge, is GATEHAMPTON MANOR,
once the home of the Whistler family.

Lower Basildon

On the right bank is LOWER BASILDON,
an attractive collection of farm buildings
grouped around the little 13th-century
church of St Bartholomew's, where
agricultural pioneer JETHRO TULL is
buried under a modern gravestone
incorrectly dated 1740 – he died in 1741.
He was born in the village, which was
the home of his mother's family, in
1674. Also in the churchyard is a beautiful sculpture of two young boys
bathing, which commemorates
teenagers HAROLD AND ERNEST
DEVERELL who drowned while swimming in the Thames in 1866. Beneath a
notable monument by John Flaxman is
SIR FRANCIS SYKES, whose Palladian
house, Basildon Park, is just visible in
the distance behind the church.

Basildon Park

BASILDON PARK was built between
between 1776 and 1783 by John Carr of
York for Sir Francis Sykes (1732–1804),
who had made a fortune in India and
was a friend of Robert Clive. Sykes
bought the Basildon estate from the
family of the 2nd Viscount Fane
and knocked down the Viscount's old
house to make way for his new Palladian

pile – alas, Sykes died before it was completed.

In 1838 the house was sold to millionaire JAMES MORRISON, the son of an innkeeper from Hampshire who built up THE WORLD'S LARGEST DRAPERY BUSINESS. Morrison was an avid art collector who was an early donor to the National Gallery in London and filled his Berkshire house with works by Constable, da Vinci, Holbein, Rembrandt, Rubens and many more.

During the Second World War Basildon became derelict, but it was rescued in the 1950s by newspaper magnate Lord Iliffe and his wife, and is now owned by the National Trust.

Childe Beale

The river now flows between the steeply wooded slopes of Hartslock Wood and a large white house, Coombe Park, on the left bank, and the flat meadows of CHILDE BEALE WILDLIFE PARK on the right. The wildlife park was formed in 1956 by GILBERT BEALE, who began with a few peacocks, and was extended by Gilbert's great-nephew Richard Howard to include nature trails, a deer park, an aviary, adventure playgrounds and a miniature railway.

Pangbourne

'O, Pangbourne is pleasant in sweet
summertime'
J. ASHBY-STERRY

PANGBOURNE is where the little River Pang joins the Thames, and is announced by the agreeable riverside dining terrace of The Swan, which overlooks the weir. The Swan is a beautiful old place established as an inn during the Civil War to serve the soldiers of the artillery units stationed on Shooters Hill, which rises behind the pub, to guard the river crossing. It was here that the Three Men in a Boat, having rowed from Kingston to Oxford and back to Pangbourne, abandoned their trip, soaked through by two days of rain. 'We have had a pleasant trip, and my hearty thanks for it to Old Father Thames, but . . . Here's to three men well out of a boat!'

The county boundary between Oxfordshire and Berkshire once ran down the middle of the bar in The

Swan. The two counties had different licensing hours, and so when the landlord called 'Time!' at one end of the bar, customers would simply pick up their drinks and walk down to the other end where they could continue their quaffing in peace.

Church Cottage

Made wealthy by the royalties from his children's tale *The Wind in the Willows*, published in 1908, KENNETH GRAHAME retired from his position as Secretary of the Bank of England and moved to Pangbourne with his wife, Elspeth, in 1924. His book is royally commemorated on the village sign, along with the Saxon king Berhtulf of Mercia, who granted the town its charter in the 9th century, which is somehow appropriate as Grahame himself was descended from the Kings of Scotland. His home, CHURCH COTTAGE, is tucked away down a quiet lane beside the church of St James the Less. It used to be the smithy and has the old round village lock-up as a garden shed. Grahame died in 1932 and at his memorial service the church was draped with willows collected from the river that morning. He was buried next to his son in Oxford (see p. 54).

Although Grahame wrote *The Wind in the Willows* when he was living downstream in Cookham, Pangbourne is strongly associated with the book's setting because E.H. SHEPARD came to Pangbourne to seek inspiration for his superlative illustrations to the popular 1931 edition. In fact, the whole stretch of river between Pangbourne and Cookham can be said to be Wind in the Willows country.

Engineer SIR BENJAMIN BAKER (1840–1907) lived in Bowden Green, a large house just outside Pangbourne, and died there in 1907. He was responsible for building the Forth Railway Bridge, the Aswan Dam in Egypt, New York's River Hudson Tunnel, the Central Line on the London Underground, and for transporting Cleopatra's Needle from Egypt and erecting it on the Thames Embankment in 1877.

Between 1917 and 1924 the writer LYTTON STRACHEY (1880–1932) lived with artist Dora Carrington at the Mill House in Tidmarsh, on the River Pang just outside Pangbourne. Here he put the finishing touches to *Eminent Victorians*, published in 1918.

Whitchurch-on-Thames

Pangbourne and WHITCHURCH have been linked by a tollbridge since 1792. The present white-painted, latticed iron bridge opened in 1902 and replaced a rickety wooden affair. It is the third bridge on the site, and ONE OF ONLY TWO TOLLBRIDGES LEFT ON THE UPPER THAMES, the other being at Swinford (see p. 40). The toll for cars is 40p and is collected from an old-fashioned booth on the Whitchurch side by the Company of Proprietors of Whitchurch Bridge, the same company that set up the original tollbridge in 1792. Pedestrians go free. The bridge gets very busy in rush hour and is due to be replaced in 2013.

The view of Whitchurch from the

bridge is almost too perfect: old mill, a cluster of half-timbered cottages, church spire, trees, all reflected in still waters – guaranteed to provoke a sigh of pleasure.

The church of St Mary was founded by the Saxons but is basically Norman and has been much rebuilt in different periods. Over the doorway within the south porch is a rare Saxon carving of a head, probably a gargoyle from the original Saxon church.

Sir John Soane

(1753–1837)

Whitchurch was the birthplace of the architect SIR JOHN SOANE, best known for his work on the Bank of England in 1788. The son of a bricklayer from Reading, he was born John Swan, changed his name to Soan and later added the 'e', which he thought added tone.

Among his architectural works are Dulwich Art Gallery, the world's first purpose-built art gallery, the dining-rooms of Nos. 10 and 11 Downing Street, and Cricket House at Cricket St Thomas in Somerset, which starred as Grantleigh Manor in the BBC television series *To the Manor Born*, starring Penelope Keith.

In his later years he bought a pair of houses in Lincoln's Inn Fields in London, which he joined together, filling them with his collection of art treasures, and left to the nation as a museum.

Sir John Soane is buried in Old St Pancras church-yard in London, beneath an elaborate tomb of his own design, on which Sir Giles Gilbert Scott modelled his iconic red telephone box.

Well, I never knew this
about
THE RIVER THAMES

For a short while in the 1970s, The SWAN AT STREATLEY was owned by the drag artist DANNY LA RUE.

Former Spice Girl GERI HALLIWELL lives in STREATLEY.

The well-known brand of writing paper, BASILDON BOND, takes its name from BASILDON PARK. In 1911 a number of the directors of stationery manufacturer Millington and Sons were staying there as guests and got into a discussion about what to call their new brand of writing paper.

BASILDON PARK starred as Netherfield Park in the 2005 film adaptation of Jane Austen's *Pride and Prejudice* starring Keira Knightley.

Within sound of the weir at Pangbourne, there is a row of splendid riverside villas known as the SEVEN DEADLY SINS. They were put up in 1896 by shopping magnate D.H. EVANS, who lived in Shooters Hill House in Pangbourne, now the Masonic Hall, and got their name because locals maintained that Evans had built them for his mistresses. One notable resident was the society hostess LADY CUNARD.

Beside the weir at Pangbourne is the luxurious BOATHOUSE where JIMMY

PAGE lived from 1967 to 1973 and where he and ROBERT PLANT met to form LED ZEPPELIN in 1968.

Up on the hill behind Pangbourne are the august buildings of PANGBOURNE COLLEGE, founded as a nautical college in 1917 to educate boys for a naval career. The college has a boat-house down on the river near to The Swan, and Pangbourne crews regularly excel at the Henley Royal Regatta. Old boys include the journalist JEFFREY BERNARD (1932–97) and film director KEN RUSSELL (b.1927).

Watching from the Oxfordshire bank below Whitchurch, while at the same time chewing the cud, are the snooty-looking residents of Europe's leading alpaca stud, BOZEDOWN ALPACAS, established in 1989 by JOY WHITEHEAD. From the river there appear to be hundreds of alpacas, brown, white and the occasional black, roaming across the plain for as far as the eye can see, as if out of a Peruvian western – and there are indeed over 800, not a bad return from the four females and one male the farm started with.

WHITCHURCH TO SONNING

Hardwick House, where Charles I played bowls

Hardwick House

Set back at the far end of a long avenue of noble trees, 1 mile downriver from Whitchurch, HARDWICK HOUSE, one of the oldest houses on the Thames valley, is easy to miss. The estate of Hard 'Wick' or 'Spring' comes down to us from the days of William the Conqueror, who gave it to his trusted friend Robert D'Oyly, builder of castles at Wallingford and Oxford. He in turn gave it to one of his underlings, whose

family adopted the name de Herdewyck or Hardwick.

The red-brick pile we see from the river conceals elements of a 14th-century house, which was greatly extended in time for Elizabeth I to stay while on one of her grand progresses around England. By the time of the Civil War Hardwick was in the hands of the Lybbe family, who were ardent Royalists and lent the King considerable sums to fight his cause. There are tales of a large stash of money being buried in the grounds at the beginning of hostilities, which family members have been looking for ever since. If the treasure was indeed hidden it was a far-sighted move, for in 1643 the house was looted by Roundhead soldiers while the owner Richard Lybbe concealed himself in a safe place – probably an old priest hole. After the war Charles I was being kept prisoner at nearby Caversham Park and was allowed to come to Hardwick on day release to play bowls on the lush lawns running down to the river in front of the house. Inside the house there is a picture of the elderly lady who was permitted to serve the captive king with refreshment.

Hardwick was given its present red-brick, gabled façade by Anthony Lybbe at the Restoration of Charles II.

In more recent times Hardwick has been owned by the Rose family. CHARLES ROSE, who bought the house in 1909, was a buccaneering business-man, a courageous militia man, an enthusiastic breeder of racehorses, a fiery politician, a sporting yachtsman and a keen flying man, president of the Royal Aero Club – and unmistakably one of the models for 'Toad' of Toad Hall. Certainly E.H. Shepard used elements of Hardwick House in his illustrations of Toad Hall.

Hardwick, amazingly enough, is still in private hands and the current owner is Sir Justin Rose, who runs the estate as an organic farming business.

The other house that has an even greater claim to be the original for Toad Hall is Mapledurham House, one of the most beautiful Elizabethan houses in England, and in one of the most beautiful locations.

Mapledurham

MAPLEDURHAM HOUSE was built by Sir Michael Blount, Lieutenant of the Tower of London, in the year of the Spanish Armada, 1588. It is clad in mellow brick and fashioned in the shape of an 'E' in honour of Elizabeth I – a shrewd move as the Queen came often to stay.

The house has suffered various minor alterations in its 420-odd years and was treated roughly in the Civil War, but remains substantially the same as when it was built and is still lived in by Blounts – one of that select band of English houses that have never been bought or sold. The Blounts were, and have remained, a leading Catholic family, and the presence of a number of priest holes dotted about behind chimneys and staircases is testament to more intolerant times when people could be endangered by their faith. In 1797 a private Catholic chapel was added to the house, designed in Strawberry Hill Gothic style.

The house is shielded from the river partly by trees and partly by the small 15th-century village church with its quaintly capped tower and Blount memorials. Down by the water is THE

ONLY WORKING WATER-MILL ON THE THAMES – driven today by electricity. On the edge of the weir and fringed by trees, the mill is 15th-century brick and timber and almost impossibly picturesque.

The whole charming ensemble of mill, church, house and river has inspired a host of artists. E.H. Shepard sketched Mapledurham for his illustrations of Toad Hall, while John Galsworthy featured the house in the closing chapters of his *Forsyte Saga*. Mapledurham Mill played a starring role alongside Michael Caine in the 1976 film *The Eagle Has Landed*, and also appears on the cover of Ozzy Osbourne's *Black Sabbath* album, released in 1970.

Pop Festival

After Mapledurham the river turns lazily westwards past PURLEY and runs towards Reading, parallel with the Great Western railway line at TILEHURST, made famous in song by Monty Python, then past the fields of LITTLE JOHN'S FARM on the right bank, site of the READING POP FESTIVAL, held every year in August. On the left bank is Caversham, and the river passes a number of enormous Victorian villas with balconies and boat-houses.

Caversham Court

Just before Caversham Bridge, St Peter's Church overlooks the lovely gardens of CAVERSHAM COURT, which contain THE OLDEST GAZEBO ON THE RIVER THAMES, dating from 1663.

This was the site, in the 12th century, of the shrine of Our Lady of Caversham which became home to 'relics' such as 'the head of the spear that pierced the side of Christ on the Cross', brought back from the Crusades by Robert, Duke of Normandy, a 'piece of rope from which Judas Iscariot hung himself' and the daggers that slew King Edward the Martyr and Henry VI. During the Middle Ages it was the most important shrine to the Virgin Mary after Walsingham in Norfolk.

After the Reformation a great half-timbered house called the Old Rectory was built on the site, which was replaced in 1840 with a castellated Gothic mansion designed by the Catholic architect Augustus Pugin for the Simonds brewing family. This was demolished in 1933 and the site is now a public park.

St Peter's Church, standing above the gardens, possesses a Norman doorway and one of Berkshire's gems, a little Norman font of Purbeck marble dug up from the gardens and thought to be from the original shrine.

Reading

READING, county town of Berkshire since 1867, is older than it looks. Reading Abbey was founded in 1121 by Henry I on high ground between the River Kennet and the Thames. He presented it with the 'Hand of St James', thereby ensuring that the abbey became rich as a place of pilgrimage and that the abbey church grew almost as big as that of Durham. HENRY I himself is BURIED BEFORE THE HIGH ALTAR, reputedly in a silver coffin, the site marked amongst the abbey ruins by a plaque. Nearby lies his daughter the EMPRESS MAUD, OR MATILDA. In 1359 John of Gaunt came to Reading Abbey to be married to Blanche, daughter of Henry, Duke of Lancaster (see Kempsford, p. 19), the ceremony being followed by 14 days of celebrations.

In 1240 a monk at Reading Abbey, JOHN OF FORNSETE, wrote down the music for a song called 'Sumer is icumen in' – THE EARLIEST RECORDED ENGLISH SONG. A memorial plaque on the wall of the ruined chapter house displays a copy of the music. The original manuscript, found in the leaves of an abbey journal from the 13th century, is now in the British Museum. The song is performed to great effect by children's voices at the climax to Benjamin Britten's 'Spring Symphony'.

The ruins of the great abbey can be explored, although only the inner gateway, home of the Abbey School attended by JANE AUSTEN, remains intact.

Standing in Forbury Gardens beside the abbey ruins is THE WORLD'S LARGEST LION, a memorial to soldiers of the Royal Berkshire Regiment killed in the Afghan Wars of the 19th century. It was sculpted by GEORGE BLACKALL SIMONDS of the Simonds brewing family.

Brewing, Bulbs and Biscuits

Reading was the birthplace of three world-famous firms and became known in the 19th century as the town built on brewing, bulbs and biscuits.

The brewing was done at SIMONDS BREWERY, founded by WILLIAM BLACKALL SIMONDS in 1785. Their brewery at Seven Bridges beside the River Kennet was designed by Simonds's old school friend and local architect John Soane – THE ONLY BREWERY SOANE EVER DESIGNED. Simonds were eventually taken over and moved away, and the site of the brewery is now occupied by the Oracle shopping centre.

The bulbs were provided by SUTTONS SEEDS, THE FIRST SEED HOUSE IN THE WORLD TO SUPPLY SEEDS BY MAIL ORDER, founded by JOHN SUTTON in 1806. In 1976 Suttons Seeds moved to Devon.

The biscuits were made by HUNTLEY & PALMERS, one of the world's first global brands, founded by Quaker JOSEPH HUNTLEY in 1722 when he opened a biscuit bakery in London Street opposite the Crown Inn, on the main London to Bristol road. His best customers were the passengers on the stage-coaches that stopped at the Crown, and so Huntley decided to package his biscuits in tins to ensure they wouldn't break when taken on the road. His younger son Joseph began to manufacture the tins, which today have become collector's items – the finest collection being found at Manderston, the present Lord Palmer's house in Berwickshire.

In 1841 a distant cousin, Quaker entrepreneur GEORGE PALMER, came on board and with his business acumen helped Huntley & Palmers to become THE WORLD'S BIGGEST BISCUIT COMPANY, with their Reading factory THE LARGEST BISCUIT FACTORY IN THE WORLD. Their product was sent across the globe and the famous tins became a widely recognised symbol of the British Empire's commercial power. In 1910 the company supplied biscuits for Captain Scott's fateful Antarctic expedition.

In 1990, after a number of mergers, the Huntley & Palmers brand disappeared, but in 2006 the name was revived and now Huntley & Palmers produce speciality biscuits from a factory in Sudbury, Suffolk.

While Reading has lost many of the great names of the Victorian era, numerous modern industries have made the town their headquarters including Oracle, Microsoft and Cisco.

Born in Reading

ARTHUR NEGUS (1903–85), TV presenter and antiques expert.

CHRIS TARRANT, *Who Wants to be a Millionaire?* presenter, born in 1946.

MIKE OLDFIELD, musician, born in 1953.

RICKY GERVAIS, writer, actor and comedian, born in 1961.

SAM MENDES, film and theatre director, born in 1965, and his former wife KATE WINSLETT, actress, born in 1975.

Kennet and Avon Canal

As the Thames departs Reading it flows under Reading Bridge, built in 1923, passing on the right what is perhaps THE ONLY

TESCO EXTRA WITH MOORINGS SO THAT
YOU CAN SHOP BY BOAT. Just beyond, also
on the right bank, is the rather ugly
Horseshoe Bridge that takes the Thames
Path over the mouth of the River Kennet,
starting point for the 87-mile (140 km)
long KENNET AND AVON CANAL which
links the Thames at Reading with the
Avon at Bath via Newbury. The canal
superseded and helped to finally kill off
the Thames and Severn Canal.

A little further on the left is the
entrance to the THAMES AND KENNET
MARINA and the new REDGRAVE AND
PINSENT ROWING LAKE, named after
Britain's Olympic gold medallists and
reserved exclusively for the British

National rowing squad and Oxford
University Boat Club.

Holme Park

On the other side of the river is HOLME
PARK, a brown and red Victorian Gothic
mansion that is the home of READING
BLUE COAT SCHOOL, founded in 1646
and alma mater of comedian RICKY
GERVAIS.

Holme Park stands on the site of the
medieval Sonning Palace inherited by
the Bishop of Salisbury from an important Saxon see, and in use until the
Reformation.

Well, I never knew this about
THE RIVER THAMES

CAVERSHAM PARK, a Victorian mansion which sits in parkland on a hill above Caversham, is the home of BBC Monitoring, which monitors news media from all over the world to provide material for the BBC's news programmes. Caversham Park began life as a castle belonging to William Marshall, 1st Earl of Pembroke and Regent to Henry III.

When CAVERSHAM BRIDGE opened in 1926 it was THE LONGEST CONCRETE BRIDGE IN THE WORLD.

Between Caversham and Reading bridges is FRY'S ISLAND, known locally as de Montfort's Island, the site in 1163 of a duel between SIMON DE MONTFORT and the EARL OF ESSEX, the latter accused of dropping the Royal Standard during a battle against the Welsh. In front of Henry II and a crowd of thousands lining the river banks Essex was run through, and his body was taken to Reading Abbey for disposal. The monks, however, found that Essex was

still alive, and he was nursed back to health and spent the rest of his life in the abbey.

In 1892 OSCAR WILDE, who was a friend of the Palmers, visited the Huntley & Palmer biscuit factory. Three years later he returned to Reading, this time to serve two years in Reading's notorious gaol, known to the inmates as the 'biscuit factory' owing to its proximity to the real thing. Wilde's awful experiences there inspired his poem 'The Ballad of Reading Gaol'.

TOAD OF TOAD HALL was also incarcerated in Reading Gaol, 'a helpless prisoner in the remotest dungeon of the best guarded keep of the stoutest castle in all the length and breadth of Merry England'.

HOLME PARK was the setting in 2001 for the film *The Hole*, starring Keira Knightley, and featured in a number of episodes of *Inspector Morse*.

SONNING TO HENLEY

Sonning – prettiest village on the Thames?

Sonning

'The most fairy-like little
nook on the whole river'
JEROME K. JEROME

SONNING, pronounced 'Sunning', is many people's choice as the prettiest village on the Thames, and certainly the combination of ancient bridge, church, lock, mill, and willow is very appealing.

The bridge, in warm red brick, has ten arches and was constructed in 1775, successor to a number of wooden bridges dating back to the Saxons. Sonning Mill, across the bridge from the village at Sonning Eye, used to supply Huntley & Palmers, and was working until 1950. It now houses a theatre and restaurant.

St Andrew's Church, largely 15th century, contains some work from the Saxon minster that previously stood there and is full of grand memorials, including a particularly splendid monument in memory of Sir Thomas Rich, owner of Holme Park in the 17th century.

Some Sonning Residents

There is nothing left to see of the sumptuous Bishop's Palace, from where the Bishop of Salisbury set out in his barge for the funeral of Henry I in Reading Abbey in 1135; and where in 1400 Henry IV imprisoned Richard II's 12-year-old widow Isabella and tried to persuade her to marry his son, the future Henry V.

The Dean of Salisbury is recalled by DEANERY GARDEN, an Arts and Crafts-style house designed and built by Edwin Lutyens in 1902 for EDWARD HUDSON, founder of COUNTRY LIFE MAGAZINE. The gardens were laid out by Gertrude Jekyll. The house is now owned by JIMMY PAGE, lead guitarist of Led Zeppelin.

HENRY ADDINGTON (1757–1844), Speaker of the House of Commons during the trial of Warren Hastings, and THE FIRST MIDDLE-CLASS PRIME MINISTER (1801–04), owned THE GROVE in Sonning. After the Battle of Trafalgar in 1805, the defeated French ADMIRAL VILLENEUVE lived in The Grove for a while and was visited there by William Pitt the Younger. GENERAL EISEN-HOWER stayed at The Grove during the Second World War, awaiting D-Day.

A cottage in the village called TURPINS is reputed to have belonged to the highwayman's aunt, and provided him with a bolt-hole from where he could escape, if necessary, across the bridge to Oxfordshire.

THE ACRE was built in 1900 for WILLIAM HOLMAN HUNT (1827–1910), founding member of the Pre-Raphaelite Brotherhood, and was where he painted his most famous work *The Light of the World*.

Playwright SIR TERENCE RATTIGAN (1911–77), author of such popular plays as *The Winslow Boy* and *Separate Tables*, lived in THE RED HOUSE in the 1940s.

Magician and psychic URI GELLER lives in a huge white house beside the river in Sonning. A regular visitor was singer MICHAEL JACKSON, who was best man when Geller and his wife Hannah renewed their vows at the house in 2001.

From the almost too perfect beauty of Sonning the river now meanders lazily past a number of small islands towards a high bluff on the Oxfordshire bank crowned by a church and two large mansions – this is the village of …

Shiplake

Vicar of this pleasant spot
Where it was my chance to marry
Happy happy be your lot
In the vicarage by the quarry.
ALFRED, LORD TENNYSON

This was the poem that LORD TENNYSON gave to the Vicar of SHIPLAKE instead of a fee for conducting his marriage to EMILY SELLWOOD in Shiplake church in June 1850.

Alfred and Emily had fallen in love and become engaged many years before, at Somersby in Lincolnshire, when she was 17 and he was 27, but at that time Tennyson was an impoverished poet and in no position to marry, so he reluctantly broke off the engagement. Fifteen years later, with Tennyson about to publish 'In Memoriam' and at the pinnacle of his career, the two were brought together again by Emily's cousin, the wife of the vicar of Shiplake, who had always been in favour of the marriage. 'The nicest wedding I have ever been at,' was how Tennyson described it. They spent their honeymoon night in Pangbourne, Tennyson became Poet Laureate that same year, and they lived happily ever after.

The church, if a bit over-restored, is certainly in a spectacular location, set upon a knoll with wonderful views along the river in both directions. On a wall inside there is memorial stone to JAMES GRANGER, vicar of Shiplake from 1746 until he died of apoplexy while delivering a sermon in 1776. His immortal legacy was a *Biographical History of England* that included blank pages for readers to fill with illustrations of their own choice. To thus 'Grangerise' became a surprisingly popular diversion.

In the churchyard lies SIR ROBERT PHILLIMORE (1810–85), politician, constitutional lawyer, judge and friend of Prime Minister Gladstone. He lived at SHIPLAKE HOUSE, the white-fronted mansion a little further east along the eminence, with grounds running down to the water. Sir Robert was responsible for adding the south front seen from the river. He died in the house in 1885 and is remembered by Phillimore Island, one of the small islands on the Thames between Shiplake and Sonning, and by the Phillimore estate in Kensington. Shiplake House remains a private residence.

Shiplake College

Between Shiplake House and the church is a large red Victorian Tudor edifice built in 1890 for Robert Harrison and now the home of SHIPLAKE COLLEGE, an independent school founded in 1959. Between the wars the house, then known as Skipwith House, was the home of Lord Wargrave, and during the Second World War and until 1953 it was used as a hostel for BBC staff working at the monitoring centre at Caversham Park (see p. 90). Shiplake College has a good reputation for rowing and maintains a number of boat-houses on the river beneath Shiplake knoll.

Wargrave

Across the river from Shiplake, the RIVER LODDON joins the Thames after a 28-mile (45 km) journey from Basingstoke, and further on, past Shiplake Railway Bridge, is WARGRAVE in Berkshire.

ST MARY'S, WARGRAVE, has a Norman doorway from the original church of 1121 and a gorgeous 17th-century brick tower, but the rest was rebuilt (very well) after the church was burned down in 1914 by Emmeline Pankhurst and her Suffragettes, angry because the vicar refused to remove the word 'obey' from the marriage service.

Also buried in the church is THOMAS DAY (1748–89) author of the children's morality tale *The History of Sandford and Merton*. Thomas Day was an abolitionist and follower of Rousseau's philosophy of virtue, hard work and simple pleasures, and his book tells the tale of how rich, spoiled, slave-owning Tommy Merton is taught the value of those qualities by honest farmer's son Harry Sandford and his saintly mentor

Mr Barlow (i.e. Thomas Day). The book, published in three volumes, became a huge bestseller. Alas, Thomas Day's goodness was to be his downfall. At his mother's home Bear Place, just outside Wargrave, he endeavoured to prove his theory that any animal could be tamed by kindness, and while attempting to mollify an untrained horse he was thrown violently and killed, aged just 41.

Wargrave Waterfront

The Wargrave waterfront consists of one gorgeous house and garden and boat-house after another, and seems particularly to attract people from the world of entertainment. Back in the 18th century the rakish EARL OF BARRYMORE built himself 'the most handsome and luxurious theatre in the country' at his home in Wargrave, and here entertained the equally rakish Prince of Wales and his court, as well as the good people of Wargrave, with performances by the finest actors in the country. Alas, the theatre quickly went bankrupt and was closed down, so the earl went off and joined the Royal Berkshire Militia, where he accidently shot himself in the eye while escorting French prisoners of war to Dover. He was laid to rest in the churchyard at Wargrave, just 24 years old.

Other entertainers who have enjoyed the delights of a waterfront abode in Wargrave include Battle of Britain pilot and *Tomorrow's World* presenter RAYMOND BAXTER (1922–2006), comedian DAVE ALLEN (1936–2005) and larger-than-life actor ROBERT MORLEY (1908–92). The TV magician PAUL DANIELS still lives there and is frequently flooded out.

Every year in August the Wargrave and Shiplake Regatta is held on this stretch of water. First held in 1867, the regatta attracts over 1,000 competitors and is the largest on the Thames after Henley Regatta.

Thames-Side

The river now heads north from Wargrave, past the George and Dragon pub, and bends lazily left and right towards a little island called Ferry Eyot. Just before that, running along-side the river on the left bank is a narrow-gauge railway, built in 1914 and described as 'a Disneyland-style park modelled on the train station at St Moritz'. The railway is in the grounds of Thames-Side Court, one of a number of properties by the river owned by Swiss financier URS SCHWARZENBACH, polo player and friend of Prince Charles.

Park Place

As the river curves gently to the left, on the right bank there is a substantial gabled boat-house and a rustic bridge, built by Humphrey Gainsborough in 1783, that still carries the main Wargrave to Henley road. These mark the entrance to Happy Valley, where striped lawns lead uphill towards PARK PLACE, a large French Renaissance-style house

that in 2007 sold for £42 million, a record at the time for a property outside London.

Park Place was begun in 1719 for the Duke of Hamilton and in 1738 was bought by Frederick, Prince of Wales, who set up his own private court at Park Place and brought up his children there, including the future George III. He planted the three cedar trees still standing in front of the house.

When the Prince died suddenly in 1751, his widow Augusta sold the house to the eccentric GENERAL HENRY SEYMOUR CONWAY (1721–95), friend and cousin of Horace Walpole, who made extensive improvements to the estate, planting THE FIRST LOMBARDY POPLARS IN ENGLAND, digging out caverns and vaulted tunnels to make a grotto and amphitheatre, and building the Conway Bridge down by the river. Most remarkable of all, though, is the DRUID'S TEMPLE, a prehistoric circle of 45 stones, shipped over from Jersey in 1785 as a gift from the grateful people of Jersey to their beloved Governor Conway, and re-erected in the grounds of Park Place to create A

MONUMENT UNIQUE IN THE SOUTH OF ENGLAND.

A subsequent owner, MR HENRY SPURLING, managed to acquire the top portion of Christopher Wren's 'wedding cake' spire from St Bride's in London's Fleet Street, which had been broken off by a lightning strike, and placed it in the garden in celebration of Queen Victoria's coronation. In 1865 Victoria herself visited Park Place in disguise, with an eye to buying it, but decided not to.

Park Place is now being developed as a private estate. Shielded from public scrutiny by trees and with no rights of way passing through the grounds, Park Place makes an ideal retreat for a reclusive billionaire ...

Humphrey Gainsborough

(1718–1776)

'One of the most ingenious men that ever lived and one of the best that ever died. Perhaps of all the mechanical geniuses this or any nation has produced, Mr Gainsborough was the first.'
GENTLEMAN'S MAGAZINE, 1785

HUMPHREY GAINSBOROUGH, brother of painter Thomas Gainsborough, was a Nonconformist minister in Henley and a brilliantly creative inventor and engineer. As well as building the aesthetically pleasing Conway Bridge at the mouth of Happy Valley, which still bears heavy traffic to this day, he also constructed eight locks on the Thames between Boulter's

Lock and Sonning. He created the most accurate sundial yet devised which was capable of use at sea – it is now in the British Museum. He developed the drill plough, advancing the ideas of Jethro Tull (see p. 68), invented the tidemill, using a mill-wheel that could rotate in either direction, and in the 1760s designed a working model of a steam engine with a separate condenser which he innocently showed to James Watt – who went away and patented his own similar design in 1769, making no mention of Gainsborough. This gentle parson living in Henley probably invented the steam-engine and thus founded the modern world, but almost no one has heard of him. Such is life. He died of a heart attack while walking in the meadows beside the river he adored, and is buried with his wife near the independent chapel in Henley where he ministered. The site is marked by a blue plaque on the gates of the new chapel that stands there now.

River and Rowing

On the left bank as the river approaches Henley, and screened by trees, is the RIVER AND ROWING MUSEUM, opened in 1998 and located in a building clad in wood designed by David Chipperfield to look like an Oxfordshire barn. In the car park are statues of Britain's greatest rowers, Olympic gold medallists SIR STEVE REDGRAVE and Sir MATTHEW PINSENT.

The Thames now reaches the most fashionable town on the Thames – Henley.

Well, I never knew this
about
THE RIVER THAMES

The poet ALGERNON CHARLES SWIN-BURNE (1837–1909), inventor of the roundel form of poetry, knew Shiplake well because his parents lived in a Georgian house called Holmwood in Binfield Heath 1 mile (1.6 km) to the west. Emily Sellwood had stayed in Holmwood on the night before her wedding to Tennyson in 1850. Swinburne usually came here to dry out after one of his notorious binges.

ERIC BLAIR, later to be known as George Orwell (see p. 62), lived as a child at Roselawn, in Station Road, Shiplake.

Shiplake seems to appeal to ageing rockers. BARRIEMORE BARLOW (b.1949), former drummer in rock band Jethro Tull, lives in Shiplake, where he has a recording studio called The Doghouse. IAN PAICE (b.1948), drummer with Deep Purple, lives in Shiplake. Sixties singer VINCE HILL (b.1937) lives in Lower Shiplake.

Inside St Mary's Church in WARGRAVE there is a tombstone to a Madame Tussaud. However, it's not the waxworks queen but the wife of her grandson, Victor Tussaud.

White-painted WARGRAVE MANOR, which dominates the river north of Wargrave, used to belong to the family of landscape gardener Gertrude Jekyll, and is now owned by the Sultan of Oman.

HENLEY TO MARLOW

Henley-on-Thames, home of the Royal Regatta

Henley-on-Thames

The view of Henley Bridge, the church and the Angel on the Bridge pub is a Thames icon. It may well be that the Angel on the Bridge actually stood on the bridge in days of yore, for the current bridge was built slightly north of a previous wooden one, and partial remains of the foundations of the wooden bridge have been found in the Angel's cellar.

The present, much admired Henley Bridge was built in 1786 by William Hayward of Shrewsbury. The keystones on either side of the central arch were sculpted with the faces of Old Father Thames looking downstream, and Isis looking upstream, by the sculptor Anne Seymour Damer, the daughter of General Conway of Park Place.

St Mary's, Henley

Henley's church of St Mary's is mainly 14th century, but the landmark flint and chequerwork tower is rumoured

Anne Seymour Damer

(1748–1828)

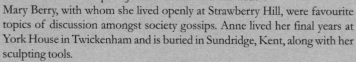

ANNE SEYMOUR DAMER was one of the most highly regarded sculptors of her day. She was encouraged in her work by her father's cousin Horace Walpole, who left her his house in Twickenham, Strawberry Hill, when he died. She led a glittering social life, becoming close friends with the likes of the Emperor Napoleon and Lord Nelson, and amongst her subjects were Nelson, George III and Charles James Fox. In 1767 she married John Damer, the son of Lord Milton, later the Earl of Dorchester, but the marriage never really gelled and they soon separated. He committed suicide in 1776 and Anne concentrated on developing her friendships with actresses such as Sarah Siddons and Elizabeth Farren. Anne's preference for wearing masculine clothing (she was THE FIRST WOMAN IN ENGLAND TO WEAR BLACK SILK STOCKINGS) and her unconcealed relationships with women such as the poet Joanna Baillie and the author Mary Berry, with whom she lived openly at Strawberry Hill, were favourite topics of discussion amongst society gossips. Anne lived her final years at York House in Twickenham and is buried in Sundridge, Kent, along with her sculpting tools.

to have been designed by Cardinal Wolsey in the early 16th century. Buried in the churchyard is RICHARD JENNINGS, master builder of St Paul's Cathedral. There is also a memorial to singer DUSTY SPRINGFIELD (1939–99), described by Elton John as 'the greatest white singer that there has ever been'. She lived in Henley during her final years and her memorial service was held at St Mary's. Her ashes were divided between Henley and the Cliffs of Moher in Ireland.

The church sits amongst a group of fine old buildings that welcome those entering the town across the bridge, among them the RED LION, where the poet WILLIAM SHENSTONE (1714–63) wrote a famous poem, four lines of which he scratched on a window pane:

Who'er has travelled life's dull round,
Where'er his stages may have been,
May sigh to think he still has found
The warmest welcome at an inn.

Charles I slept at the Red Lion in 1632 and again in 1642; and, rather fittingly, across the road is the Tudor oak-beamed birthplace of WILLIAM LENTHALL (1591–1662), Speaker of the House of Commons who refused Charles's demand to give up five Members of Parliament with the immortal words, 'May it please Your Majesty, I have neither eyes to see, nor tongue to speak in this place, but as the House is pleased to direct me, whose servant I am.'

Although the BRAKSPEAR BREWERY in New Street closed in 2002, the Georgian brewery buildings survive as restaurants and craft centres, while the KENTON THEATRE, founded in 1805, is housed in a wonderful Georgian building and is BRITAIN'S FOURTH OLDEST WORKING THEATRE.

Friar Park

Just to the west of the town centre is FRIAR PARK, the 120-room Victorian Gothic mansion where Beatle George Harrison lived from 1971 until his death in 2001.

Friar Park sits in the midst of 30 acres (12 ha) of garden, which were laid out originally by eccentric lawyer SIR FRANK CRISP, who lived at Friar Park from 1895 until 1919. He created an extraordinary world of subterranean waterways, cascades and lakes, linked by passageways to underground caverns and grottoes filled with vines and skeletons. One of the caverns was occupied by Crisp's unrivalled horde of garden gnomes, some of whom appear on the cover of George Harrison's album *All Things Must Pass*.

Crisp also built a rock garden in the shape of the Matterhorn, complete with an alpine meadow and topped with a piece of rock from the summit of the real thing, and a lake with stepping stones just beneath the surface so that his butler, when summoned to serve Crisp's incredulous guests, could appear to be walking on the water with the drinks tray.

When they bought Friar Park, George Harrison and his wife Olivia set about restoring many of Crisp's features, which had been neglected by the Catholic nuns who had owned it previously. At first they let the people of Henley wander through the grounds at will. However, after the shooting of John Lennon in 1980, Harrison became understandably more reclusive, the gates were locked and the estate was surrounded by barbed wire and security cameras. In 1999 an intruder managed to break into the house and attack Harrison, badly injuring the former Beatle before being felled by Olivia with a poker.

The house and grounds remain well fortified despite complaints from neighbours, including former TV Likely Lad RODNEY BEWES.

Henley Royal Regatta

The stretch of river north from Henley Bridge is THE LONGEST NATURALLY STRAIGHT STRETCH OF RIVER IN BRITAIN, almost 1 mile (1.6 km) long, and hence perfect for rowing races, and when all is said and done, what Henley is known for across the world is rowing.

Facing the Angel on the Bridge across the river from Berkshire is the Henley Royal Regatta headquarters, designed by Terry Farrell.

On the downstream side of the bridge, in Berkshire, is the social headquarters of the regatta, the smart clubhouse of THE WORLD'S OLDEST ROWING CLUB, LEANDER CLUB, founded in London in 1818. The Henley clubhouse opened in 1897, and 101 years later women were admitted. Leander Club has WON MORE OLYMPIC AND WORLD CHAMPIONSHIP GOLD MEDALS THAN ANY OTHER ROWING CLUB IN THE WORLD. Leander Club colours were originally red but were altered to the now famous pink (or more correctly cerise) to distinguish them from Marlow Rowing Club's red.

The origins of the Henley Regatta go back to 1829 with THE FIRST OXFORD AND CAMBRIDGE BOAT RACE, which was rowed between Hambleden Lock and Henley Bridge, a distance of 2 miles (3.2 km). It was arranged by two friends from Harrow, CHARLES MERIVALE, who went to Cambridge, and CHARLES WORDSWORTH, nephew of the poet William Wordsworth, who was at Oxford. The two boats collided at the off and had to start again. Oxford won.

Although Cambridge chose to stage the next Boat Race in London, other rowing races were run over the same course at Henley and started to attract large crowds of spectators. The town decided to raise money for a GRAND CHALLENGE CUP FOR MEN'S EIGHTS, which remains the most prestigious event to this day, and THE FIRST HENLEY REGATTA was held in 1839.

In 1851 PRINCE ALBERT travelled up the Thames from Windsor to attend, whereupon the regatta became Henley Royal Regatta, and it has been an integral part of the 'Season' ever since. Since 1986 the regatta has been a five-day event and takes place over the first weekend in July.

The regatta course runs from Temple Island to just short of Henley Bridge, a distance of 1 mile, 550 yards.

Downstream from Henley Bridge

Now begins what some regard as the loveliest stretch of the Thames, supremely English, a wide, slow river valley lined with lush green meadows backed by gentle wooded hills that come and go.

Since Lechlade the left bank has been Oxfordshire. About halfway down the regatta course it becomes Buckinghamshire, and here a short stretch of tree-lined canal leads away from the left bank to Fawley Court.

Fawley Court

FAWLEY COURT was occupied in Norman times by Walter Giffard, the Earl of Buckinghamshire, but during the Civil War in the 17th century it was the home of Parliamentarian Sir Bulstrode Whitelock and was ransacked by the Royalist cavalry under Prince Rupert. In 1684 new owner plantation merchant William Freeman had the house rebuilt, some claim by Sir Christopher Wren, others by Inigo Jones, although without proof in either case. What is known is that in 1770–71 the house was refashioned by James Wyatt as his first country house commission.

In 1953 the estate was bought by the Congregation of Marian Fathers as a school for Polish boys. The house was badly damaged by fire in the 1970s but was restored with the help of the Polish community, and a new church was built in the grounds funded by Prince Radziwill, ex-husband of Lee Bouvier Radziwill, younger sister of Jacqueline Kennedy Onassis. When the Prince died in 1976 he was interred inside the church.

In 2008 Fawley Court was purchased by Iranian Heiress AIDA HERSHAM, reportedly for £13 million.

Remenham

REMENHAM sits on the opposite bank from Fawley Court and consists of a church, a rectory and a rather pleasant Georgian farmhouse now owned by the Copas Partnership and used for hospitality during the regatta and at other events throughout the year. The church dates from the 13th century but was greatly restored in 1870 and is famous for its iron gates from Sienna, presented in 1875 by John Noble from Park Place. In 1990 actress JENNY AGUTTER, star of *The Railway Children*, was married in the church to Johan Tham, director of the Cliveden Hotel.

Temple Island

TEMPLE ISLAND marks the start of the regatta course and takes its name from the miniature temple which was built there by James Wyatt in 1771 as a fishing lodge for Fawley Court. The temple can boast ENGLAND'S FIRST ETRUSCAN INTERIOR. The island is now owned by Henley Royal Regatta and can be hired for weddings and private functions.

Greenlands

At the end of the Henley straight on the Buckinghamshire bank, with a glorious view past Temple Island back to Henley, there sits a long white house, in the middle of manicured lawns, called GREENLANDS. During the Civil War the property here belonged to Royalist Sir John D'Oyley, descendant of the Robert D'Oyly who built Oxford Castle, and the house was reduced to rubble by Roundhead artillery positioned on the opposite bank.

The house was later rebuilt and in 1868 became the home of WILLIAM HENRY (W.H.) SMITH (1825–91), the newsagent who in 1848 had opened the first railway bookstall, at Euston Station in London. Jerome K. Jerome described Greenlands as 'the rather uninteresting looking residence of my newsagent, a quiet unassuming old gentleman, who may often be met with about these regions . . . sculling himself along in easy, vigorous style . . .'

Greenlands is now the campus of the Henley Business School, part of the University of Reading.

Hambleden Mill

The river continues in a sweeping curve round Remenham Hill, and soon white-timbered picture postcard HAMBLEDEN MILL appears, the centrepiece of one of the most photographed scenes on the upper river. 'Hambledene Mill' is mentioned in the Domesday Book and remained in use until 1955. It has now been sympathetically converted into luxury apartments and remains as picturesque as ever.

After Hambleden Mill and Lock the river flows past the village of Aston, where there is a pleasant brick inn called the Flower Pot, which used to run a ferry here. Also on the right bank, set on a small hill above the plain, with panoramic views of the Thames valley, is Culham Court, built in 1770 and another property of Swiss financier Urs Schwarzenbach, which he bought for £35 million in 2007.

Medmenham Abbey

Next up on the Buckinghamshire side is the somewhat mock-ruined MEDMEN-HAM ABBEY, founded in 1201 for Cistercian monks, although practically nothing survives from the original building. In the 18th century Medmenham Abbey was owned by the rakish SIR FRANCIS DASHWOOD (1708–81) of West Wycombe Park, a wealthy London merchant, THE ONLY CHANCELLOR OF THE EXCHEQUER TO ADMIT DELIVERING HIS BUDGET SPEECH WHILE DRUNK, and founder of the Knights of St Francis of Wycombe or, as it became known, the HELLFIRE CLUB. The club would hold secret meetings at Medmenham to which only ladies of 'a cheerful and lively disposition' were invited, and which would invariably descend into Bacchanalian orgies.

One night at Medmenham in 1763, as so often happens, rough house turned to tears. One of the members, Sir Henry Vansittart, the Governor of Bengal, brought along as his guest a baboon that had accompanied him back from India. Another member, John Wilkes, the cross-eyed radical journalist and MP for Aylesbury, thought what fun it would be

to dress the animal up as the Devil and conceal it in a box. At just the right moment he released the creature, which sprang out from the box on to the back of the Earl of Sandwich, First Lord of the Admiralty. 'Spare me gracious Devil,' cried out the noble earl in terror, 'thou knowest I was only fooling, I am not half as wicked as I pretended!' And with that, earl and baboon fled from the abbey into the night. The baboon was never seen again, while the Earl of Sandwich retired into private life to work on his new invention, the sandwich. The Hellfire Club moved their headquarters to the caves at West Wycombe and continued their debauched ways underground for a while, but the members slowly grew old and weary and began to prefer a quiet night in to orgies, and the club finally closed down in 1774.

Medmenham Abbey is now a private home.

Danesfield House

Gleaming white, high up on a chalk bluff on the Buckinghamshire side is DANESFIELD HOUSE, built on the site of the Danish encampment that protected the river crossing here. The late Victorian Tudor pile was designed in 1899 for ROBERT WILLIAM HUDSON (1856–1937), the son of ROBERT 'SOAPY' HUDSON (1812–84), who INVENTED SOAP POWDER by grinding coarse bar soap with a mortar and pestle, and was THE FIRST TO USE MASS ADVERTISING TO POPULARISE HIS PRODUCT, with posters on public transport saying 'A Little of Hudson's goes a long way'. Hudson's

Dry Soap was taken over by Lever Brothers in 1908.

Between 1941 and 1977 Danesfield was owned by the Air Ministry and known as RAF Medmenham, then became headquarters of the Carnation Milk Company, and in 1991 was converted into a luxury hotel.

Hurley

On the other side of the river from Danesfield House is the secret village of HURLEY, hidden from both the river and the road. The church here was founded in about AD 635 by St Birinius (see p. 65), who established chapels at the places where he preached, and the remains of a Saxon church can be seen in the foundations of the present St Mary's. PRINCESS EDITHA, sister of Edward the Confessor, is buried somewhere beneath the floor of the Norman nave, which is all that survives of the church of St Mary's Priory, founded for Benedictine monks in 1086. Some of the monastic buildings have been incorporated into private homes, there is a fabulous 12th-century barn, and the Priory guesthouse is now the crooked and quaint YE OLDE BELL – dating from 1135, it has a claim to be England's oldest inn.

Ladye Place

On top of the monastery ruins RICHARD LOVELACE, who sailed the Spanish Main with Sir Francis Drake, built the original LADYE PLACE, paid for with Spanish gold. He was later created Lord Lovelace of Hurley, and his spectacular brightly coloured family tomb is in the church.

The 3rd Baron Lovelace of Hurley used the crypt of Ladye Place to hold secret meetings with his Whig friends at which they plotted the downfall of James II, and it was here that they signed the proposal to send for William of Orange, which brought about the Glorious Revolution of 1688. King William came to Hurley after his accession to see for himself the vaults where his destiny had been determined. Those same vaults are all that survives of the Elizabethan Ladye Place, which was demolished in 1837 and later replaced by an Edwardian mansion.

Harleyford Manor

The Thames at Hurley divides into numerous channels and over on the Buckinghamshire side, by Hurley Lock, is HARLEYFORD MANOR, a handsome red-brick house built in 1755 by Sir Robert Taylor for SIR WILLIAM CLAYTON, MP for Marlow. His descendant, also Sir William, fought at Waterloo and used the field to the east of Harleyford Manor to graze his warhorses, or chargers; hence the field is known as Chargers Paddock. There is a commemorative plaque in the walled garden telling the story of Sir William's favourite horse, Skirmisher, who was fatally wounded while serving in France.

Harleyford Manor is now the headquarters and offices of the Harleyford Leisure Estate and Marina.

Temple Lock

Where Temple Lock now is, there was once a mill run by the Templar Knights of Bisham Abbey. The mill was enlarged in the 18th century to incorporate a copper foundry, taking advantage of cheap copper brought from Swansea along the Thames and Severn Canal. This business got caught up in the South Sea Bubble and afterwards the mill was used for making paper. At one time the mill here had THE BIGGEST MILL-WHEEL ON THE THAMES, but it closed in 1969 and is now converted into a marina and apartments.

Bisham Abbey

BISHAM ABBEY, one of the Thames's most historic jewels, is well known today as the NATIONAL SPORTS CENTRE and headquarters of the England football team.

The house is set proudly above the river with gardens coming down to the water, its venerable old tower and gables and mullioned windows a magnet for artists who throng the towpath on the far side of the river. In the days of Henry III, the manor of Bisham belonged to the Knights Templar, who added a refectory, or dining hall, in 1260. The present building is constructed around this great hall, which survives inside. When the Templars were suppressed in 1307, Edward II took over the hall and used it as a place of confinement for Robert the Bruce's wife and daughter, Elizabeth and Marjorie, who had been captured on the Isle of Rathlin.

The EARL OF SALISBURY bought the manor in 1335 and established a priory next door. Six Earls of Salisbury are buried in the priory, including the 2nd Earl, who fought at Poitiers, and the 4th Earl, who fought at Agincourt. Through the 4th Earl's daughter Bisham passed to WARWICK THE KINGMAKER, who was buried here in 1471 after his defeat at the Battle of Barnet.

At the Dissolution of the Monasteries the priory was briefly refounded as a Benedictine abbey, but this in turn was dissolved six months later. The Abbot, JOHN CORDERY, as he was being dragged away, laid a curse on the building: 'As God is my witness, this property shall ne'er be inherited, for its sons will be hounded by misfortune.' And with one or two exceptions the curse seems to have held.

Henry VIII next gave Bisham Abbey to Anne of Cleves as part of her divorce settlement, and she passed it on to SIR

PHILIP HOBY, who restored the house using materials from the abandoned abbey. The property he left, which is much what we see today, took the name Bisham Abbey.

Lady Elizabeth Hoby

Princess Elizabeth (later Elizabeth I) was confined at Bisham during her sister Bloody Mary's cruel reign and would sit for hours at the bow window gazing at the river. She was befriended by the lady of the house, ELIZABETH HOBY, and when the Princess became Queen, Lady Hoby was rewarded with a place at Court.

Lady Elizabeth Hoby was a stern mother who liked to attend to her children's education herself. One of her sons, William, was slower than the rest and she would regularly beat him about the head until his face ran red with blood. One day poor William literally blotted his copybook, so his frustrated mother took him by the ear and marched him up to the top of the tower and locked him in, telling him that he wouldn't be allowed out until he had finished his homework.

A little later Lady Hoby received a message from the Queen ordering her to attend the Court without delay, and joyously she galloped away, not returning for over a week. 'Why is William not here to meet me?' she demanded on her return, and suddenly her heart froze. She ran to the tower room, unlocked the door and there was William – starved to death.

To this day Lady Elizabeth Hoby is said to haunt the tower at Bisham Abbey, frantically rubbing away at her bloodstained hands – and, spookily enough, when the house was being restored at a later date, some old copybooks were found under floorboards in the tower.

Bisham Church

Lady Elizabeth Hoby's magnificent tomb is one of a number of grand Hoby monuments to be found in BISHAM CHURCH, which stands a little way downriver from Bisham Abbey. Although much restored, the church boasts a magnificent Norman tower that is set right beside the water and creates an unforgettable

spectacle. Also inside is the sculpted figure of an Eton schoolboy kneeling at his desk with his trusty spaniel curled up beside him. This is a Vansittart, the last heir of Bisham Abbey who died at the age of 14 – a victim of the abbot's curse?

From Bisham Church it is but a short boat ride into Marlow.

Well, I never **knew this**
about
THE RIVER THAMES

On first leaving Henley the river passes a large white house, set back a little from the river on the right bank, known as BARN ELMS, which was the last home of actress GLADYS COOPER (1888–1971), the Force's pin-up in the First World War. She was often seen walking the towpath.

MISS FREEMAN, the daughter of the house at Fawley Court, was used by Anne Damer as model for her sculpture of the head of Isis on Henley Bridge.

HAMBLEDEN village, about 2 miles (3.2 km) from the river and formerly owned by W.H. Smith, is today the property of Swiss financier Urs Schwarzenbach. He bought the Hambleden estate for £38 million in 2007.

In the 18th century LADYE PLACE in HURLEY was owned by the brother of ADMIRAL KEMPENFELT, whose ship, the *Royal George*, largest warship in the world when it was launched in 1756, sank at Spithead in 1782 with the loss of over 800 lives, including that of the Admiral. The story is told that a hawthorn tree planted by Admiral Kempenfelt at Ladye Place shrivelled and died on the night the *Royal George* went down.

TV sports presenter STEVE RIDER lives in a cottage by the river at HURLEY.

Just downstream from Hurley Lock is the family-run FREEBODY'S BOATYARD, THE LARGEST SURVIVING BUILDERS OF WOODEN BOATS IN ENGLAND. The Freebody family have been making wooden boats on the Thames since the 13th century.

TEMPLE BRIDGE, arching over the Thames for 150 ft (46 m) near Temple Lock, is THE LONGEST HARDWOOD BRIDGE IN BRITAIN.

MARLOW TO
MAIDENHEAD

Marlow, birthplace of Frankenstein

Marlow

'Marlow is one of the pleasantest
river centres I know of.
It is a bustling, lively little town.'
JEROME K. JEROME

MARLOW is an attractive 18th-century
market town with plenty of fine old
buildings and provides another wonderful Thames spectacle of church spire
and bridge – in this particular case, THE
ONLY SUSPENSION BRIDGE ACROSS THE
NON-TIDAL THAMES.

MARLOW BRIDGE was erected in 1832
by WILLIAM TIERNEY CLARK, designer
of THE FIRST SUSPENSION BRIDGE
ACROSS THE THAMES at Hammersmith.
Clark's bridge at Marlow was a prototype for his much larger Szechenyl
Chain Bridge, linking Buda and Pest
across the Danube, which was
Budapest's first permanent bridge and,
when it was built in 1849, the longest
suspension bridge in the world.

ALL SAINTS CHURCH, Marlow, was
built in 1835 on the site of a 12th-
century predecessor whose foundations
were rotted away by flooding. Inside

there is an interesting memorial to SIR
MILES HOBART, MP for Marlow who, as
Speaker of the House of Commons in
1628, began the tradition of shutting the
door of the Commons in Black Rod's
face by locking the door to the King's
Messenger and pocketing the key until
the resolution of the 'illegal tonnage and
poundage' debate. For this he was
thrown briefly into the Tower, and not
long afterwards he died in a coach accident on Holborn Hill. The memorial
depicts this unfortunate event and was
THE FIRST MONUMENT EVER ERECTED AT
PUBLIC EXPENSE IN BRITAIN.

Preserved in Marlow's Roman
Catholic Church of St Peter, built by
Pugin at the expense of Charles Scott-
Murray of Danesfield, is the 'Hand of
St James', which was removed from
Reading Abbey at the Dissolution and
found its way here via Scott-Murray's
private chapel at Danesfield (see p.
104).

THAMES LAWN, a big three-storey
house by the river behind All Saints, was
the home of Captain Morris, who
commanded the three-decker battleship
HMS *Colossus* at the Battle of Trafalgar.
Thames Lawn played the home of MI6
chief 'M' (played by Bernard Lee) in the
James Bond film *On Her Majesty's Secret
Service*.

The novelist and poet THOMAS LOVE
PEACOCK wrote the novel *Nightmare
Abbey* while living at No. 47 West Street
in Marlow. In 1816, after PERCY BYSSHE
SHELLEY's young wife Harriet had
drowned herself in the Serpentine in
London, Peacock encouraged Shelley
and his girlfriend Mary Godwin to
marry and move to Marlow, which they

did, taking up residence in a Gothic-
style cottage ALBION HOUSE, also in
West Street, early in 1817. While living
there, Shelley spent his time drifting
down the river to Bisham in his skiff,
composing *The Revolt of Islam*, while his
wife Mary sat in the house writing her
horror novel *Frankenstein*. Their house is
marked by a plaque.

Another poet, T.S. ELIOT (1888–1965),
lived at No. 31 West Street at the end of
the First World War – the house is now
called The Old Post Office House.

A famous resident of Marlow in the
18th century was DR WILLIAM BATTIE
(1703–76) who wrote the first book on
the treatment of mental illness and gave
his name to the expression 'batty'. He
lived at COURT GARDEN HOUSE, now
part of Higginson Park, by the river on
the west side of town. There is a statue
in Higginson Park of SIR STEVE
REDGRAVE, who was born in Marlow in
1962, looking across the park to the
finishing line of the Marlow regatta in
which he used to compete. He is THE
ONLY BRITISH ATHLETE EVER TO WIN A
GOLD MEDAL AT FIVE CONSECUTIVE
OLYMPIC GAMES (1984–2000).

JEROME K. JEROME wrote some of *Three Men in a Boat* at the TWO BREWERS, just downstream from the bridge. The two brewers in question were THOMAS WETHERED, founder of the brewery at Marlow, and SAMUEL WHITBREAD, who took over Wethered's, and there used to be a picture of them on the pub sign, one on either side.

A short walk from the Two Brewers is a house by Marlow Lock bearing a blue plaque to indicate the home of SIR EVELYN WRENCH (1882–1966), editor of the *Spectator* from 1925 until 1932 and founder of the English Speaking Union.

Across the bridge from Marlow, on the Berkshire side and right next to the weir, is the COMPLEAT ANGLER, named after Izaak Walton's famous book of 1653, and THE FIRST RESTAURANT OUTSIDE LONDON TO BE VISITED BY THE QUEEN. She was invited to dine there with the President of Hungary in 1999. It is now a hotel.

Kenneth Grahame

On leaving Marlow the river flows around the steep slopes of Winter Hill, thick with the trees of Quarry Wood, the 'Wild Wood' of KENNETH GRAHAME'S *The Wind in the Willows*. Grahame was sent here to live with his grandmother when he was five years old, after his mother had died, and he grew up in a wonderful, rambling old house called The Mount, in Cookham Dean, just on the other side of the woods. The grounds of the house came down to the river here, and it was

Grahame's youthful memories of the woods and riverside scenery around Cookham Dean that would later form the background to his stories. Grahame married in 1899 and had a son, Alastair, and in 1906 he moved his family back to Cookham Dean where he had been so happy as a child. They bought a house called MAYFIELD, not far from his childhood home, and it was at Mayfield that he composed the bedtime stories for Alastair that would become *The Wind in the Willows*, which was first published in 1908.

Dame Nellie Melba

Australian opera star DAME NELLIE MELBA (1861–1931) lived in a cottage in Quarry Wood, and her voice could often be heard wafting through the trees as she practised her arias. Dame Nellie was THE FIRST ARTISTE TO BROADCAST ON BRITISH RADIO, in June 1920, and THE FIRST AUSTRALIAN TO APPEAR ON THE COVER OF *TIME* MAGAZINE, in 1927. And then, of course, there was the PEACH MELBA, named in her honour by the head chef at the Savoy Hotel, Auguste Escoffier.

Cock Marsh

On the Berkshire side Winter Hill now gives way to Cock Marsh, an area of lowland marsh wonderful for birds and rare flowers that has been common grazing land since the 13th century. Most of it is now looked after by the National Trust.

Bourne End

A ferry used to ply between Cock Marsh and the Spade Oak pub on the left bank. Here Buckinghamshire now into BOURNE END, where the River Wye joins the Thames, an area popular with sailing clubs. Among those fortunate enough to have lived in Bourne End are:

LOUIS BLERIOT (1872–1936), THE FIRST MAN TO FLY ACROSS THE ENGLISH CHANNEL, who lived at NEW YORK LODGE, a large property beside the Thames at Bourne End, from 1916 to 1926. The house was destroyed by fire in 1926.

ENID BLYTON (1897–1968), children's author, who lived in a delightful 16th-century home called OLD THATCH COTTAGE at Bourne End from 1929 to 1938.

KENNETH CONNOR (1916–93), Carry On films actor.

Sir TOM STOPPARD, playwright, born in 1937.

Cookham

'A village in Heaven'
STANLEY SPENCER

South of Bourne End, on the opposite bank, is COOKHAM, a large, sprawling, still pretty village made famous by the paintings of SIR STANLEY SPENCER (1891–1959), who was born in FERN-LEA, a semi-detached Victorian house in the High Street. The Stanley Spencer Gallery is located nearby in the former Methodist chapel where he attended Sunday School. Spencer lived his last 28 years in Cookham and was often seen pushing a tatty old pram about the place, filled with all his easels and paints and canvases.

Spencer's best-known works depict biblical scenes set in Cookham, his 'village in Heaven', and a diverting hour or two can be passed trying to find the actual setting for the paintings. For instance, the unfinished *Christ Preaching at Cookham Regatta* is clearly set beside the Ferry Inn, although the pub has since been modernised and is virtually unrecognisable; *The Crucifixion* is set in the High Street; and *The Resurrection* in Cookham Churchyard, in which the good folk of Cookham are seen rising from their graves, is set in the churchyard close to where Spencer now lies buried.

Spencer's *Swan Upping* shows Cookham Bridge, a flimsy-looking Victorian iron bridge of 1867 – its predecessor of 1840 was the first bridge here for 1,400 years since the Romans left in the 5th century.

Formosa

FORMOSA ISLAND just downstream of Cookham Bridge covers 50 acres (20 ha) and is THE LARGEST ISLAND IN THE NON-TIDAL THAMES.

After Cookham Lock, on the right bank and difficult to see through trees, is FORMOSA PLACE. The original house here was built in 1785 for Sir George Young, 1st baronet, and the property, now redeveloped, has descended to Sir George Young, 6th baronet (b.1941), Conservative Secretary of State for Transport under John Major.

Cliveden Reach

Just after the island of Formosa the river encounters the great chalk cliff of Cliveden and is forced to turn sharply south to flow along CLIVEDEN REACH, a gorgeous sweep of river flanked by magnificent beechwoods and described by Jerome K. Jerome as 'perhaps the sweetest stretch of all the river'. Indeed, as Stanley Spencer, who spent his last years in a house at Cookham called Cliveden View, put it, 'You can't walk by

the river at Cliveden Reach and not believe in God.'

About halfway down Cliveden Reach, on the Buckinghamshire bank, behind a small patch of lawn and half hidden by trees, is a little chalet that looks like something out of *Hansel and Gretel* – the notorious Spring Cottage on the Cliveden estate where the 'Swinging Sixties' began.

Spring Cottage

At the start of the 1960s, SPRING COTTAGE was let out by Lord Astor, owner of Cliveden, to the society osteopath Dr Stephen Ward, who used it as somewhere for his rich and famous friends to indulge themselves with ladies who – and this is the key point – were not their wives. One such couple were a leggy young lovely called CHRISTINE KEELER, who was 19, and JOHN PROFUMO, Secretary of State for War, who was considerably older, but not wise enough to resist Keeler's topless antics in Cliveden's swimming pool. Unfortunately for Profumo, Keeler was friends with some unsavoury characters and got involved with the police, which brought the affair out into the open, along with the explosive fact that Keeler was also sleeping with a naval attaché at the Soviet embassy called Yevgeny Ivanov. Profumo stupidly claimed in the House of Commons that there was 'no impropriety whatever' in his relationship with Keeler, but in the end he had to admit that he had misled the House and was forced to resign. The scandal led ultimately to the fall of Harold Macmillan's government and in many people's opinion caused the breakdown of trust and respect for authority that ushered in the 'Swinging Sixties'. Profumo eventually restored his reputation by working for a charity at Toynbee Hall in London's East End. Spring Cottage is now available as a holiday let – but it may be a good idea to draw the curtains, since it is among the most photographed houses on the Thames.

Cliveden House

CLIVEDEN HOUSE, which glides slowly and gloriously into view, high on a plateau at the end of a long avenue of trees above this most majestic sweep of the Thames, was, it must be said, no stranger to scandal. The original house was built in 1666 for George Villiers,

later the 2nd Duke of Buckingham, who used the house to entertain his mistresses, notably Anna, Countess of Shrewsbury. Anna's husband, the 11th Earl of Shrewsbury, challenged Villiers to a duel and was fatally run through as his faithless wife held the reins of her lover's horse. Then, apparently, the triumphant couple frolicked in the dead earl's blood. George Villiers survived the duel unscathed but he was banished from Society, and Cliveden's reputation for high jinks was established.

From 1737 to 1751 the house was leased to Frederick, Prince of Wales, who divided his time between Cliveden and Park Place, up the river at Henley. It was during a party thrown by the Prince at Cliveden in 1741 that 'RULE BRITANNIA' WAS PERFORMED FOR THE FIRST TIME, as part of a masque about Alfred the Great written by JAMES THOMSON and set to music by THOMAS ARNE.

It was also while at Cliveden that the Prince of Wales became THE FIRST PERSON TO BE KILLED BY A CRICKET BALL, when he was struck on the chest by one, causing an abscess which became fatally infected.

In 1795 the house burned down, as did the next one, and in 1851 the new owner, the Duke of Sutherland, commissioned Sir Charles Barry, architect of the Houses of Parliament, to build the huge Italianate pile we see today.

In 1893 Cliveden was bought by the American billionaire WILLIAM WALDORF ASTOR (later 1st Lord Astor), who gave it to his son as a wedding present. The 2nd Lord Astor and his wife

Nancy, who in 1919 became THE FIRST WOMAN TO TAKE HER SEAT AS A MEMBER OF PARLIAMENT IN THE BRITISH HOUSE OF COMMONS, held lavish parties at Cliveden for the glitterati, writers, artists, politicians and world leaders.

It was the 3rd Lord Astor who leased Spring Cottage to Stephen Ward, and around whose swimming pool John Profumo met Christine Keeler.

Today Cliveden is owned by the National Trust and leased out as a luxury hotel, although Trust members may wander through the grounds and enjoy the celebrated views of the Thames from the terraces.

Boulter's Lock

One of the first big houses to appear on the right bank as the river heads for Boulter's Lock is ISLET PARK HOUSE where GERRY ANDERSON, creator of *Thunderbirds*, produced his first puppet shows.

Just before Boulter's Lock a channel cuts away to the left, the beginning of BRITAIN'S LARGEST EVER MAN-MADE RIVER PROJECT, the JUBILEE RIVER. Completed in the Queen's Jubilee year of 2002, the Jubilee River runs for 7 miles (11 km) between Cliveden Reach and Black Potts Bridge east of Windsor and acts as an overflow for the Thames to alleviate flooding around Maidenhead and Windsor.

Cliveden Reach comes to an end at BOULTER'S LOCK, made famous by Edward Gregory's riotous painting, *Boulter's Lock – Sunday Afternoon 1895*, showing the lock packed with gaily coloured craft of every sort. The lock is the most easily accessible of all the Thames locks, with a road running alongside it and a bridge across it from which to watch all the action and bustle. It was a popular day out for Victorian and Edwardian families who would come down to watch the Prince of Wales pass through on his way to visit the Astors at Cliveden, or see Oscar Wilde and Dame Nellie Melba wave imperiously from their yacht. Today the crowds come to watch the chaos and with luck to see somebody fall in – it happens regularly.

Taplow Court

Hidden in the trees above Boulter's Lock is TAPLOW COURT, once owned by the 1ST EARL OF ORKNEY (1666–1737), the FIRST BRITISH SOLDIER TO BE MADE A FIELD MARSHAL. In 1852 the house was remodelled in its present Victorian Tudor style for Lord Desborough, who hosted meetings at Taplow of the 'Souls', a group of intellectuals and politicians who would get together to talk about matters of the Soul.

Since 1988 Taplow Court has been

the headquarters of SGI-UK, a lay Buddhist society.

The name Taplow comes from the Saxon chief Taeppa who was buried on

the hill here, and this great hill, or 'mai dun', gives it name to Maidenhead, or 'mai dun hythe', meaning wharf.

Well, I never knew this
about
THE RIVER THAMES

Not far from All Saints Church in Marlow, beside the war memorial, is a drinking fountain erected in honour of CHARLES FROHMAN, the American theatrical manager who put on the first performances of J.M. Barrie's *Peter Pan* at the Duke of York's theatre in 1904. He was played by Dustin Hoffman in the 2004 film *Neverland* which starred Johnny Depp as Barrie. Frohman loved Marlow and spent all his summer holidays in the town. He was drowned when the liner *Lusitania* was torpedoed by a German submarine and sunk off the coast of Ireland in 1915.

If LULLEBROOK MANOR in Cookham's Ferry Lane was not one of the inspirations for Toad Hall from the *The Wind in the Willows*, then maybe the owner of the house was a model for Mr Toad – he was very proud of being THE FIRST PERSON IN COOKHAM TO OWN A CAR.

Comedian JOYCE GRENFELL (1910–79) was a niece of Nancy Astor, spent much of her child-

hood at CLIVEDEN and lived in one of the cottages on the Cliveden estate with her husband after she married in 1927.

CLIVEDEN HOUSE played the home of Lady Penelope in the 2004 live action film *Thunderbirds*.

The PROFUMO AFFAIR gave rise to one of the most famous quotes of the 1960s when Mandy Rice-Davies, a friend of Christine Keeler, was in the witness box giving evidence. On being told by the prosecuting counsel that Lord Astor denied having met her, she replied, 'Well, he would, wouldn't he?'

A blue plaque on the covered wooden bridge across to BOULTER'S ISLAND by Boulter's Lock tells us that legendary TV broadcaster RICHARD DIMBLEBY (1913–65) lived on the northern tip of the island. Apparently he would often come out of the house and shout at boats to slow down.

MAIDENHEAD
TO WINDSOR

The Sounding Arch – the world's widest and flattest brick arch

Maidenhead

MAIDENHEAD was an important coaching stop on the Great West Road between London and Bath because it was exactly one day's ride from London. In addition, people didn't want to risk the next stage of the journey in the dark, because the notorious Maidenhead Thicket was plagued by highwaymen.

'Are you married or do you live in Maidenhead?' was the quip on everyone's lips in the late 19th, early 20th century, such was Maidenhead's reputation for high jinks and sauciness at the time.

Much of the fun was centred on SKIN-DLES HOTEL, situated right next to Maidenhead Bridge, and founded in 1833 by William Skindle. The introduction of the railways brought Maidenhead within easy reach of London, and once the Prince of Wales (future Edward VII) started taking Lillie Langtry there his rackety set soon followed. Later, in the 1920s and 30s, playboys and debutantes would flock there for parties and dirty weekends in their open-top sports cars. In the 1960s and 70s Skindles became a music venue hosting performances from bands such as the Rolling Stones and the Beatles, but the glamour soon faded and the place eventually turned into a down-market disco club. Alas, Skindles is now closed, cobwebbed and boarded up, no doubt to be demolished to make way for executive waterside apartments.

What the elegant, Portland Stone MAIDENHEAD BRIDGE of 1777 thought of all the goings-on at Skindles, no one knows, but she has outlived it all and still carries the Great West Road over the Thames.

The Sounding Arch

A quarter of a mile (400 m) downstream is Maidenhead's famous railway bridge, built in 1838 by ISAMBARD KINGDOM BRUNEL to take the Great Western Railway over the Thames. It has THE FLATTEST AND WIDEST BRICK ARCH IN THE WORLD, with a span of 128 ft (39 m) that rises by just 24 ft (7.3 m). Few people thought it would take the weight of a locomotive, but it proved so strong that an exact copy was later built to extend the bridge westwards. Brunel's original is known as the SOUNDING ARCH because of the PERFECT ECHO that can be experienced when standing on the path underneath. The bridge was the subject of a painting by J.M.W. Turner called *Rain, Speed and Steam* which now hangs in the National Gallery in London.

Millionaire's Row

The river continues on past the magnificent villas of Maidenhead's 'MILLIONAIRE'S ROW', before rounding a bend that brings the chalk and stone tower of Bray church into view. Among the residents of these delightful properties are singer ROLF HARRIS, chat show host MICHAEL PARKINSON and at one time, before he unwisely described the products sold in his jewellery shops as 'total crap', GERALD RATNER.

Bray

BRAY is a lovely place and it's no wonder that SIMON ALLEYN, the infamous VICAR OF BRAY, clung to his position, twice as a Catholic and twice as a Protestant during the reigns of Henry VIII and his three children.

> And this is law, I will maintain,
> Unto my dying day, Sir
> That whatsoever King shall reign,
> I'll still be the Vicar of Bray, Sir!

In fact, he never did leave, and had to be carried out of the vicarage feet first and now lies for all eternity in the churchyard.

Bray has been dubbed BRITAIN'S GASTRONOMIC CAPITAL since it can boast TWO OF THE FOUR MICHELIN 3-STAR RESTAURANTS IN THE UK. By the water, and identified by a jetty full of expensive gin palaces, is MICHEL ROUX'S WATERSIDE INN, while HESTON BLUMENTHAL'S FAT DUCK is just up the road.

Monkey Island

After passing under the M4 the river comes to the secret retreat of MONKEY ISLAND, originally 'monks eyot', which belonged to monks from a cell of Merton Abbey located upstream near Bray. In 1738 the 3rd Duke of Marlborough, a keen angler, bought the island and built a couple of fishing pavilions, one of them decorated with ceiling paintings depicting monkeys engaged in human activities.

Since 1840 the pavilions have been expanded and transformed into a discreet luxury hotel. EDWARD VII and QUEEN ALEXANDRA once came here to take tea on the lawn with their family, which included three future monarchs, George V, Edward VIII and George VI.

Dames CLARA BUTT and NELLIE MELBA sometimes sang for the hotel guests. From 1912 H.G. WELLS would often row up the river from the Royal Oak, his uncle's pub at Windsor, for trysts with REBECCA WEST, who set her novel *The Return of the Soldier* on the island.

In 1910 SIR EDWARD ELGAR composed his Violin Concerto while staying in THE HUT, a house on the Berkshire riverbank overlooking Monkey Island that had been bought by banker Frank Schuster as a creative retreat. Among those who also stayed there were GABRIEL FAURÉ, SIEGFRIED SASSOON, WALTER SICKERT and GEORGE BERNARD SHAW. In the 1930s The Hut, by now called Long White Cloud, was bought by the Moss family and was the childhood home of legendary racing driver STIRLING MOSS. GERRY AND SYLVIA ANDERSON, the creators of the hugely popular

television show *Thunderbirds*, own a house on the estate that surrounds Long White Cloud.

Dorney Court

Just past Monkey Island, a footpath on the left bank leads to DORNEY COURT, a glorious piece of Olde England perched on a slight rise above the flood plain. Begun in about 1450, it came into the Palmer family by marriage in the mid 16th century and has remained in the family ever since.

In a corner of the Great Hall there stands a carved stone pineapple which commemorates the fact that THE FIRST PINEAPPLE EVER GROWN IN ENGLAND was grown at Dorney Court. The story goes that Charles II, at a dinner in the Mansion House in London, cut the top off a pineapple sent over from Barbados and handed it to Roger Palmer to give to his gardener. Said gardener planted the top at Dorney and the pineapple that grew from it was presented to the Merrie Monarch in 1661. Roger Palmer just happened to be married to the most notorious of Charles II's many mistresses, BARBARA VILLIERS.

Down Place

Next up on the right bank is the slightly
dingy, lumpen back wall of what used
to be DOWN PLACE, now BRAY
STUDIOS. Down Place was built in 1750
for JACOB TONSON (1655–1736), one of
the first publishers to bring literature to
ordinary people by publishing modestly
priced editions of John Dryden, John
Milton and Shakespeare. Jacob was
founder of the KIT KAT CLUB, which
would occasionally meet at Down Place
– it was while staying there that Kit Kat
member the Duke of Marlborough
discovered Monkey Island and decided
to buy it.

In 1951 HAMMER FILM PRODUCTIONS
bought the by now derelict Down Place
as a production base for their low-
budget films, with the house serving as a
ready-made film set. In 1952 Hammer
Films built a studio in the grounds of

Down Place, calling it Bray Studios, and
here they made many of their early films
including *The Curse of Frankenstein* (1957)
and *Horror of Dracula* (1958). The last
Hammer film made at Bray was *The
Mummy's Shroud* in 1966, and the studios
were sold in 1970.

Throughout the 1970s Bray Studios
were used for the special effects in series
such as *Doctor Who* and Gerry Anderson's *Space 1999* and are now used
regularly for TV productions and music
videos.

Oakley Court

A little further downstream is OAKLEY
COURT, a fantastical Victorian pile that
was built in 1857 for RICHARD HALL-
SAYE next door to Down Place.
Apparently, he chose to build the house
in Gothic style in the hope that his
French wife would no longer feel home-

Kit Kat Club

The Kit Kat Club was founded in the early 18th century, both to promote
literature and the arts and to further the cause of the Protestant succession.
Its members were prominent 'Whigs' who had supported the Glorious
Revolution of 1688 that brought the Protestant William of Orange to the
throne, and were determined to ensure that the Catholic Stuarts could never
return. Included in the cast list were future Prime Minister Robert Walpole
(1676–1745), dramatist William Congreve (1670–1729) and co-founders of
the Spectator Joseph Addison (1672–1719) and Richard Steele (1672–1729),
along with any number of dukes and earls. The name Kit Kat was derived
from that of Christopher (Kit) Catling, the keeper of a pie house near
Temple Bar where the club first met.

timber-framed tower standing on a mound, all alone at the end of a track. ST MARY'S BOVENEY dates from the 12th century and served what was once the large village of Boveney. It was declared redundant in 1975 and is now being cared for and restored by The Friends of Friendless Churches. St Mary's was another location used by Hammer Films when they occupied Bray Studios.

sick. In 1919 Oakley Court was bought by ERNEST OLIVIER, Turkish Consul-General in Monte Carlo, who was a friend of General de Gaulle, and during the Second World War Oakley became THE SECRET HEADQUARTERS OF THE FRENCH RESISTANCE, with de Gaulle a frequent visitor.

When Olivier died in 1965 and left Oakley Court uninhabited, the spooky-looking house served as a splendidly atmospheric setting for a number of productions from the Bray Studios next door, including the Hammer horror films. Oakley Court also became St Trinian's School in *The Wildcats of St Trinians*, Tommy Steel's home in *Half a Sixpence* and the mansion in *Murder by Death*, and it featured in *The Rocky Horror Picture Show*.

In 1981 Oakley Court opened as a luxury hotel.

St Mary's Boveney

Just upstream from Boveney Lock there is a little deserted church with a small,

Clewer

After a series of tight bends, the river reaches the ancient village of CLEWER, built here to guard a fording place well before Windsor existed. The present St Andrew's Church is very early Norman and would have been attended by William the Conqueror while Windsor castle was being built. There is a Saxon font inside from the earlier Saxon church.

Buried in the churchyard is SIR DANIEL GOOCH, who was THE FIRST CHIEF MECHANICAL ENGINEER OF THE GREAT WESTERN RAILWAY and was responsible for the development of Swindon as a railway centre. He was also the engineer that organised the laying of the first transatlantic cable from Brunel's SS *Great Eastern* in 1866, for which he was knighted.

Leaving Clewer, the Thames passes under the A332 and Windsor Railway Bridge, and suddenly there opens up what is possibly (except maybe for Greenwich) the most majestic Thames view of them all.

Well, I never knew this
about
THE RIVER THAMES

In 1991 the 'BIRMINGHAM SIX', who were sentenced to life imprisonment for a series of pub bombings in Birmingham in 1974 and were then freed by the Court of Appeal in 1991, spent their first night of freedom on MONKEY ISLAND, in great secrecy.

Occupying the left bank between Dorney and Boveney is the spectacular DORNEY ROWING LAKE, an eight-lane 1.4-mile (2,200 m) long course with a separate return lane that was completed in 2006 and has been chosen to host the rowing and canoeing events at the London 2012 Olympics. It was constructed by Eton College as somewhere for their rowing and canoeing teams to practise away from the crowded and choppy waters of the Thames, and sits in the midst of a 450-acre (182 ha) park that is open to the public.

Occupying a large island site on the right bank between Boveney and Clewer is WINDSOR RACECOURSE, ONE OF ONLY TWO FIGURE-OF-EIGHT RACECOURSES IN BRITAIN, the other being Fontwell Park.

In the 19th century there was a House of Mercy at CLEWER to which Prime Minister WILLIAM GLADSTONE sent the fallen women he had rescued from the streets of London.

The MILL HOUSE at Clewer has been home to Led Zeppelin guitarist JIMMY PAGE, actor SIR MICHAEL CAINE and singer NATALIE IMBRUGLIA.

WINDSOR RAILWAY BRIDGE, opened in 1849, IS THE OLDEST WROUGHT-IRON BRIDGE STILL IN REGULAR USE IN THE WORLD.

WINDSOR TO STAINES

Windsor Castle – the largest inhabited castle in the world

Windsor Castle

WINDSOR CASTLE, the English Royal Family's weekend cottage, rises above the Thames in a sublime vision of towers and turrets and battlements and flags that is breathtaking – and seen at its very best from the river itself. One can scarcely imagine what it must have been like when the river was full of royal barges and pageantry. In fact Windsor matches everyone's idea of a fairy-tale castle so exactly that it is sometimes hard to remember that it is actually real and not some Disney film set. As one awe-struck tourist was heard to say, 'Wow, it's real dandy – but why the heck did they build it so close to the airport?'

Indeed, one consolation for the interminable noise of aircraft overhead is the heartening thought that for many of the millions who fly over on their way into Heathrow, Windsor Castle is their first glimpse of England.

The first castle at Windsor, a motte and bailey, was built by William the Conqueror in 1070 to take advantage of the strategic bluff above the River Thames and guard the western approaches to London.

Putting a round tower on the mound fed conveniently into the widely held belief that this was the site of King Arthur's Round Table, thus helping William to portray himself as the natural heir to the legendary English hero. The walls of Windsor Castle today follow the same shape and enclose the same area as William's original castle, which was rebuilt in stone by Henry II in 1170. It is now THE OLDEST AND LARGEST INHABITED CASTLE IN THE WORLD.

Order of the Garter

Edward III, who was responsible for the distinctive Round Tower, was born in the castle in 1312. It was he who set up the NOBLE ORDER OF THE GARTER at Windsor, THE FIRST AND MOST PRES-TIGIOUS ENGLISH ORDER OF CHIVALRY, originally consisting of Edward, his son the Black Prince, and 24 of his most courageous and trustworthy knights. The Order was based on King Arthur's Knights of the Round Table, dedicated to St George, the patron saint of England, and intended both as a mark of royal favour and a reward for loyalty.

The symbol of the Garter was derived from an item of military dress, and the Order's motto referred to

Edward's claim to the French throne. There is, however, a much more romantic tale of how they both came about. During a dance at Windsor, Joan, Countess of Salisbury, a noted beauty rumoured to be among the King's mistresses, dropped one of her garters. To cover her embarrassment Edward picked it up and tied it around his own leg, much to the shock and amusement of the assembled court. 'Honi soit qui mal y pense,' he declared, and this became the Order's motto – 'Shame on him who thinks evil of this.'

St George's Chapel

The banners of the Garter knights hang above the stalls of the Choir in ST GEORGE'S CHAPEL at Windsor, and every June a special Garter Service is held there, attended by all the current members of the Order.

St George's Chapel was begun by Edward IV and completed by Henry VIII, and is regarded as THE FINEST MEDIEVAL GOTHIC CHURCH IN BRITAIN.

Buried in St George's Chapel, Windsor

Edward IV, Henry VII, Henry VIII (with Jane Seymour), Charles I, George II, George III, George IV, William IV, George V, George VI, Queen Elizabeth the Queen Mother.

Windsor Town

The town that grew up under the mighty castle walls is one of England's show towns and has stories of its own to tell. In 1597 WILLIAM SHAKESPEARE stayed at the Garter Inn while writing *The Merry Wives of Windsor*, and the play was FIRST PERFORMED AT WINDSOR FOR QUEEN ELIZABETH I HERSELF.

WINDSOR GUILDHALL was built in 1689 by Sir Christopher Wren, whose father was the Dean of Windsor. He modelled his design on the old market hall he was replacing, which had open arcades, but the good burgesses of Windsor didn't trust the slender columns Wren had used to support the upper floors and they insisted he put in more. Wren complied, but those with a keen eye will spot that the extra columns stop just short of the ceiling, to prove they were unnecessary.

Prince Charles married Camilla Parker-Bowles in the Guildhall in April 2005, and Sir Elton John and David Furnish were united in a civil partnership there in December 2005.

Eton

Windsor Bridge, built in 1822, links Windsor with ETON and extends west straight into Eton High Street, which is quaint and full of antique shops, and you might think this is more or less all there is of Eton except, of course, for 'the most famous school in the world'. In fact, Eton was THE FIRST TOWN IN BRITAIN TO HAVE A COMPLETE MODERN DRAINAGE SYSTEM, and the High Street possesses THE OLDEST VICTORIAN PILLAR BOX STILL IN USE IN THE WORLD.

Eton College

ETON COLLEGE was founded in 1440 by the pious Henry VI, who was only 18 years old at the time, as a charity for poor boys who would then go on to King's College, Cambridge, which Henry founded the following year. He intended the chapel to be bigger than a cathedral, at least twice its present length, but was toppled by Edward IV in 1461 before the chapel was completed – a plaque on the wall of the building opposite the west end marks where the chapel was intended to end. Even so, Eton College chapel is an impressive example of Perpendicular architecture and forms a distinctive landmark for miles around. It is best seen from Romney Lock.

Eton has educated 19 British Prime Ministers. Fictional Old Etonians include Bertie Wooster, Tarzan, Captain Hook from *Peter Pan* and James Bond.

Old Etonian the Duke of Wellington never actually said, 'The Battle of Waterloo was won on the playing fields of Eton.' According to Sir Edward Creasy, he did say, while watching a cricket match at Eton, 'There grows the stuff that won Waterloo,' referring to the toughness of character engendered by sports generally, not specific to Eton.

Gone Fishing

On leaving Windsor the river passes underneath Black Potts Railway Bridge, which carries the trains from Waterloo to Windsor and Eton Riverside, and is soon joined by the waters

of the Jubilee River from Cliveden Reach (see p. 115). It then passes under the Victoria Road Bridge, a 1967 concrete replacement for the original cast-iron bridge built in 1851 when Datchet Bridge was closed down (see opposite). This was, and still is, a popular fishing spot, enjoyed by Charles II and that complete angler IZAAK WALTON and his fishing friend CHARLES COTTON, who were sometimes accompanied by the poetic Dean of St Paul's, JOHN 'NO MAN IS AN ISLAND' DONNE.

Home Park

The Thames now affords a unique view of Windsor's HOME PARK, the section of Windsor Great Park east of the castle that is only open to the public on a few days each year – the Queen's private back garden, if you will. And it looks very much like a private garden of extraordinary beauty, with avenues, lawns, noble trees and that unmistakable feel of an English country garden. It is easy to understand why the Queen and her predecessors have all loved the Home Park so much, and it is easy to picture the Queen tramping through the park in her very English head scarf and wellies with the dogs scampering beside her. The only slight blot on this ravishing landscape is the occasional hatchet-faced security man, usually at the wheel of a Range Rover, glaring from the high walled bank.

Frogmore

As well as gardens Windsor Great Park also includes HOME FARM, producing fresh food for the castle, some playing fields and the Frogmore estate.

It is possible just to catch a glimpse of FROGMORE HOUSE, built in 1680 and then enlarged by James Wyatt for George III's wife Queen Charlotte. Many members of the Royal family have since enjoyed Frogmore as an informal retreat. EARL MOUNTBATTEN OF BURMA was born in Frogmore House in 1900.

Behind the house is the resplendent ROYAL MAUSOLEUM, built in the shape of a Greek cross by Queen Victoria for her husband Albert, who died in the Blue Room at Windsor Castle in 1861. Queen Victoria joined him in the mausoleum in 1901. The Romanesque exterior is of granite and Portland Stone, and the roof is copper. The opulent interior is decorated with paintings by Raphael, the sarcophagus is of Aberdeen granite, and there are splendid effigies of Victoria and Albert in marble. The Mausoleum is open to the public very occasionally, usually on bank holidays.

Datchet

Overlooking Home Park from the opposite bank is DATCHET, where Falstaff was dumped in the river at 'Datchet Mead' in *The Merry Wives of Windsor*. A ferry from Datchet used to provide a short cut to Windsor Castle from the main London road, but in 1706 Queen Anne had a bridge built instead. When the time came for it to be replaced, Buckinghamshire and Berkshire couldn't agree who should pay for it, so Bucks made their half in wood while Berks built theirs in iron, with their final span cantilevered out from the last stone pier so that it didn't need any support from Buckinghamshire. This must have been quite a sight, but it was notoriously precarious and offended the sensibilities of Prince Albert, who decreed in 1848 that the ridiculous contraption should be taken down and two new bridges built, the Victoria Bridge upstream and the Albert Bridge downstream – hence there are now two Albert Bridges across the Thames. DATCHET BRIDGE IS THE ONLY MAJOR BRIDGE EVER BUILT ACROSS THE THAMES THAT HAS COMPLETELY DISAPPEARED, with only the truncated High Street in Datchet and a small Victorian cottage on the Home Park side recalling its existence.

England's First Car

THE FIRST PERSON IN BRITAIN TO OWN A
MOTOR CAR, the HONOURABLE EVELYN
ELLIS (1843–1913), lived at ROSENAU in
Datchet. The car was a PANHARD-LEVAS-
SOR with a Daimler engine, which Ellis
picked up at Micheldever station in
Hampshire, to where it had been trained
over from France. He drove it back to
Datchet on 6 July 1895 – THE FIRST CAR
JOURNEY EVER MADE IN BRITAIN. In
February 1896 the car was honoured to
have as a passenger Edward VII, for THE
KING'S FIRST RIDE IN A MOTOR CAR,
making Edward VII THE FIRST REIGN-
ING BRITISH MONARCH EVER TO RIDE IN
A MOTOR CAR. Ellis went on to found the
RAC. Rosenau burned down in 1930 but
the Panhard-Levassor can be seen in the
Science Museum in South Kensington.

Silent movie star LAURA LA PLANTE
(1904–96), THE FIRST ACTRESS TO HAVE
HER SINGING DUBBED IN A MOTION
PICTURE (SHOW BOAT, 1929), lived in
Datchet House from 1932 until 1935.

Actress BILLIE WHITELAW (b.1932)
lived in Riverside Corner in the 1960s,
while her friend the actor DONALD
PLEASANCE (1919–95), a very creepy
Blofeld in the 1967 James Bond film *You*

Only Live Twice, lived across the road in the
Willows.

The river now flows under Albert
Bridge, once the twin of the Victoria
Bridge upstream but now a brick affair
built in 1928, and boats continue along
New Cut (1822), which avoids the 1 mile
(1.6 km) loop around Ham Island and
passes through Old Windsor Lock.

Friday Island

FRIDAY ISLAND, just below Old Windsor
Lock, is so named because it resembles
Man Friday's footprint. There is a little
thatched two-bedroom cottage hidden
amongst the willows on the island, and
between 1966 and 1991 this was the
home of DR JULIUS GRANT (1901–91),
the forensic scientist who proved in
1984 that the infamous Hitler Diaries,
declared authentic by Hugh Trevor-
Roper and published in the *Sunday Times*,
were in fact a forgery.

Old Windsor

OLD WINDSOR was a most important
town in Saxon Berkshire, site of a minster
and of the original Windsor Castle, a
royal palace belonging to Edward the
Confessor, which sat right on the river.
Nothing remains of the palace, but the
minster's successor survives, a 13th-
century church surrounded by trees in a
pretty corner between the sprawling new
village and the river. Inside there is a brass
memorial to THOMAS SANDBY (1721–98),
secretary to 'Butcher' Cumberland, who
was responsible for laying out Windsor

Great Park and Virginia Water and was a founder of the Royal Academy in 1768, becoming its FIRST PROFESSOR OF ARCHITECTURE.

Buried outside in the churchyard is a great beauty of her day, MARY 'PERDITA' ROBINSON (1757–1800), poetess and THE FIRST PUBLIC MISTRESS OF GEORGE IV, who made her name, and caught the King's eye, playing Perdita in *Florizel and Perdita*, an adaptation of Shakespeare's *A Winter's Tale*. She was later the mistress of Banastre Tarleton, the British officer upon whom Mel Gibson unfairly based his villain Colonel William Tarvington in his scurrilous film about the American Revolutionary War, *The Patriot*.

SIR ELTON JOHN has a fine house in Old Windsor called WOODSIDE, on the edge of Windsor Great Park, from where he went forth to marry DAVID FURNISH at Windsor Guildhall in December 2005. Just across the road is the DOWER HOUSE, home of golfer NICK FALDO.

The river departs Old Windsor past the BELLS OF OUZELEY, a pub whose name recalls a legend that goes back to the Dissolution of the Monasteries, when the bells of Osney Abbey in Oxford were supposed to have been lost in the mud of the river bed here by monks who were trying to escape with them from Henry VIII's agents. The balls have never been found.

Into Surrey

The right bank, Berkshire up to this point, now becomes Surrey. Once in Surrey, a pair of gatehouses by Lutyens

guards the lush green meadows of that sacred place where 'the idea of human rights was born', the place where English liberties and freedoms took their first faltering steps, the place where the rights of free-born Englishmen were for the first time, if not guaranteed, at least reluctantly acknowledged. The place that is . . .

Runnymede

'No freeman shall be seized, or imprisoned, or disseised, or outlawed, or any way destroyed, nor will we go upon him, nor will we send upon him, except by the lawful judgement of his peers, or by the law of the land. To none will we sell, to none will we deny, to none will we delay right of justice.'

On the 15th day of June in the summer of 1215, King John angrily stamped his royal seal (he couldn't write) on the preliminary draft of the Great Charter that forms, or used to form, the foundation stone of English liberty.

MAGNA CARTA was the result of King John's abject misrule. The profligacy of John's brother King Richard the Lionheart had left the coffers empty, and John was forced to raise exorbitant taxes to pay for his own disastrous foreign wars. He compounded this with boorish behaviour and any number of injustices until finally even his squabbling barons had had enough and united against him, fortunate that in Stephen Langton, Archbishop of Canterbury, they had a brilliant and articulate champion. King John was summoned to Windsor, and for several days the King, representatives of the noblemen, the Church and the merchants of London, and even some ordinary English yeomen, gathered beside the Thames on the broad green sward of Runnymede to thrash out an agreement that would answer 49 grievances drawn up by the barons.

Although Magna Carta is limited in its aspirations and effect, it is nonetheless THE VERY FIRST RECORDED ATTEMPT TO ESTABLISH SOME FORM OF BASIC RIGHTS and is therefore most revered. It is the raw template from which all others draw their inspiration and forms the basis for the constitutions and statutes of all the countries in the English-speaking world. It underlies the American Constitution and Bill of Rights and even the European Convention for Human Rights.

On the lower slopes of Cooper's Hill, below which the meadows of Runnymede are spread out, sit the simple yet classical MAGNA CARTA MEMORIAL presented in 1957 by the American Bar Association as a tribute to 'freedom under law', and the KENNEDY MEMORIAL, set on an acre (0.4 ha) of land given to the people of America in 1965 in memory of President John F. Kennedy. At the summit of the hill is the COMMONWEALTH AIR FORCES MEMORIAL, designed by Sir Edward Maufe in 1953 and dedicated to 20,456 airmen who have no known grave.

The greater part of Runnymede was rather fittingly donated to the National Trust by the American-born wife of English civil engineer Urban H. Broughton, in her husband's memory.

Magna Carta Island

No one knows exactly where Magna Carta was sealed, but while the barons were mustered on Runnymede meadows King John and his men occupied the opposite bank, on a stretch of land now called Magna Carta Island. Inside the Gothic cottage on the island, which was built in 1834, there is a flat stone slab called the Charter Stone inscribed with the words:

'BE IT REMEMBERED, THAT ON THIS ISLAND, 25 JUNE 1215, JOHN KING OF ENGLAND SIGNED MAGNA CHARTA; AND IN THE YEAR 1834, THIS BUILDING WAS ERECTED, IN COMMEMORATION OF THAT GREAT AND IMPORTANT EVENT, BY GEORGE SIMON HARCOURT, ESQ LORD OF THIS MANOR, AND THEN HIGH SHERIFF OF THIS COUNTY.'

Ankerwyke

A little further downstream on the left bank are the scant remains of ANKERWYKE PRIORY, founded in the reign of Henry II for Benedictine nuns.

The priory was built right next to the venerable ANKERWYKE YEW, still standing but anything up to 2,000 years old and ancient even in 1215. It seems a credible theory that the barons may

have set up the stone on which Magna Carta was sealed under this great yew.

From the historic meadows of Runnymede the river now runs under the M25, which is carried by Runnymede Bridge, built of concrete in the 1980s and ingeniously incorporating the elegant brick bridge of Sir Edwin Lutyens that was already there.

Next the river skirts HOLM ISLAND, with a little house on it called THE NEST, once used as a secret hideaway by the future Edward VIII and Wallace Simpson, and enters Staines.

Well, I never knew this
about
THE RIVER THAMES

For 1,000 years WINDSOR has been at the heart of the English monarchy. In 1917, during the First World War against Germany, George V chose Windsor as the new family name for the English Royal family to replace the Germanic-sounding Saxe-Coburg-Gotha.

In addition to the Royal family, Windsor gives its name to a brown soup, the perfect knot for a tie and a kind of chair. Windsor is also the reason why Berkshire is THE ONLY ENGLISH COUNTY TO BE ACCORDED THE PREFIX 'ROYAL'.

In 1781 WILLIAM HERSCHEL discovered the planet we now know as Uranus and named it Georgium Sidus in honour of George III. Naturally the King was most

pleased and made Herschel 'King's Astronomer'; and so in 1782, to be close to the King at Windsor, Herschel moved to DATCHET with his sister Caroline and built what was at the time THE WORLD'S LARGEST TELESCOPE in the garden of his house, THE LAWNS. After four years the damp got too much and they moved briefly to Old Windsor and then Slough, where Herschel spent the rest of his days, and where he is buried, in St Laurence's Church, Upton.

Under an arch in the church at OLD WINDSOR is the effigy of SIR CHARLES 'HIPPOPOTAMUS' MURRAY, a diplomat who in 1850 introduced into England THE FIRST HIPPOPOTAMUS SINCE PREHISTORIC TIMES – indeed THE FIRST

HIPPOPOTAMUS SEEN ANYWHERE IN EUROPE SINCE ROMAN TIMES. The hippo, a noble creature from Egypt called Obaysch, went to live at London Zoo, where he was visited almost every day by his kindly benefactor Hippopotamus Murray.

Just downstream from Old Windsor Lock in WRAYSBURY, on the left bank, is the thatched HONEY POT COTTAGE where actress BERYL REID (1919–96) lived from the late 1950s until her death. She loved cats and gave a home to any passing stray, often giving house-room to up to 20 cats at one time. Her ashes were scattered in the garden.

STAINES TO
HAMPTON COURT

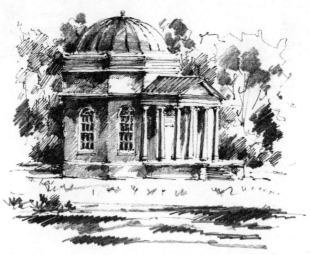

Garrick's Temple, Hampton – David Garrick's tribute to William Shakespeare

London Stone

Over the top of the trees on Church Island to the left, as the river reaches Staines, there is sometimes a glimpse of the lovely brick tower of St Mary's Church, part designed by Inigo Jones in 1633. Then, also on the left bank just before Staines Bridge, can be seen LONDON STONE, put there in 1285 to indicate the western limit of the Corporation of London's authority over the Thames. Richard I sold the rights of the river to

the Corporation in 1197 to raise funds for his Crusades. These included fishing rights and the right to license watermen.

In addition, the stone marks the dividing point between the upper and lower Thames, and before the locks were built downstream this was the upper limit of the tidal river. It also marks the meeting point of Buckinghamshire and Middlesex. The stone there now is a replica, with the original one held in the Old Town Hall Arts Centre. This London Stone should not be confused with the much older

London Stone on display near Cannon Street station in the City, nor the London Stone that marks the end of the River Thames in Kent.

Staines

The name STAINES comes from the Saxon 'stana', or 'stones', and is thought to refer to a group of nine ancient stones mentioned in a 12th-century charter of Chertsey Abbey, which marked the boundary of the abbey lands. There was a Roman town here called 'Ad Pontes', or 'by the bridges', at the point where the London to Silchester road crossed the Thames, about halfway between the two towns.

There was indeed a Roman bridge at Staines – and a Saxon one and a Norman one. The present STAINES BRIDGE, handsomely designed by George Rennie, son of the John Rennie who built the original Waterloo Bridge, has three arches in white granite and was opened in 1832.

Just downstream from the bridge the RIVER COLNE joins the Thames, and then the Old Town Hall comes into view, built on the site of the Market Hall where the founder of the British Empire, Sir Walter Raleigh, was condemned for treason in 1603, his trial held outside London to avoid the plague.

St Peter's Church nearby was built in 1894 by SIR EDWARD CLARKE, the lawyer who represented Sir William Gordon-Cumming, the plaintiff in the Royal Baccarat scandal, during which Clarke cross-examined the Prince of Wales. Clarke would go on to represent Oscar Wilde at his trial against the Marquess of Queensberry. He lived in a big house, which he built himself next door to the church, and which is now the Vicarage.

Staines Lino

Staines was the home of THE WORLD'S FIRST LINOLEUM FACTORY, opened in 1862 by the inventor of linoleum, FREDERICK WALTON. For over 100 years this factory produced the world-famous 'STAINES LINO', which was shipped from Staines all over the world. Extremely durable and made entirely from natural ingredients – solidified linseed oil, crushed limestone, wood flour and cork dust, with a burlap or hemp backing – linoleum is impeccably 'green' and in recent years has become fashionable again. Staines linoleum factory closed in 1969 and the site is now occupied by the Two Rivers shopping centre, but the industry is commemorated with a bronze statue of two lino workers in the High Street.

Penton Hook Lock

The river now runs through a land of bungalows for many miles. Penton Hook Lock is the first of the locks controlled by the Corporation of London and cuts off a huge loop of the river notorious for flooding and now occupied by a vast marina. Shortly afterwards the low, 18th-century brick tower of Laleham's 12th-century All Saints Church appears on the Middlesex side.

Laleham

LALEHAM means 'village of twigs or willows', an apt description as the village is almost hidden from the river by willows, many of them newly planted after the hurricane of 1987 wreaked its havoc.

In 1803 the 2ND EARL OF LUCAN bought the manor and much of the village of Laleham and built himself LALEHAM HOUSE, cream painted and neo-classical with a huge Doric porch.

All Saints Church dates from the 12th century and retains its massive Norman pillars inside, while the Lucan Chapel is Tudor. Buried in the churchyard is the 3RD EARL OF LUCAN, under whose orders Lord Cardigan, born upstream at Hambleden, led the Charge of the Light Brigade at the Battle of Balaclava in 1854.

Also buried in the churchyard, under a simple stone shaded by trees, is the poet and literary critic MATTHEW ARNOLD (1822–88), the man who described Oxford as 'the city with its dreaming spires'. He was born in Laleham in the house where his father Thomas Arnold ran a private school, perhaps ENGLAND'S FIRST PREP SCHOOL. The house is no more, demolished to help build a new school, and the site is now occupied by Glebe House. Thomas Arnold went on to become the legendary headmaster of Rugby School, where he set the standard for modern private schooling and achieved immortality in *Tom Brown's Schooldays*.

In 1928 Laleham House was bought by the nuns of the Community of St Peter and became Laleham Abbey. Since 1981 it has been divided into executive apartments.

The Lucan family still has strong links with Laleham and the 7th Lord Lucan, who disappeared in 1974 in mysterious circumstances, was a patron of the church.

From Laleham the river runs through a flat landscape with reservoirs on the left and meadows on the right as far as the handsome seven-arched Chertsey Bridge, built from Purbeck stone by James Paine in 1785.

Chertsey

CHERTSEY is one of England's ancient places, the site of a great Benedictine abbey founded in 666 by St Erkenwald on what is now Abbey Mead, upstream of the bridge. The abbey was sacked by the Danes but refounded by King Edgar in 964 and grew to be one of the biggest and richest abbeys in the country. After Henry VI was murdered in the Tower of London in 1471, his body was brought to Chertsey Abbey for burial in the Lady Chapel and his tomb became a great place of pilgrimage. In 1485 his body was moved upstream to St George's Chapel at Windsor Castle.

Chertsey Abbey was dissolved by Henry VIII in 1537. The monks moved up the river to Bisham, the abbey buildings were demolished and the materials used for Henry VIII's new home at Weybridge, Oatlands Palace. There is practically nothing left of the abbey today except ENGLAND'S FINEST COLLECTION OF 13TH-CENTURY LETTER TILES, an early form of movable type printing used for decoration and illustration in medieval abbeys. The great curfew bell from the abbey, dated 1380, now hangs in the parish church of St Peter, where it still rings the curfew at 8pm from Michaelmas (29 September) to Lady Day (25 March).

Blanche Heriot

This curfew bell features in the heart-warming tale of Chertsey's great heroine, BLANCHE HERIOT. During the Wars of the Roses, Blanche's lover, a Lancastrian soldier called Neville, was captured by Yorkist soldiers and thrown into prison, condemned to die at the sounding of the curfew bell. A rider was dispatched to beg pardon of the King in London, and a reprieve was duly granted, but the messenger carrying the pardon was seen waiting on the opposite bank for the Laleham ferry with only five minutes to curfew. Blanche realised he wouldn't make it across in time, so she sprang into action, ran up the steps of the bell tower and flung herself on to the clapper of the great bell, preventing it from sounding until the pardon arrived and her lover's life was saved.

There is a splendid bronze statue of Blanche Heriot by Sheila Mitchell standing near Chertsey Bridge.

On leaving Chertsey the river flows around PHARAOH'S ISLAND, presented to Lord Nelson after the Battle of the Nile in 1798, and used by the admiral as a fishing retreat. Today the island is thick with large houses despite being accessible only by boat.

River Wey

After Shepperton Lock the Thames is joined by the RIVER WEY at the end of its journey from the North Downs via Guildford to Weybridge. The River Wey WAS THE FIRST OF ENGLAND'S RIVERS TO BE MADE NAVIGABLE, and its course between Godalming and the Thames is still intertwined with the WEY NAVIGA-TION CANAL, which was constructed by SIR RICHARD WESTON of Sutton Place near Guildford in 1635.

Weybridge – Oatlands Palace

WEYBRIDGE began life, appropriately enough, as a bridge over the River Wey, but truly started to grow in the 16th century when Henry VIII built OATLANDS PALACE by the Thames there, using stones from the demolished Chertsey Abbey and creating a vast complex covering 35 acres (14 ha). It was meant as a gift for his unwanted fourth wife Anne of Cleves, but she rejected it, and so instead Henry kept it and married his fifth wife Catherine Howard there on 28 July 1540.

Much of the palace was knocked down after the execution of Charles I in

1649, and the bricks were used to line the new Wey Navigation (see above), but the house that remained came down to the Duke of Newcastle, who expanded the grounds, constructed THE FINEST GROTTO IN ENGLAND at the time and created the lake now called Broad Water. The grotto, alas, was demolished in 1948.

Grand Old Duchess of York

Between 1794 and 1820 Oatlands was owned by PRINCE FREDERICK, THE GRAND OLD DUKE OF YORK, second son of George III. His Duchess made herself a hugely popular figure in Weybridge, and after she died in 1820 the good burghers purchased the tall column from Seven Dials in London, where it was obstructing traffic, and erected it as a monument to the Duchess at the foot of the fortuitously named Monument Hill. The Duchess lies in Weybridge Church under a beautiful memorial sculpted by Francis Chantrey.

The house at Oatlands, by now Goth-icised, was bought in 1820 by a bright young thing called EDWARD BALL HUGHES, who was so bright and so rich he was known as the Golden Ball, and then in 1856 it became a hotel. Today it is the OATLANDS PARK HOTEL, its chimneys just visible from the river, poking above the trees. In front of the hotel is ONE OF THE FIRST CEDAR OF LEBANON TREES IMPORTED INTO ENGLAND, planted by Charles I to celebrate the birth of his son, Henry of Otelands.

The pedestrian ferry that takes the towpath across the Thames from Weybridge to Shepperton, as mentioned in H.G. Wells's 1898 novel *The War of the Worlds*, still runs from 8am until 5.30pm every day and can be summoned by a bell.

D'Oyly Carte Island

Leaving Weybridge and the ferry behind, the river flows around D'OYLY CARTE ISLAND, named after the impresario and hotelier Richard D'Oyly Carte, who bought the island after discovering it on a rowing trip with his sons in 1887. He put up a large house on the island, intended as a country wing of his Savoy Hotel in central London, but he was unable to secure a drinks licence and so decided to use it as a country retreat for himself and his family. Many famous guests visited, including D'Oyly Carte's protégés GILBERT AND SULLIVAN, who wrote the song 'Tit Willow', from *The Mikado*, while staying on the island.

Richard D'Oyly Carte
(1844–1901)

RICHARD D'OYLY CARTE was born in London into a musical family. In 1875 he took over as manager of the Royalty Theatre in Soho and brought together the librettist WILLIAM GILBERT and composer ARTHUR SULLIVAN to devise a comic opera to fill the theatre. *Trial by Jury* was a huge success, and D'Oyly Carte formed the D'Oyly Carte Opera Company to produce more Gilbert and Sullivan operas. He also built the Savoy

Theatre to host the productions. D'Oyly Carte then moved into hotels, opening the Savoy in 1889 and eventually owning Claridges, Simpsons-in-the-Strand and the Berkeley.

Lord Desborough
(1855–1945)

Just after D'Oyly Carte Island the river divides between its original winding 3-mile (4.8 km) course past Shepperton and the dead straight Desborough Cut, created in 1935 and named after the extraordinary LORD DESBOROUGH of Taplow Court, who was head of the Thames Conservancy for 32 years, amateur punting champion, member of the Oxford Boat Race crew in the famous dead heat of 1877 and the one that won the race in 1878, and President of the 1908 London Olympics. He also swam the Niagara rapids twice, the second time to confound those who didn't believe he had done it the first time, climbed the Matterhorn three times and rowed across the English Channel. He was predeceased by all three sons, two of whom died in the First World War, and his title thus became extinct.

Shepperton

On its original, winding course the river runs by the delightful backwater of CHURCH SQUARE, the heart of old SHEPPERTON, somewhat detached from its newer offspring to the north. The former church was ruined by floods in 1606 and the new one built in 1614, with a brick tower added in 1710.

There are two noted old inns in Church Square, the KINGS HEAD, where Charles II dallied with 'witty, pretty' Nell Gwyn, and the 16th-century ANCHOR HOTEL, well known to stars working at the nearby Shepperton Studios, including RICHARD BURTON and ELIZABETH TAYLOR, who enjoyed romantic evenings there and apparently threw sausage rolls at each other, while filming *Cleopatra* in 1962–3.

Just across the road from Church Square, in the new cemetery, lies the poet THOMAS LOVE PEACOCK (1785–1866), who grew up in Chertsey and later persuaded Shelley to join him in Marlow (see p. 110). Peacock lived his

last years in a lovely cream-painted house called ELMBANK (now Peacock House), on a bend in the river just downstream from Shepperton at LOWER HALLIFORD. He died there from injuries sustained while trying to save his library from a fire. Peacock's daughter married the novelist George Meredith, author of *Anne of Green Gables*, and they lived in Lower Halliford in a house on the green called Vine Cottage.

Shepperton Manor

Downriver from Church Square, set high on a green platform above shaven lawns sweeping down to the river, is the white-painted SHEPPERTON MANOR, where GEORGE ELIOT (1819–80) stayed while writing *Scenes from Clerical Life*. Liberal politician JOHN BRIGHT (1811–89), considered THE GREATEST ORATOR OF HIS DAY, was a frequent visitor to the manor and it was here that he prepared his famous House of Commons speech against the Crimean War: 'The Angel of Death is abroad in the land; we can almost hear the beating of his wings.' It was John Bright who first uttered the phrase 'England is the Mother of Parliaments'.

Walton Bridge

After Lower Halliford the river reaches the downstream end of the Desborough Cut and turns east for WALTON BRIDGE. Actually, that should be Walton Bridges, for although the latest road bridge is the fifth on the spot, the fourth one is still in use for cyclists and pedestrians. Canaletto did a wonderful painting, now hanging in the Dulwich Picture Gallery, of the first Walton Bridge of 1747, a picturesque latticework of timber described as 'the most beautiful wooden arch in the world' and designed 'so that a damaged timber could be removed without having to dismantle the whole structure'. J.M.W. Turner painted the equally pretty second Walton Bridge, constructed of brick and stone in 1788, but no one, alas, could possibly want to paint the fourth and fifth Walton Bridges, strictly functional affairs that are due for replacement in 2011.

Walton-on-Thames

Although WALTON is mostly new, it has an old church, St Mary's, a Saxon foundation with Norman pillars and a 15th-century tower. There is a fine memorial sculpted by Chantrey to his patroness SARAH D'OYLEY, granddaughter of the physician Sir Hans Sloane, and an enormous marble monument by Louis Roubillac to the last VISCOUNT SHANNON, who fought at the Battle of the Boyne and died in 1740. He was the great-nephew of Robert Boyle the scientist. Buried outside in the churchyard is the cricketer EDWARD 'LUMPY' STEVENS (see Chertsey).

A bit further downstream is the garden of the SWAN, where American songwriter JEROME KERN ('Ole Man River', 'A Fine Romance', 'Smoke Gets in Your Eyes') met his future wife Eva, who was the landlord's daughter. They married in St Mary's Church in Walton in 1910.

Screened from the river by trees is RIVER HOUSE (now council property), where composer SIR ARTHUR SULLIVAN lived between 1894 and 1898.

Between Walton-on-Thames and Hampton Court the riverbanks are crowded with uninteresting houses, reservoirs and sports fields, interrupted on the north side by the villages of Sunbury and Hampton. On the river itself there are a number of large wooded islands, or aits, and houseboats of all shapes and sizes.

Sunbury

SUNBURY is announced by the strange tower of St Mary's Church, which is topped by a cupola. The churchyard is where Oliver Twist and Bill Sykes slept under a yew tree before going on to the robbery in Shepperton.

Monksbridge

A rash of fine Georgian houses line the riverbank at Sunbury, the most interesting of which overlooks Rivermead Island and is called MONKSBRIDGE. A topiary teddy bear in the garden is thought to have been created as a love token from the Prince of Wales, later Edward VIII, to his mistress FREDA DUDLEY WARD, who lived at Monksbridge with her husband Liberal MP William Dudley Ward. In the 1920s the Prince would rent a cottage nearby in Thames Street in Sunbury as cover for his dalliances at Monksbridge with Freda. They were apparently regularly seen taking a dip in the river together. In the 1950s the house became LE CLUB DE CLIO, where actress DIANA DORS was wont to dance on the tables, and then in the 1980s Monksbridge became the home of DAVID GILMOUR, lead singer and guitarist with rock band Pink Floyd. The wall around the tennis court at Monksbridge is said to be the wall of Pink Floyd's iconic album *The Wall*.

SUNBURY COURT AIT takes its name from the adjacent Sunbury Court, a big red and white 18th-century house that is now the Salvation Army Youth Centre.

Hampton

HAMPTON is dominated by its church, rebuilt in 1831 on the site of a 14th-century building. In 1754 the actor DAVID GARRICK (1717–79) moved into HAMPTON HOUSE and commissioned Robert Adam to remodel it for him. In the garden, which was laid out by Capability Brown, is GARRICK'S TEMPLE. This was possibly also designed by Robert Adam and is Garrick's tribute to William Shakespeare. It once housed a Roubillac sculpture of the Bard (based on Garrick), which is now in the British

Museum. Dr Johnson remarked after a visit to the temple, 'Ah, David, it is the leaving of such places that makes a death-bed terrible.' In 1758 the REVD ALEXANDER 'JUPITER' CARLYLE performed THE WORLD'S FIRST RECORDED TRICK GOLF SHOT here in Garrick's garden, when he chipped a ball through an ornamental archway into the river.

Hampton House is now called Garrick's Villa and is divided into apartments.

Astoria

Moored on the river just down from Garrick's Temple is the ASTORIA, a houseboat built for impresario FRED KARNO in 1913. It was later sold to music-hall star VESTA VICTORIA (1873–1951), who became famous in 1892 with the song 'Daddy Wouldn't Buy Me a Bow Wow'. In 1986 Pink Floyd's DAVID GILMOUR (see Monksbridge) bought the Astoria and turned it into a recording studio. His 2006 album *On an Island* was recorded there in 2005.

Hurst Park

On the Surrey bank, across the river from Garrick's Temple, is HURST PARK, once known as Moulsey Hurst and once a significant sporting venue. ONE OF THE VERY EARLY CRICKET MATCHES was played here in 1723 between the Gentlemen of London and the Gentlemen of Surrey. Both teams afterwards took tea with the Prince of Wales (later George II) at Hampton Court.

In 1758 the Revd Alexander 'Jupiter' Carlyle and John Hume played ONE OF THE FIRST RECORDED GOLF MATCHES here before retiring to David Garrick's house for tea and trick shots.

Hurst Park was also a popular venue for bare-knuckle fights, including one in 1816 when a pugilist was bludgeoned to death – prize fighting was banned here not long afterwards. Hurst Park then became a racecourse, but most of the area is now housing.

Tagg's Island

The biggest of the islands in this stretch of Thames, TAGG'S ISLAND, is named after boat-builder TOM TAGG who used the profits from his boatyard to build a hotel on the island in 1872. It became a popular retreat for the famous and the well-to-do: the Prince of Wales brought LILLIE LANGTRY and ALICE KEPPEL here, French actress SARAH BERNHARDT lived there for a while, and *Peter Pan* author J.M. BARRIE rented one of the hotel's comfortable houseboats.

The lease was bought next by impresario FRED KARNO (1866–1941), who commissioned the great theatre designer Frank Matcham to convert the hotel into the 'Karsino' music hall and casino. Karno also built himself a luxurious houseboat called the *Astoria* to live on (see previous page). Karno, who began life as a plumber, started to produce comedy sketches with a variety of artists and grew to be one of the great comedy music-hall impresarios. He invented the 'custard pie in the face' gag and was responsible for discovering, amongst others, Charlie Chaplin, Stan Laurel, Will Hay, Flanagan and Allen and Max Miller. They were the original 'Karno's Army', a phrase still used today to describe a chaotic or shambolic group or organisation. Karno went bankrupt in 1926 and the hotel never regained its former glory and was eventually demolished in 1971. Tagg's Island is now a houseboat community and belongs to the owners of the houseboats that are moored around it.

Across from Tagg's Island on the Middlesex bank is the SWISS CHALET, a genuine chalet that was shipped in from Switzerland in 1899 to serve as a boathouse for a big villa called Riverholme, now demolished. It has recently served as a boatyard.

Bushy Park

Beyond the Swiss Chalet and the busy A308 are the trees of Bushy Park, covering 1,100 acres (445 ha) and THE SECOND LARGEST OF LONDON'S EIGHT ROYAL PARKS, created in the early 16th century as a hunting ground for Hampton Court Palace. Sir Christopher Wren laid out the magnificent Chestnut Avenue and Diana Fountain as a grand approach to the palace, and in spring people still come from all over London on Chestnut Sunday to see the chestnut trees in blossom. From 1871 onwards the rules of the modern game of (field) hockey were largely devised at Bushy Park, which is the home of THE WORLD'S OLDEST SURVIVING HOCKEY CLUB, TEDDINGTON HOCKEY CLUB.

Hampton Court Bridge

HAMPTON COURT BRIDGE, opened in 1933, is the fourth bridge on the site and was built by Sir Edwin Lutyens to blend in with Hampton Court Palace. The first bridge, an extraordinary and picturesque Chinese-style timber bridge of seven arched spans built in 1753 by Samuel Stevens and Benjamin Ludgator, was THE LARGEST CHINOISERIE BRIDGE EVER BUILT and included a central span guarded by four Chinese pagodas. It looked better than it worked, alas, and had to come down in 1778.

Well, I never knew this about
THE RIVER THAMES

Grey-painted STAINES RAILWAY BRIDGE is decorated with a yellow stripe, apparently to stop swans flying into it.

LAGONDA CARS were founded in STAINES in 1906 and built in a small factory there until the company was taken over by Aston Martin in 1947. The founder was expatriate American WILBUR GUNN, who named the company after the Indian name for a river near his home town of Springfield, Ohio. In 1935 a 4.5-litre Lagonda car built at Staines won the Le Mans 24-Hour Race.

Near to the river in LALEHAM is an unusual house called THE BARN, which was built by SIR EDWARD MAUFE in 1909 as a home for the Edwardian musical star MARIE STUDHOLME (1872–1930). It was named after her hit song 'The Little Dutch Barn'.

Actress GABRIELLE ANWAR from the American television series *Burn Notice* was born in LALEHAM in 1970.

BRITAIN'S FIRST FOREIGN SECRETARY, the radical Whig politician CHARLES JAMES FOX (1749–1806), lived in a big house (demolished between the wars) on St Ann's Hill in CHERTSEY from 1780 until his death. He planted many trees on the surrounding estate which was named Foxhills after him. Fox wanted to be buried in Chertsey, but his wish was not granted and he lies in Westminster Abbey. There is a bust of him near the railway station in Chertsey.

CHERTSEY CRICKET CLUB was founded in 1737 and is ONE OF THE OLDEST CRICKET CLUBS IN BRITAIN. Its most celebrated player was EDWARD 'LUMPY' STEVENS, regarded as CRICKET'S FIRST GREAT BOWLER. His extraordinary accuracy was responsible for THE INTRODUCTION OF THE MIDDLE STUMP TO THE GAME. During a single-wicket match in 1775 he beat the Hambleden batsman John Small with three consecutive balls that passed through the middle of the two-stump wicket traditionally used at that time – since the wicket was not touched Small remained in, much to Stevens' annoyance, and it was eventually agreed that a third stump should be added.

In 1906 THE WORLD'S FIRST LEISURE CAMPSITE was set up near Weybridge by THOMAS HOLDING, founder of the

Camping and Caravan Club in 1901 and author of the *Camper's Handbook* of 1908.

J.M. NEALE (1818–66), who wrote the carol 'Good King Wenceslas', spent his childhood in SHEPPERTON and was educated at the rectory in Church Square.

Writer J.G BALLARD, best known for his novel *Empire of the Sun*, lived in a run-down semi-detached house in SHEPPERTON from 1956 until his death in 2009.

Film director JOHN BOORMAN (*Deliverance, Zardoz, Excalibur, The Emerald Forest*), father of actor and traveller Charlie Boorman, was born in SHEPPERTON in 1933.

HERSHAM AND WALTON MOTORS in New Zealand Avenue in Walton-on-Thames was THE WORLD'S FIRST ASTON MARTIN DEALER. From 1951 until 1955 they built HWM racing cars here, which were driven by many of the leading British drivers including Stirling Moss.

Actress DAME JULIE ANDREWS was born in WALTON-ON-THAMES in 1935.

MOLESEY LOCK by Hampton Court Bridge is THE SECOND LONGEST LOCK ON THE THAMES, 268 ft (82m) long.

HAMPTON COURT
TO TEDDINGTON

Hampton Court – once the largest royal residence in Britain

Hampton Court

The only way to approach the marvellous jumble of chimneys and turrets that is HAMPTON COURT PALACE is by boat, the same way in which kings and queens from Henry VIII to Queen Anne arrived. Britain's answer to Versailles, Hampton Court is really two palaces in one, the Tudor palace of Henry VIII and Sir Christopher Wren's baroque splendour built for William and Mary – sharply contrasting styles yet beautifully harmonised in rose-red brick. The palace is framed from the river by the beautiful late 17th-century wrought-iron gates and railings of Jean Tijou.

Henry VIII confiscated Hampton Court from the disgraced Cardinal Wolsey, who had hoped to build himself the finest private house in England at Hampton. Instead it became Henry's favourite home and THE LARGEST ROYAL RESIDENCE IN BRITAIN.

Among the highlights of Henry's palace are the enormous TUDOR KITCHENS where food was prepared, not just for the king and his guests but also for his retinue of 500 servants.

The sumptuous CHAPEL ROYAL was where in 1540 Henry learned from Archbishop Cranmer of his new young wife CATHERINE HOWARD's 'unchaste' behaviour. The Queen was led away from the gallery screaming, but was executed at the Tower in 1542. She is reputed to haunt the gallery to this day. In 1543 Henry married CATHERINE PARR, his sixth and final wife, at Hampton Court.

The GREAT HALL of 1535, with its mighty carved hammer beam roof, was THE LAST MEDIEVAL HALL OF ITS KIND BUILT FOR AN ENGLISH MONARCH. Henry was so impatient for the hall to be finished that the workmen had to work in shifts for 24 hours a day, and by candlelight at night. Over Christmas and New Year in 1603–4 WILLIAM SHAKESPEARE and his company the 'King's Men' performed in front of James I in the Great Hall.

THE ROYAL TENNIS COURT, started by Wolsey in 1526, is THE OLDEST SURVIVING REAL TENNIS COURT IN ENGLAND. Henry is said to have been playing tennis here when he heard of Anne Boleyn's execution upriver at the Tower. The court is still used today by the 500 members of the Hampton Court Real Tennis Club.

In 1540 ENGLAND'S FIRST ASTRONOMICAL CLOCK was installed on the gatehouse to the inner court, known as Anne Boleyn's Gate. The clock was essential as a means of calculating the times of high and low water on the Thames for those travelling on the river between Hampton and London.

Henry's longed-for son, later EDWARD VI, was born at Hampton Court in 1537, and his mother, JANE SEYMOUR, died there two weeks later. Henry's eldest daughter, QUEEN MARY, honeymooned at Hampton Court with PHILIP OF SPAIN after their marriage at Winchester.

In 1604 JAMES I hosted the HAMPTON COURT CONFERENCE, which resulted in the AUTHORISED KING JAMES BIBLE.

In 1625 Charles I honeymooned with Henrietta Maria at Hampton Court and in 1647 was held prisoner at the palace. He escaped by river but was recaptured later and executed in 1649.

In 1689 William and Mary commissioned Christopher Wren to replace Henry's Tudor palace with a baroque building, leaving just the Great Hall. However, when Mary died in 1694 William lost interest and work stopped, leaving half the Tudor palace still standing, along with the new south front and Fountain Court. In 1702 William fell from his horse when it stumbled on a mole-hill in the park at Hampton Court and not long afterwards died from the resulting injuries.

Hampton Court's famous MAZE was planted in 1690 and is THE OLDEST HEDGE MAZE IN BRITAIN. It covers a third of an acre (0.13 ha) and has half a mile (800 m) of paths.

GEORGE II was the last monarch to reside at Hampton Court. George III had bad memories of being bullied there by his father and never set foot in it as king. It was during his reign, however, in 1768, that the GREAT VINE was planted at Hampton Court by Capability Brown. Today the vine has a trunk 85 inches (216 cm) thick and branches up to 115 ft (35 m) long, and is THE BIGGEST AND OLDEST VINE IN BRITAIN. It still produces a crop of black grapes every year.

QUEEN VICTORIA opened Hampton Court Palace to the public in 1838.

On leaving Hampton Court the Thames is joined by the RIVER MOLE, thought to be so named because it keeps disappearing underground on its journey through Surrey from Gatwick Airport.

On the right bank are Thames Ditton, then Surbiton, and on the left bank the 700 acres (283 ha) of Hampton Court Park, open to the public and home to the WORLD'S LARGEST FLOWER SHOW, first held in 1990.

Thames Ditton

THAMES DITTON, centred around the pretty shrub-embowered 11th-century church of St Nicholas, with its quaint spirelet, still retains a village atmosphere. There are a couple of picturesque riverside pubs. The 13th-century Olde Swan grew up to serve the river crossing place provided by Thames Ditton Island and was visited by Henry VIII on his progress to Hampton Court Palace.

The Pavilion

Opposite Thames Ditton Island, on the edge of Hampton Court Park, is THE PAVILION, a smart red-brick house designed in 1700 by Sir Christopher Wren as a superior kind of summerhouse for William of Orange. Queen Victoria often stayed there when it belonged to her father, Prince Edward, Duke of Kent, fourth son of George III. Between 1935 and 1958 the Pavilion was occupied by CECIL KING, chairman of Daily Mirror Newspapers Ltd, who built the *Daily Mirror* into THE BEST-SELLING DAILY NEWSPAPER IN THE WORLD. In 1968 Cecil King instigated a meeting with Lord Mountbatten at which he apparently floated the idea of a military coup to bring down the then Prime Minister Harold Wilson and replace him with Mountbatten. King was himself replaced as chairman of THE WORLD'S LARGEST PUBLISHING EMPIRE, the INTERNATIONAL PUBLISHING

CORPORATION (IPC), not long afterwards.

Surbiton

SURBITON is a Victorian railway suburb built on the site of a farm south of Kingston, or 'southern homestead'. It shot to fame in the 1970s as the home of the self-sufficient Tom and Barbara Good and their horrified strait-laced neighbours Jerry and Margot from the BBC television sit-com *The Good Life*, although the exterior scenes were actually shot in nearby Northwood.

Those who have lived in Surbiton include ALFRED BESTALL (1892–1986), author and illustrator of Rupert Bear for 30 years from 1935, who lived in Ewell Road, between 1966 and 1978, anti-apartheid campaigner DONALD WOODS (1933–2001), who settled in Surbiton after fleeing from South Africa in 1977, and HELEN SHARMAN, THE FIRST BRITON IN SPACE.

Kingston Bridge

In 1745 KINGSTON BRIDGE was the scene of ONE OF THE LAST DUCKINGS EVER RECORDED IN BRITAIN when, as reported in the *London Evening Post* of 27 April, 'a woman that keeps the Queen's Head ale-house at Kingston, in Surrey, was ordered by the court to be ducked for scolding, and was accordingly placed in the chair, and ducked in the river Thames, under Kingston Bridge, in the presence of 2,000 or 3,000 people'. The present Kingston Bridge with its five arches of Portland Stone was opened in 1828.

Kingston upon Thames

Before Putney Bridge opened in 1729, KINGSTON WAS THE FIRST PLACE YOU COULD CROSS THE THAMES BY BRIDGE UPSTREAM FROM LONDON BRIDGE. There was a ford here in Roman times and the Saxons erected a number of timber bridges to serve their 'King's Town', whose regal heritage dates back to 838 when KING EGBERT, Alfred the Great's grandfather, held a Great Council under the trees here. Kingston's proudest possession, the KING STONE, or CORONATION STONE, can be found open to the wind and rain in front of the modern Guildhall, set upon a crude base and surrounded by ornamental railings. This is THE EARLIEST THRONE OF ENGLAND, on which seven Saxon kings, THE VERY FIRST KINGS OF ENGLAND, were crowned.

The dimensions of the Saxon chapel of St Mary where the coronations actually took place are marked out beside the present church of All Saints, built by the Normans next to the Saxon structure and much restored. Undermined

Saxon Kings crowned at Kingston

902 Eadweard the Elder, Alfred the Great's son
925 Athelstan, who won Northumbria at the Battle of Brunanburh in 937 to become the first king to control all of England
940 Edmund I (the Magnificent)
946 Eadred, brother of Edmund
958 Edgar the Peaceful, later confirmed by St Dunstan of Glastonbury at Bath Abbey as the first true King of England
975 Eadweard the Martyr, murdered at Corfe Castle by his stepmother Elfrida to clear the way for her son . . .
979 Ethelred the Unready (or 'ill advised'), who established the disastrous Danegeld to buy off the Danish invaders

by grave digging, St Mary's chapel collapsed in 1730, killing the sexton and injuring his daughter.

Modern Kingston hides its royal past well but in 1977, on the occasion of her Silver Jubilee, Queen Elizabeth II, now THE-LONGEST-LIVING ENGLISH MONARCH IN HISTORY, came to the town where her royal line began and unveiled a stone commemorating her Saxon predecessor Eadweard the Elder . . .

Born by the Thames in Kingston

JOHN CLELAND (1709–89), author of *Fanny Hill, or the Memoirs of a Woman of Pleasure.*

EADWEARD MUYBRIDGE (1830–1904), the pioneer cinema photographer who made the famous series of photographs of a galloping horse that proved for the first time that all four hooves of a horse leave the ground at the same time during a gallop. His name was spelt so as to match the spelling of Eadweard on the plinth of Kingston's coronation stone.

JOHN GALSWORTHY (1867–1933), author of *The Forsyte Saga*, who won the Nobel Prize for Literature in 1932.

DONALD CAMPBELL (1921–67), THE ONLY PERSON TO HOLD THE WORLD WATER AND LAND SPEED RECORDS IN THE SAME YEAR, 1964.

JOHN COOPER (1923–2000), builder of racing cars who invented the rear-engined single-seater racing car and developed the Mini Cooper.

JONNY LEE MILLER (b.1972), actor, grandson of Bernard Lee ('M' in the James Bond films) and former husband of Angelina Jolie.

Teddington Lock

TEDDINGTON LOCK, where the Thames becomes tidal, is THE LAST AND LARGEST LOCK SYSTEM ON THE THAMES, with a barge lock built in 1904 of 650 feet (198 m) in length, making it THE LONGEST LOCK ON THE THAMES. In 1940 a huge flotilla of 'Little Ships' from all along the Thames assembled at Teddington Lock before taking part in the Dunkirk Evacuation. The headquarters for the flotilla was set up in THE TIDE END, a small cottage pub on the Middlesex bank beside the lock. The pub, now called The Tide End Cottage, is still there.

A few hundred yards downstream from the lock is an obelisk that marks the point where the Port of London Authority takes over control of the Thames from the Environment Agency, who now look after the non-tidal river (in succession to the Thames Conservancy).

Teddington

Looming over the Victorian villas of TEDDINGTON is the mighty, if truncated church of ST ALBAN'S, 'Cathedral of the Thames Valley', built in 1889 and intended to resemble the 13th-century Cathedral of Notre Dame in Clermont Ferrand in France. Alas, the funds ran out, and only the nave was completed. The congregation eventually returned to the much smaller Tudor church of ST MARY across the road and St Alban's became the Landmark Arts Centre. Someone who sang in the choir at ST ALBAN'S was actor and writer NOËL COWARD, who was born at No. 131 Waldegrave Road in Teddington in 1899. Coward was Ian Fleming's choice to play arch-villain Dr No in the first James Bond movie of the same name in 1961.

Buried at St Mary's, Teddington

DR STEPHEN HALES (1677–1761), 'perpetual curate' at Teddington from 1708 until his death in 1761, buried beneath the church tower. Known as the FATHER OF PLANT PHYSIOLOGY, Hales was THE FIRST PERSON TO STUDY THE FUNCTIONING OF PLANT LIFE, plants' rate of growth, evaporation, the fact that plants draw their nourishment from the air and that sap rises, conclusions he laid down in his pamphlet 'Upon the Effect of ye Sun's warmth in raising ye Sap in trees'. He was also the first person to study and accurately record blood pressure in animals and humans. He invented surgical forceps and a ventilator to cleanse the air of public buildings such as hospitals and prisons, and developed a water cleansing system for Teddington that doubled the life expectancy of his parishioners.

MARGARET 'PEG' WOFFINGTON (1720–60), Irish actress and mistress of David Garrick (see Hampton, p. 141), considered the most beautiful woman of her day, outshining even her friend the 'beautiful Miss Gunnings', also from Ireland. She moved to Teddington in 1744 and lived there for the rest of her life. She donated funds for a row of almshouses in the High Street, which were completed in 1759. They bear a plaque to 'Peg Woffington'.

Teddington Studios

Overlooking Teddington Lock is TEDDINGTON STUDIOS. In the early 1900s stockbroker Henry Chinnery, who owned Weir House next door to the Anglers Hotel, allowed some local film enthusiasts to use the greenhouse in his garden as a studio. Equipment was brought in and the greenhouse grew into a proper studio, which was purchased in 1931 by Warner Bros, to make their 'quota quickies', British-made films that American companies were required to make before they could show their American-made movies in Britain. ERROL FLYNN MADE HIS FIRST MAJOR FILM, *Murder at Monte Carlo*, at Teddington in 1934. In 1958 the studios were taken over by independent television and during the 1970s and 80s many of Thames Television's most popular programmes were made at Teddington, such as all of Tommy Cooper's shows, *The Benny Hill Show*, *This is Your Life*, *Opportunity Knocks* and *Minder*. Recent productions include *Pop Idol*, *The Office* and *Harry Hill's TV Burp*.

Part of the studio building is occupied by the HAYMARKET MEDIA GROUP, founded in 1952 by Michael Heseltine and now THE LARGEST INDEPENDENT PUBLISHING COMPANY IN BRITAIN (What Car? Autocar, Practical Caravan, What Hi-Fi? and BBC Magazines).

Well, I never knew this
about
THE RIVER THAMES

CAPTAIN W.E. JOHNS, author of the Biggles books, and the most prolific writer of children's stories of his era other than Enid Blyton, lived at Park House, HAMPTON COURT, from 1953 until his death in 1968.

Between 1911 and 1984 THAMES DITTON was the home of AC CARS and was thus, according to their slogan, 'the Savile Row of Motordom'. AC stands for Auto Carriers and they were famed particularly for the AC Cobra sports car.

The HOGSMILL RIVER, setting for Sir John Millais's painting *Ophelia*, joins the Thames at KINGSTON.

Lloyds Bank in KINGSTON sports a plaque to NIPPER, the dog featured on the HMV (His Master's Voice) logo, who was buried under a willow tree in Kingston in 1895 by the widow of Nipper's owner MARC BARRAUD. The burial site was eventually built over to become a car park for the bank.

In 1857 R.D. BLACKMORE (1825–1900), author of *Lorna Doone*, inherited enough money to buy a 16-acre (6.5 ha) plot of land near Bushy Park, where he built GOMER HOUSE, named after his favourite dog, and set up a market garden to supply London with fresh fruit. The market garden wasn't very successful but the royalties from *Lorna Doone*, published in 1869, enabled Blackmore to indulge his passion for fruit for the rest of his life. Gomer House was demolished in 1938, but Blackmore is remembered in the road names of Gomer Place, Blackmore's Grove and Doone Close. He is buried in Teddington Cemetery.

TEDDINGTON TO RICHMOND

The view from Richmond Hill – the only view in England protected by an Act of Parliament

Strawberry Hill

On the Middlesex side, set on a slight rise and just visible from the river is STRAWBERRY HILL, perhaps the most extraordinary house of the many extraordinary houses on the Thames. In 1747 HORACE WALPOLE (1717–97), wit, letter-writer, author and son of Britain's first Prime Minister, Sir Robert Walpole, bought a cottage outside Twickenham called Chopped Straw Hall, renamed it Strawberry Hill after a field in the grounds and set about creating his own

fantasy castle. The result, which took 30 years to complete, is an astonishing, wondrous confection of towers and turrets and arches both inside and out that became famous throughout Europe and even spawned its own style of architecture, Strawberry Hill Gothic. Although quite small, the house was like a miniature castle, richly exotic and full of atmosphere.

One June evening in 1764, Walpole fell asleep while alone in the eerie gloom of Strawberry Hill and experienced a nightmare which inspired him to write what is acknowledged as THE

FIRST GOTHIC NOVEL, *The Castle of Otranto.*

Strawberry Hill has now been restored by the Friends of Strawberry Hill and is open to the public on pre-booked tours.

Pope's Villa

Just as the river begins to turn east again towards Twickenham it passes a small park and then a red-brick building with many windows and a curious Chinese pagoda that sits on the site of the poet Alexander Pope's villa and garden.

ALEXANDER POPE (1688–1744) won renown for his translation of *Homer's Iliad*, and with the money he made from that he bought himself three cottages and a plot of land beside the Thames and set about building himself a Palladian-style villa. In the garden he planted THE FIRST RECORDED WEEPING WILLOW TREE IN ENGLAND, using a sprig from a willow basket sent to him from Turkey containing figs. The tree enjoyed the plentiful supply of water from the Thames and flourished, and legend has it that from this tree came all the weeping willows in England today.

Pope also created a much-admired grotto in a tunnel leading from the base-ment of his house to the garden, which he filled with mirrors, mineral stones, crystals and shells, and running water from a fortuitously uncovered spring.

The house was demolished in 1808 and replaced by the Chinese Pagoda, itself later subsumed into the present building. Pope's grotto survives under-neath and can sometimes be visited – amongst the features that can be seen are a section of the Giant's Causeway from Northern Ireland, given to Pope by Sir Hans Sloane, and the preserved trunk of Pope's celebrated weeping willow.

Eel Pie Island

One of the larger Thames islands, EEL PIE ISLAND sits between Ham and Twickenham and is attached to the latter by a footbridge. The island's lasting legacy is as a cradle of British rock music – 'the place where the Sixties began'.

In the 1950s and 60s the Eel Pie Island Hotel was a concert venue, first for jazz players (GEORGE MELLY, ACKER BILK, KENNY BALL), and then for emerging rock bands. In 1963 THE ROLLING STONES had a weekly residency on the island and attracted the attention

Pope Dicta

Alexander Pope, who is buried in St Mary's Church in Twickenham, is not much read today but he is the third most quoted writer in the *Oxford Dictionary of Quotations*, after Shakespeare and Tennyson, and many of his sayings have passed into the language.

Damn with faint praise

A little learning is a dangerous thing

To err is human, to forgive divine

For fools rush in where angels fear to tread

Hope springs eternal in the human breast

of impresario Robert Stigwood. In 1964 David Jones played his first gig on the island and, to avoid confusion with Davy Jones of the Monkees, changed his name to DAVID BOWIE. Amongst the Who's Who of British music who were discovered or played some of their first gigs on Eel Pie Island in the Sixties were ROD STEWART with Long John Baldry's Hoochie Coochie Men, ERIC CLAPTON with John Mayall's Bluesbreakers, JEFF BECK with the Tridents,

the YARDBIRDS, THE WHO, GENESIS, and PINK FLOYD.

Eel Pie Island's days as a music venue are long gone, the hotel having burned down, and today it is occupied by small houses and workshops. A current resident is TREVOR BAYLIS, who invented THE WIND-UP RADIO in the house he built for himself on the island 30 years ago.

Twickenham

The heart of TWICKENHAM village is gathered around the unusual red-brick church of St Mary, protected from the river and Eel Pie Island by a high brick wall. Only the tower survives from the medieval building, most of which collapsed in 1713, and the new church is classical in style. The vicarage next door, which was built in 1726 as Dial House

(from the sundial above the front door), was once the home of THOMAS TWINING, the tea merchant.

York House

Next door to the church is YORK HOUSE, which now belongs to Richmond Borough Council. It was built in 1633 and takes it name from the local landowning family of the time, the Yorkes. Over the years the house has had a number of interesting owners, including the sculptress ANNE SEYMOUR DAMER (see Henley, p. 99), who lived there from 1818 to 1828, the Orleans Pretender the COMTE DE PARIS, from 1864 to 1871, and from 1906 until 1917 SIR RATAN TATA (1871–1918), youngest son of the Indian industrialist Jametsi Tata who founded what would become the Tata Group, India's largest private company, which now owns Corus (previously British Steel) as well as Jaguar and Land Rover cars. Sir Ratan was responsible for acquiring the remarkable Naked Ladies statue, which adorns the cascade in the York House gardens.

Orleans House

Peeping over the treetops a little further downstream is THE OCTAGON, built in 1718 by James Gibbs as a summerhouse for the garden of the new house being built here for JAMES JOHNSTON (1643–1737), the Secretary of State for Scotland. For two years from 1815 the house was leased by the exiled King of France, LOUIS PHILIPPE, DUC D'ORLÉANS, from whom it took its name. In 1926 the main house was demolished, but the Octagon was saved and now houses the Orleans House Gallery, run by the local council.

Marble Hill House

Downstream, still on the Middlesex side, framed by an avenue of trees and set back from the river in 66 acres (27 ha) of beautiful parkland is MARBLE HILL HOUSE, a pure and simple Palladian villa, cute as a doll's house and built in the 1720s as a pay-off to Henrietta Howard, Countess of Suffolk, former mistress of George II. Despite being banished from Court,

Lady Suffolk determined to enjoy life to the full at Marble Hill and held celebrated soirées in the first-floor drawing-room attended by the likes of her neighbour Alexander Pope and Jonathan Swift, author of *Gulliver's Travels*.

Towards the end of the 18th century Marble Hill House was the temporary home of another royal mistress, MRS FITZHERBERT, who in 1785 illegally married the Prince of Wales, later George IV. The marriage was illegal on two counts – firstly an Act of Parliament passed 13 years before had made it unlawful for a member of the Royal Family under the age of 25 to marry without the consent of the sovereign, and secondly Mrs Fitzherbert was a Roman Catholic. During a debate in the House of Commons about paying off George's debts, the Prince's friend Charles James Fox was forced to lie to the house and deny that the Prince and Mrs Fitzherbert were married, when everyone knew they were – Fox never recovered his previous reputation for honesty. Mrs Fitzherbert retired to Twickenham in 1795, when George was obliged to marry Caroline of Brunswick, but the two continued to meet frequently at Marble Hill House to carry on with their relationship.

Marble Hill House is now run by English Heritage, who hold summer concerts in the grounds every year.

A ferry runs across the river from Marble Hill to Ham House on the Surrey side.

Ham House

Directly opposite Orleans House on the Surrey bank, lurking behind imposing iron gates, is the enormous red-brick HAM HOUSE, built in 1610 for SIR THOMAS VAVASOUR, Knight Marshal to James I. In 1628 the house passed to Charles I's whipping boy WILLIAM MURRAY, who had taken punishment on behalf of the future king and was rewarded for his loyalty during the Civil War with the title Earl of Dysart. He remodelled the interior of the house to more or less how we see it today.

Murray's daughter Elizabeth married JOHN MAITLAND, THE 1ST DUKE OF LAUDERDALE. He was the 'L' in the secretive CABAL Cabinet which met at Ham House during the reign of Charles II.

After Elizabeth died the house was passed on to her son by her first marriage to Sir Lionel Tollemache, and the Tollemache family continued to own Ham House until 1948, when it was handed over to the National Trust.

Ham House and its contents are considered to be one of England's finest examples of a complete, unaltered 17th-century house and garden.

Cabal

The Cabal Ministry was made up of five Privy Councillors who met in private to run the affairs of Charles II's government between 1668 and 1674: Sir Thomas Clifford, Lord Arlington, the Duke of Buckingham, Lord Ashley, the Earl of Lauderdale.

The word cabal has come to mean a clique who meet in secret to make decisions or gain power through intrigue and conspiracy. The origin of the word is actually derived from the Hebrew Kabbalah, meaning 'secret doctrine', and the fact that the names of the cabinet members could be arranged into the acronym CABAL is purely serendipitous.

Petersham

Across the meadows is Petersham's pretty little Norman church, rebuilt in Georgian days, where the explorer GEORGE VANCOUVER (1757–98) lies in a simple churchyard grave. He discovered Vancouver Island, and the Canadian city of Vancouver is named after him. In poor health, he retired to Petersham and lived his final years in a small cottage in River Lane.

Richmond Hill

The view from the Thames at this point is of Richmond Hill, crowned by the huge landmark ROYAL STAR AND GARTER HOME for disabled ex-Servicemen, built in 1916 on the site of the Star and Garter Hotel popular with Charles Dickens.

The dazzling view from Richmond Hill, of the 'silvery' Thames meandering away towards Windsor through a twinkling, wooded landscape of heath and meadows and great houses, has been immortalised by numerous artists and poets.

> Here let us sweep
> The boundless landscape;
> not the raptur'd eye,
> Exulting swift, to huge Augusta send,
> Now to the sister-hills that skirt her plain
> To lofty Harrow now, and then to where
> Majestic Windsor lifts his princely brow.
> In lovely contrast to this glorious view,
> Calmly magnificent.

Those words are from JAMES THOMSON'S poem 'Summer', written in 1727. Thomson, who also wrote the words for 'Rule Britannia' (see Cliveden, p. 114) later came to live by the Old Deer Park in Richmond from 1736 until his death in 1748. He is buried in Richmond Parish Church.

J.M.W. Turner's painting *England: Richmond Hill on the Prince Regent's Birthday* was exhibited at the Royal Academy in 1819 and now hangs in the Tate Gallery.

The view from RICHMOND HILL is THE FIRST AND ONLY VIEW IN ENGLAND TO BE PROTECTED BY AN ACT OF PARLIAMENT, the Richmond, Ham and Petersham Open Spaces Act of 1902.

MICK JAGGER lived at DOWNE HOUSE on Richmond Hill in the 1990s. It now belongs to his former partner JERRY HALL.

Across the road is WICK HOUSE, built for SIR JOSHUA REYNOLDS, who painted HIS ONLY LANDSCAPE 'A View from Richmond Hill' while living there. Next door is THE WICK, where the actor JOHN MILLS and his wife MARY HAYLEY BELL brought up their daughters JULIET and HAYLEY, and later where RONNIE WOOD of the Rolling Stones lived.

Richmond

RICHMOND BRIDGE, built between 1774 and 1777 to a design by James Paine, is THE OLDEST SURVIVING BRIDGE ACROSS THE THAMES IN LONDON.

Just downstream is modern Richmond, a riverside panorama of 17th to 19th-century style classical architecture created by Quinlan Terry in the 1980s.

Richmond grew up around its palace, originally the Manor of Sheen, first used

as a royal residence by EDWARD I in 1299. After 'Braveheart' William Wallace was executed in London in 1305, the Scottish Commissioners came to Sheen to ask Edward to choose between the contenders for the Scottish throne.

EDWARD III died at Sheen in 1377. In 1501, following a fire, Henry VII rebuilt the palace and renamed it RICHMOND after the town in Yorkshire of which he was the earl. HENRY VIII was born at Richmond, and ELIZABETH I had THE WORLD'S FIRST FLUSH WATER CLOSET installed there, invented by her godson SIR JOHN HARINGTON and which, to avoid embarrassment, they agreed to refer to as her 'throne'. Elizabeth died at Richmond in 1603 and CHARLES I brought his court to Richmond to escape the plague.

After Charles I was executed in 1649, Richmond Palace was allowed to decay, and all that remains of it today is the Wardrobe, Trumpeter's House and the Gatehouse, all located on the south-west side of Richmond Green. The Green can also boast one of London's finest early Georgian terraces, MAIDS OF

HONOURS ROW, built in 1724 for the maids of honour of George II's wife. Victorian explorer SIR RICHARD BURTON lived at No. 2.

Novelist Mary Anne Evans lived at No. 8 Park Shot in Richmond, now the site of the Magistrate's Court, and while there began to write under the name GEORGE ELIOT. LEONARD AND VIRGINIA WOOLF lived in Hogarth House in Paradise Road and founded the HOGARTH PRESS there in 1917.

Film director and actor SIR RICHARD ATTENBOROUGH lives on Richmond Green, while his brother the naturalist SIR DAVID ATTENBOROUGH lives on Richmond Hill.

Asgill House

Just before flowing under the Twickenham rail and road bridges the river passes ASGILL HOUSE, a Palladian villa built on the river wall of the palace in 1758 as a weekend house for merchant banker and Lord Mayor of London SIR CHARLES ASGILL (1713–88). The Lord Mayor's coach used today was built for his inauguration in 1757. The house is now part of the Crown Estate.

St Margarets

Across the river on the Middlesex bank is ST MARGARETS, where CHARLES DICKENS lived at No. 2 Ailsa Park Villas while writing *Oliver Twist* in 1838. The house is now called Downes Close and is very near to TWICKENHAM STUDIOS, founded in 1912, and where *The Italian Job* and the two Beatles movies *A Hard Day's Night* and *Help!* were filmed. The Turks Head pub featured in *A Hard Day's Night*, while Ailsa Gardens was the Beatles' home in *Help!*.

Old Deer Park

The OLD DEER PARK was the original hunting ground for Richmond Palace before Richmond Park was enclosed. An obelisk by the towpath is a marker for the true north point by which to align the telescope in KEW OBSERVATORY, built for George III to view the transit of Venus in 1769. The Observatory can be glimpsed through the trees and is now used by the Meteorological Office for weather observations.

Well, I never knew this about
THE RIVER THAMES

HORACE WALPOLE of Strawberry Hill coined the word SERENDIPITY, meaning a fortunate discovery of something while looking for something else, after reading a story called 'The Three Princes of Serendip'. Serendip is the Persian name for Sri Lanka.

HENRY FIELDING (1707–54) wrote *Tom Jones* while living in a cottage in the lane that ran along the top of Alexander Pope's garden in TWICKENHAM.

GERALD HOLTOM (1914–85), the artist who designed the Campaign for Nuclear Disarmament (CND) logo, lived in TWICKENHAM.

In 1807 the painter J.M.W. TURNER (1751–1843) built a house for himself and his father in Sandycoombe Road just behind Marble Hill Park. He sold it in 1826 and the house is still there today.

In 1851, not long after his marriage upstream at Shiplake (see p. 92), ALFRED, LORD TENNYSON, by now Poet Laureate, moved into Chapel House in Montpelier Row on the edge of MARBLE HILL PARK with his new wife Emily. Their son HALLAM was born in the house, and baptised at St Mary's Church in Twickenham on 5 October 1852. They removed themselves to the Isle of Wight in 1853, leaving Chapel House to Tennyson's widowed mother Elizabeth.

WILLIAM BYRD II, who founded Richmond, Virginia, in America in 1737, called his new settlement Richmond because he found the view of the James River similar to the view from RICHMOND HILL, which he had come to love while a schoolboy in England.

RICHMOND GREEN was the site of THE SECOND RECORDED COUNTY CRICKET MATCH, played between Middlesex and Surrey in 1730, and THE EARLIEST RECORDED TIED CRICKET MATCH, between London and Surrey in 1741.

Actor EDMUND KEAN (1789–1833), regarded as the greatest actor of his day, is buried in Richmond Parish Church.

RICHMOND TO HAMMERSMITH

Old Isleworth – a pleasing riverside scene

Old Isleworth

Once the wooded Isleworth Ait, now a 10-acre nature reserve, is cleared, OLD ISLEWORTH comes into view on the left bank, providing a pleasing village scene with church, a variety of handsome houses and an old pub, the London Apprentice, so called because it was a favourite destination for the apprentices of the City livery companies who would row up the river to enjoy its hospitality.

The little domed pavilion by the water belongs to FERRY HOUSE, which until 2008 was the home of Conservative MP IAN GILMOUR, who hosted a hugely popular annual garden party there and who was related by marriage to the Duke of Northumberland, owner of next door Syon Park. Ferry House is a Georgian-style rebuild of a dower house where the artist J.M.W. Turner lived for a while in the early 19th century.

The river now flows between two green spaces, the last of any size until it leaves London again. On the left bank is Syon Park and on the right is Kew Gardens.

Syon Park

SYON PARK is the London seat of the Dukes of Northumberland. It was originally Syon Abbey, named after Mount Zion in the Holy Land, and the abbey church, of which there is nothing left, was the size of a cathedral, THE LARGEST ABBEY CHURCH IN ENGLAND. When Henry VIII dissolved the abbey in 1539 a curse was laid upon him, foretelling that dogs would one day lick at his blood – and indeed, after his death, when Henry's body was resting here overnight on its way to Windsor, the corpse burst open, spilling blood and guts on to the ground which were voraciously licked up by the household dogs.

Syon was given to EDWARD SEYMOUR, DUKE OF SOMERSET, Lord Protector of the young Edward VI, and Seymour built SYON HOUSE in Italian Renaissance style over the foundations of the abbey church. When Seymour was executed in 1552, Syon passed to JOHN DUDLEY, 1ST DUKE OF NORTHUMBERLAND (no relation to the present family who at that time were Earls of Northumberland) and it was at Syon that his daughter-in-law LADY JANE GREY was offered the crown. From Syon she went up to London by river to be proclaimed Queen but only nine days later she was toppled by Mary I and beheaded.

Dudley was stripped of his Dukedom and later was himself executed.

In 1594 HENRY PERCY, 9TH EARL OF NORTHUMBERLAND, acquired Syon by marriage and it has remained in possession of the Percy family ever since.

In 1762 Hugh Percy, Earl of Northumberland, who was created Duke of Northumberland in 1766, commissioned Robert Adam to remodel the interior of Syon House, and the result is considered to be Adam's earliest English masterpiece. Capability Brown laid out the park. The lion on top of the east front of Syon House is the Northumberland crest and came here after Northumberland House in London's Trafalgar Square was demolished in 1874.

The GREAT CONSERVATORY in the grounds of Syon House was built by Charles Fowler in 1826 and was THE FIRST LARGE CONSERVATORY IN THE WORLD TO BE MADE FROM METAL AND GLASS.

Brentford

BRENTFORD has a history older than London itself, with evidence of neolithic flint workings and a Bronze Age trading settlement. In AD 54, Julius Caesar is said to have crossed the Thames at Brentford, overcoming the forces of tribal chief Cassivellaunus.

Today, the waterfront area of Brentford is undergoing an astonishing regeneration, with the old docks, railway yards, gasworks and warehouses being replaced with plush new riverside apartments, shops and restaurants. The

RIVER BRENT joins the Thames here, and Brentford Dock is the southern terminus of the Grand Union Canal, connecting the Thames with Northamptonshire and the Midlands.

There have been two BATTLES OF BRENTFORD. The first, in 1016, saw the English King Edmund Ironside rout the forces of Danish King Canute. In November 1016 Edmund suffered a horrible death at the hands of a treacherous earl called Edric, who concealed himself in the pit below Edmund's latrine and thrust a pike through the King's bowels, a callous act that took place in the yard of what was to become the RED LION INN at Brentford.

The second Battle of Brentford was fought in 1642, during the Civil War, when Prince Rupert's cavalry, advancing on London, won a skirmish against the Parliamentary soldiers defending Brentford.

Brentford's most unexpected treasure is a superb painting of the *Last Supper* by the artist JOHANN ZOFFANY (1733–1810), which can be found high up on the wall of the original chancel in the remodelled church of St Paul, and which was inherited from nearby St George's Church when the latter closed. The face of St Peter is said to be that of the artist himself, while those of the disciples are based on the local fishermen of Strand on the Green, where Zoffany lived. The painting was intended for Kew Church, across the river, but the gift was rejected when someone spotted that the portrait of Judas Iscariot looked remarkably like one of the churchwardens, a local lawyer Zoffany didn't like very much.

Kew Gardens

The ROYAL BOTANIC GARDENS at KEW began life in 1759 as a garden for PRINCESS AUGUSTA, the grieving widow of Frederick, Prince of Wales, killed by a cricket ball upriver at Cliveden, as somewhere she could console herself by putting her green fingers to good use. It has expanded to become a World Heritage Site (2003) covering 300 acres (120 ha) and responsible for THE LARGEST COLLECTION OF LIVING PLANTS IN THE WORLD.

The octagonal ten-storey PAGODA was built in 1761 by Sir William Chambers as a gift for Augusta from her son George III. At the same time George built a cottage in the garden at Kew as a wedding present for his wife Charlotte, which can still be seen.

In the latter half of the 18th century botanist SIR JOSEPH BANKS (1743–1820) contributed huge numbers of plants to

Kew, gathered during his voyages around the world with Captain Cook. These helped to form the basis of the plant collection owned by the Royal Botanic Gardens today. In 1775 Francis Masson, another of Kew's early plant collectors, presented Kew with an ENCEPHALARTOS ALTENSTEINII from the Eastern Cape region of South Africa, which still survives in the Palm House and is now THE OLDEST POT PLANT IN THE WORLD. It has an average growth rate of just under 1 inch (2.5 cm) per year and has only ever produced one cone at Kew, in 1819. This was such a momentous occurrence that the frail, 76-year-old Sir Joseph Banks insisted on coming to see it, for what proved to be his last ever visit to Kew. He died the following year.

Two of the conservatories at Kew were built by DECIMUS BURTON in the 19th century. The PALM HOUSE was completed in 1848 and was THE FIRST LARGE-SCALE BUILDING IN THE WORLD TO BE MADE FROM WROUGHT IRON. THE TEMPERATE HOUSE, completed in 1899, is THE LARGEST VICTORIAN GLASSHOUSE ANYWHERE IN THE WORLD.

Kew's Herbarium was begun in 1853, and eventually Sir Joseph Banks's entire herbarium was brought to Kew from the British Museum. The KEW GARDEN HERBARIUM is now THE LARGEST HERBARIUM IN THE WORLD.

Kew Palace

KEW PALACE, THE SMALLEST OF THE ROYAL PALACES, was built in 1631 by a Dutch merchant called Samuel

Fortrey and was originally known as the Dutch House. In 1729 it was purchased by GEORGE II as a country home for his daughters Anne, Caroline and Amelia. George III's wife, QUEEN CHARLOTTE, died there in 1818. Queen Victoria's parents were married there later that same year. Kew Palace was restored in time for PRINCE CHARLES to host a dinner to celebrate the Queen's 80th birthday there in 2006 and the palace is now open to the public.

St Anne's, Kew

Red-brick ST ANNE'S CHURCH on Kew Green was built on land donated by Queen Anne in 1714, and is the burial place of two legendary artists, THOMAS GAINSBOROUGH (1727–88), painter of *The Blue Boy*, and German classical painter JOHANN ZOFFANY (1733–1810), who lived just across the river at Strand on the Green. Zoffany, along with Sir Joseph Banks, was pall-bearer at the funeral here of William Aiton, the much-respected first royal gardener at Kew Gardens.

Kew Bridge

The present KEW BRIDGE, officially the Edward VII Bridge, was opened in 1903. The first bridge across the Thames here was built in 1759 and dedicated to George, Prince of Wales and his mother Augusta. The following year the Prince was riding across the bridge from a visit to Kew Palace when he was met by a messenger with the news that his grandfather George II was dead and he had become George III.

Strand on the Green

Immediately after passing under Kew Bridge the Thames flows by a cluster of picturesque, brightly coloured 18th-century houses on the Middlesex side, liberally interspersed with pubs. This is STRAND ON THE GREEN, once a community of fishermen, now the preserve of the very wealthy.

Artist JOHANN ZOFFANY (1734–1810), known for his portraits of George III, lived from 1790 until his death at No. 65, now ZOFFANY HOUSE, and entertained the Prince Regent in his garden there. During the 1980s television writer CARLA LANE (*Liver Birds*, *Butterflies*, *Bread*) lived in Zoffany House. Welsh poet DYLAN THOMAS often stayed with friends at Ship Cottage behind Ship House during the 1940s and early 50s, while NANCY MITFORD lived at ROSE COTTAGE in the 1940s and there wrote *The Pursuit of Love*, published in 1945. From 1959 to 1964 film director JOHN GUILLERMIN (*The Blue Max*, *The Towering Inferno*) lived at No 60. During the 1960s humorist JOHN BIRD (*Bremner, Bird and Fortune*) lived at No. 31. Actor DONALD PLEASANCE (1919–95), Ernst Blofeld in the James Bond film *You Only Live Twice*, lived at No. 10 from 1969 until 1973 and then purchased No. 11, BULL COTTAGE, where he stayed until 1985.

The CITY BARGE pub began life in the 1480s as the Navigator's Arms and was given its present name in the 18th century, when it became the mooring place for the Lord Mayor of London's barge.

The folk at the BULL'S HEAD maintain that OLIVER CROMWELL often drank there and on one occasion, during the second Battle of Brentford in 1642, was trapped in the pub by the advancing Royalist soldiers of Prince Rupert. He escaped through a secret tunnel to the island in the middle of the Thames adjacent to the Bull's Head – which extraordinarily enough is called Oliver's Island

EAMONN ANDREWS (1922–87), host of, television's *This is Your Life*, lived from 1961 to 1970 at No. 61 Hartington Road with a 60 ft (18 m) garden on the Thames.

National Archive

Just beyond Kew Railway Bridge of 1869, on the Surrey bank is the Public Record Office, now called the NATIONAL ARCHIVE, some 15 acres (6 ha) of public records, court proceedings going back to the Middle Ages, the original manuscript of the Domesday Book, birth certificates, wills, marriage certificates, and pretty much anything else recorded on paper in England and Wales over the last 1,000 years.

Chiswick Bridge

When CHISWICK BRIDGE was built in 1933, carrying the new Great Chertsey Road over the river, its central span of 150 feet (46 m) was THE LONGEST CONCRETE SPAN OVER THE THAMES, taking the accolade away from Caversham Bridge upstream. Exactly 370 feet (113 m) downstream can be found a stone bearing the letters UBR on the Surrey bank and a blue and black marker on the Middlesex side, designating the end of the University Boat Race course.

Mortlake

IN MORTLAKE, a little further on in Surrey, is the delightful, gaily painted pub THE SHIP, which gleams against the looming brown bulk of THE STAG BREWERY, LONDON'S LARGEST BREWERY, once Watneys, then Courage and now Budweiser. Mortlake has been associated with brewing since the 15th

century, when the local monastery operated a brewhouse.

The village of Mortlake first came to prominence in the early 17th century, when James I established THE FIRST ENGLISH TAPESTRY WORKS there in 1619, employing Flemish weavers. Mortlake tapestries became highly sought after, particularly by Charles I, but the factory closed in 1703 and only rare examples can now be found in stately homes (such as Hardwick House, see page 84) and museums.

St Mary's, Mortlake

The next distinctive landmark after the brewery on the Surrey side is the 16th-century tower and cupola of ST MARY'S CHURCH, resting place of the first scientists, a Prime Minister and a great reformer.

Buried in the chancel is DR JOHN DEE (1527–1608), an influential if controversial advisor and astrologer to Elizabeth I who often came by barge to his house on the river at Mortlake. A mixture of alchemist, mathematician and scholar, he was one of the very early scientists who attempted to understand the world around him through research and analysis, developing theories and methods of experimentation that were copied by the likes of Isaac Newton more than 50 years later. He was a passionate advocate of imperialism and in a work of 1576 was first to coin the terms 'BRITISH ISLES' and 'BRITISH EMPIRE'.

On the north wall is a tablet to HENRY ADDINGTON (1757–1844), 1st Viscount

Sidmouth, Prime Minister from 1801 to 1804. He was THE FIRST MIDDLE-CLASS PRIME MINISTER, signed the Treaty of Amiens with France in 1802, agreeing terms unfavourable to Britain, and in the same year opened the docks at Canary Wharf, where he is today commemorated by the Henry Addington pub, which has THE LONGEST PUB BAR IN BRITAIN.

Buried in the churchyard is SIR EDWIN CHADWICK (1800–90), a single-minded philanthropist and reformer whose *Report on an Enquiry into the Sanitary Condition of the Labouring Population of Great Britain* is considered THE BIBLE OF MODERN PUBLIC SANITA-TION.

Just behind St Mary's is the Roman Catholic church of St Mary Magdalen, in whose cemetery is a huge tent-shaped tombstone. Within, and visible through a window, is the coffin containing the remains of the great explorer SIR RICHARD BURTON (1821–90), who discovered Lake Tanganyika and introduced PYJAMAS and the KAMA SUTRA into England.

Barnes

BARNES means what it says, because this was the site of the barns used for storing grain for the manor at Mortlake. Today it is an affluent area, much sought after by established media types, with a distinctly villagey conservation centre grouped around pond, pub and church. HENRY FIELDING, author of *Tom Jones*, lived in Barnes's oldest house MILBOURNE HOUSE, which faces the green, a Georgian front hiding its 15th-century origins.

BARNES RAILWAY BRIDGE (1895) provides a significant landmark for the University Boat Race, as whoever is leading at this point usually wins the contest.

Just past the bridge is Barnes's show-piece, THE TERRACE, lined with handsome early Georgian houses. Composer GUSTAV HOLST lived at No. 10 from 1908 until 1913 before moving to Thaxted in Essex to write his orches-tral suite *The Planets*. NINETTE DE VALOIS (1898–2001), founder of the Royal Ballet, lived at No. 14 from 1962 to 1982. She stayed in Barnes, albeit in a smaller apartment, until she died aged 102 in 2001.

The riverside BULL'S HEAD is an inter-nationally famous jazz venue, while Queens Ride by Barnes Common was the site in 1977 of the car crash that killed T. Rex rock star MARC BOLAN. It is marked by a bronze bust and recognised by the English Tourist Board as a 'Site of Rock 'n' Roll Importance'.

Cheese Farm

Across the river from Barnes, the green recreation fields of Dukes Meadows, once part of the gardens of Chiswick House, give way to townhouses and then the elegance of CHISWICK MALL, marked at its upstream end by the 15th-century tower of ST NICHOLAS'S CHURCH, around which the original fishing village of CHISWICK or 'cheese farm' began.

The owners of two of Chiswick's most famous houses are buried at St Nicholas.

William Hogarth
(1697–1764)

In the churchyard, underneath a tomb surmounted by an urn and sporting an epitaph by David Garrick, lies the painter and satirist WILLIAM HOGARTH, THE ONLY MAJOR ENGLISH ARTIST TO HAVE A ROUNDABOUT NAMED AFTER HIM. The roundabout, a busy junction on the A4, sends traffic right past HOGARTH'S HOUSE, built in 1700 on the northern edge of what was then the quiet village of Chiswick. The house provided a summer retreat for Hogarth from the noise and bustle of his main house and studio in Leicester Square, and he would often arrive here by river. A mulberry tree which Hogarth loved still grows in the garden.

William Hogarth was famous for his narrative pictures that told moral tales, an early form of the comic strip. The eight pictures of his celebrated *Rake's Progress* (now in the Soane Museum in Lincoln's Inn Fields) illustrate the life of wealthy Thomas Rakewell who throws away his inheritance on drinking, whoring and gambling and ends up in Bedlam. Hogarth loved to poke fun at self-serving politicians and at affectation, and he was especially good at capturing real life, as he had a photographic memory and could remember and recreate scenes he had witnessed in the most precise detail.

Earl of Burlington

Lying in the great family vault of the Earls of Burlington (whose London abode was Burlington House in Piccadilly, now the Royal Academy) in St Nicholas's Church is the 3rd Earl, creator of one of London's most beautiful and important houses, Chiswick House, which sits in lovely gardens across the road from the church.

Chiswick House

CHISWICK HOUSE was designed by the 3rd Earl between 1724 and 1729, not as a residence but as 'a temple to the arts', somewhere to display his fine collection of paintings. Burlington was influenced by the buildings of ancient Rome and by the work of Andrea Palladio as well as England's first Palladian architect Inigo Jones, and Chiswick House is now considered one of the finest examples of Palladian architecture anywhere.

The interiors, which are exquisite, were designed by WILLIAM KENT (1685–1748), a friend of the earl, who also laid out the garden, which is considered to be THE FIRST ENGLISH LANDSCAPE GARDEN. William Kent is buried alongside his patron in the Burlington vault.

After Burlington's death in 1753 Chiswick House passed to his daughter, who was married to the 4th Duke of Devonshire, and the house remained with the Devonshires until 1929. Georgiana, wife of the 5th Duke and a dazzling hostess, entertained Whig society at Chiswick and it was in Chiswick House that CHARLES JAMES FOX died in 1806 while Foreign Secretary. GEORGE CANNING died in the very same room 21 years later in 1827, after just 119 days as Prime Minister, THE SHORTEST TERM AS PRIME MINISTER IN BRITISH HISTORY.

From 1892 until 1929 Chiswick House was leased out as a mental asylum. It was then acquired by Middlesex Council, and is now being restored and run by English Heritage.

Chiswick Burial Ground

Buried in the centre of the Burial Ground behind St Nicholas's Church, under a huge tomb crowned with a carved soldier's helmet, is FREDERICK HITCH (1856–1913), who was presented

with a Victoria Cross by Queen Victoria personally, for courage displayed during the Battle of Rorke's Drift, as depicted in the 1964 film *Zulu*. When he returned to England he became a cab driver, THE ONLY LONDON CABBIE EVER TO HAVE WON A VC.

Close by lies HENRY JOY, the trumpeter who sounded the Charge of the Light Brigade. He died in 1893.

Also lying in the churchyard, inside a large bronze classical tomb, is the artist J.M. WHISTLER (1834–1903).

Thornycroft & Co.

Right in front of the church on the river is Church Wharf, now occupied by Georgian-style townhouses built in the 1980s. Between 1864 and 1909 this was a huge shipbuilding yard belonging to THORNYCROFT AND CO., builders of high-speed launches and torpedo boats. When he was 17, John Thornycroft built *NAUTILUS*, THE FIRST STEAM LAUNCH THAT COULD KEEP UP WITH THE UNIVERSITY BOAT RACE CREWS.

Chiswick Mall

Looming over the nice houses of CHISWICK MALL is FULLERS BREWERY, which originated in the 16th century as a brewhouse belonging to Bedford House on Chiswick Mall. In 1701 the brewhouse was bought by THOMAS MAWSON, founder of what became Fullers in 1845 and later expanded to incorporate the Lamb Brewery next door. Fullers Brewery is particularly known for London Pride, ESB (Extra Special Brew) and Chiswick Bitter.

Right in front of the brewery is BEDFORD HOUSE, built in the middle of the 17th century by the Russells, Earls of Bedford. Between 1945 and 1954 the house was lived in by the actor SIR MICHAEL REDGRAVE (1908–85) and his acting family, wife RACHEL KEMPSON and children Vanessa, Lynn and Corin.

Walpole House

The grandest house on Chiswick Mall is the 17th-century WALPOLE HOUSE named after THOMAS WALPOLE (1727–1803), nephew of Britain's first Prime Minister Sir Robert Walpole. Before Walpole, the house was the last home of BARBARA VILLIERS, mistress of Charles II, whom we met upriver at Dorney Court (see p. 119). It was later run as a boarding house, during which time the Irish politician DANIEL O'CONNELL, known as 'The Liberator', lodged there while studying law at Lincoln's Inn – Dublin's main street is named after him. A young WILLIAM MAKEPEACE THACKERAY attended Walpole House when it was run as a school in 1817 and later made it Miss Pinkerton's Seminary for Young Ladies in his novel *Vanity Fair*. In 1885 shipbuilder JOHN THORNYCROFT owned Walpole House, and between 1903 and 1910 it was the home of actor-manager SIR HERBERT BEERBOHM TREE (1853–1917). In 2008 Walpole House became the most expensive house in Chiswick when it was sold to HADEEL IBRAHIM for £12,500,000. The vendor was fashion designer JASPER CONRAN,

who bought it in 2006 for £7,250,000 and completely redesigned the interior.

Hammersmith Terrace

At the eastern end of Chiswick Mall is HAMMERSMITH TERRACE, where lived SIR SAMUEL MORLAND (1625–95), inventor of the MEGAPHONE. Independent MP and humorous writer A.P. HERBERT (1890–1971) lived at No. 12 for 50 years and could often be seen sculling on the river in the boat he kept moored at the bottom of his garden. He was known to enjoy a drink or two at The Dove too (see below). As an MP Herbert drove the divorce laws through Parliament, while amongst his most popular works as a writer were his *Misleading Cases*, adapted for television by the BBC as *A.P. Herbert's Misleading Cases* starring an incomparable Alastair Sim as the bewildered judge Mr Justice Swallow.

Upper Mall

UPPER MALL boasts some of London's most enticing Thames-side residences all built on the site of RIVERCOURT, the home of Charles II's widow Catherine of Braganza. At No. 18 is The DOVE, a cosy little 17th-century pub that boasts a delightful terrace right on the river. The Dove is always packed on Boat Race day despite having THE SMALLEST BAR IN BRITAIN. In 1740 JAMES THOMSON (1700–48) wrote the words to 'RULE BRITANNIA' in an upstairs room here.

He would walk to The Dove from his home in Richmond, and on returning home by boat some years later he caught a chill and died.

Kelmscott House

At No. 26 is KELMSCOTT HOUSE, where WILLIAM MORRIS lived from 1879 and where he died in 1896. Morris named the house after Kelmscott Manor, his country home upriver in Oxfordshire (see p. 30), and described the location as 'certainly the prettiest in London'. In 1880 he made a grand, much talked

about progress up the Thames from his London home to his country house in his eccentric houseboat, a voyage which took over a week. In 1891 Morris set up the KELMSCOTT PRESS at No. 16. Morris was something of a socialist, and the Hammersmith branch of the Socialist party would meet at Kelmscott House to hear lectures by Ramsay MacDonald and to sing under the baton of Gustav Holst.

Before Morris arrived on the scene the house was the home of SIR FRANCIS RONALDS (1788–1873), who invented THE WORLD'S FIRST ELECTRIC TELE-GRAPH in the back garden in 1816.

After Furnival Gardens, Upper Mall becomes LOWER MALL, where we find the BLUE ANCHOR pub, licensed in the days of George I and where GUSTAV HOLST wrote his *Hammersmith Suite*. The pub appeared on the end credits of the 1980s television series *Minder*.

Well, I never knew this
about
THE RIVER THAMES

VINCENT VAN GOGH lived in ISLE-
WORTH briefly in 1876, when he was
working as a teacher at a private school,
HOLME COURT HOUSE. There is a blue
plaque on the house which is near the
village centre.

THOMAS PERCY, a cousin of the 9th Earl
of Northumberland, dined at SYON
HOUSE on 4 November 1605, the night
before he joined Guy Fawkes in the
attempt to blow up James I and the
Houses of Parliament. Thomas was
shot dead trying to escape and the earl
was sent to the Tower for 15 years.

As a boy, J.M.W. TURNER (1775–1851)
lived with his uncle in a house beside
THE WEIR pub (formerly The White
Horse) in BRENTFORD. Walks along the
river here are said to have sparked his
interest in painting.

BRENTFORD'S MUSICAL MUSEUM houses
THE LARGEST COLLECTION OF ANCIENT
MUSIC ROLLS IN THE WORLD.

Just upstream of Kew Bridge on the
left bank is a tall brick chimney that
marks the site of THE KEW BRIDGE
STEAM MUSEUM. The museum boasts
THE LARGEST COLLECTION OF STEAM
PUMPING ENGINES IN THE WORLD, as
well as THE LARGEST WORKING BEAM
ENGINE IN THE WORLD, built in 1846 to
pump water to west London, and also
THE ONLY OPERATING STEAM RAILWAY IN
LONDON.

CHISWICK EYOT IS THE MOST EASTERLY OF
LONDON'S EYOTS and THE ONLY ONE ON
THE UNIVERSITY BOAT RACE COURSE.

Novelist and poet NAOMI MITCHISON
(1897–1999) lived at RIVERCOURT HOUSE.

HAMMERSMITH
BRIDGE TO PIMLICO

Hammersmith Bridge – the lowest bridge across the Thames in London

Hammersmith Bridge

The elegant and distinctive cast-iron HAMMERSMITH BRIDGE, with a central span of 422 ft (128 m), was designed by Sir Joseph Bazalgette, creator of London's sewer system, and opened in 1887. It replaced LONDON'S FIRST SUSPENSION BRIDGE, which William Tierney Clarke built across the Thames here in 1827. The green and gold paintwork reflects the colours of Harrods, whose depository is nearby in Barnes. At high tide, the bridge has a clearance of just 12 ft (3.6 m), making it THE LOWEST BRIDGE ACROSS THE THAMES IN LONDON.

Riverside Studios

RIVERSIDE STUDIOS, just downstream of Hammersmith Bridge, on the left bank, began life in the 19th century as a factory, then became film studios which, in 1954, were bought by the BBC who made them into THE FINEST AND BIGGEST TELEVISION STUDIOS IN EUROPE. THE FIRST COLOUR TELEVISION

PROGRAMMES were broadcast from here in 1967. The BBC moved out to their new Wood Lane studios in the early 1970s. Today Riverside Studios is a multi-purpose arts centre, home to film and television studios, dance and theatre.

Brandenburgh House

Just beyond the studios is CHANCELLOR'S WHARF, the site in the 17th century of BRANDENBURGH HOUSE, home of Caroline of Brunswick, ill-treated wife of the Prince Regent, who was said to be so shaken on first meeting her that he called for brandy. After Caroline died there, the King ordered the house to be razed to the ground.

Next, at THAMES WHARF, is the futuristic headquarters of RICHARD ROGERS, controversial architect of the Lloyds Building. On the ground floor is the RIVER CAFÉ, opened in 1987 by Rogers' wife Ruth and the late Rose Grey, authors of *The River Cafe Cook Book*. Naked Chef JAMIE OLIVER was 'discovered' while working at the River Café.

Harrods Village

Across the river in Barnes is another Boat Race landmark, the old Harrods Furniture Depository, built in 1894 and looking unnervingly like Harrods itself. Customers who were posted overseas would deposit their furniture and possessions here (bought at Harrods

naturally) while they were away. This is now Harrods Village, a development of high-security luxury apartments.

Wetlands

Downstream from the Depository the reservoirs of Barn Elms Water Works have been turned into the LONDON WETLAND CENTRE, 105 acres (42 ha) of lakes, water meadows and reed beds that are home to a huge variety of wildlife, including water voles, butterflies and moths, bats and over 180 species of birds. It is THE FIRST URBAN PROJECT OF ITS KIND IN BRITAIN.

Craven Cottage

Back on the north bank sits CRAVEN COTTAGE, home of LONDON'S OLDEST FIRST-CLASS FOOTBALL CLUB, FULHAM FC, founded in 1879. The riverside location is the most picturesque of all London's football grounds and takes its name from an 18th-century cottage built for Lord Craven that once stood on the site but burned down in 1888. The novelist LORD LYTTON (1803–73) lived in the original cottage during the 1840s. A popular writer of his time, he gave a number of expressions to the English language such as 'the great unwashed', 'the pen is mightier than the sword', 'in pursuit of the mighty dollar' and the classic first line for a novel 'It was a dark and stormy night . . .', as plagiarised by Snoopy, the 'Peanuts' cartoon character.

Fulham Palace

trees. Bishop Grindal, Bishop of London from 1559 to 1570, planted THE FIRST TAMARISK TREE IN EUROPE here in 1560. Bishop Compton, in office from 1675 to 1713, INTRODUCED THE ACACIA, THE MAGNOLIA and THE MAPLE INTO ENGLAND, growing the first examples here at Fulham. The CEDAR OF LEBANON he planted was thought to be THE LARGEST EVER SEEN IN LONDON.

The University Boat Race begins just upstream of Putney Bridge.

Embowered in the 27 luscious acres (11 ha) of Bishop's Park is one of the least known and most beautiful historic buildings in London, FULHAM PALACE, country home of the Bishops of London since the 11th century. There is a lovely, mellow, red-brick Tudor quadrangle built by Bishop Fitzjames in the early 16th century, with a fountain, a great porch and bell tower, and some 17th-century windows. To the left of the porch is the Great Hall of 1480. The Bishops of London vacated Fulham Palace in 1973 and the site is now managed by Hammersmith and Fulham Council as a museum, with a café and offices.

A Place for Trees

The palace was originally surrounded by THE LONGEST MOAT IN ENGLAND, thought to have been dug by the Danes in the 10th century. The gardens themselves were once noted for their unusual

Putney Bridge

The first PUTNEY BRIDGE, constructed in 1729, was made of wood, had 26 arches, and was THE FIRST BRIDGE EVER TO BE BUILT ACROSS THE THAMES BETWEEN KINGSTON AND LONDON BRIDGE. Apparently it was put there on the orders of Sir Robert Walpole after he had got stranded on the Putney side one night while the ferryman was carousing in a hostelry on the other side.

In 1795 the feminist MARY WOLL-STONECRAFT threw herself off the bridge in despair after her lover ran off with an actress. She was pulled unconscious from the water by a boatman and went on to marry William Godwin, with whom she produced two daughters, the younger of whom, Mary, grew up to marry the poet Shelley and write the novel *Frankenstein*.

The present bridge was designed by Sir Joseph Bazalgette of sewer renown and opened in 1886.

Two Churches

PUTNEY BRIDGE IS THE ONLY MAJOR
BRIDGE IN BRITAIN WITH A CHURCH AT
BOTH ENDS – All Saints in Fulham and St
Mary's in Putney. It is said that the
churches were built by two sisters who
lived on opposite sides of the river.
When being ferried across to visit each
other, one would say to the ferryman
'Full home, my man', while the other
would cry 'Put nigh!'

ALL SAINT'S, Fulham, with a splendid
tower that dates from 1440, is the
mother church of Fulham and burial
place of ten Bishops of London. All
Saints was used for a particularly grue-
some scene in the 1976 film *The Omen*,
where a priest is speared by a flagpole
falling from the church tower.

St MARY's, Putney, was the scene of the
groundbreaking PUTNEY DEBATES of
1647, when, in talks held around the
altar table between Oliver Cromwell
and the Levellers, there was discussion
for the first time of such radical
innovations as 'one man one vote',
parliamentary constituencies defined by
population size rather than wealth,

authority to be vested in the Commons
rather than the Crown or the Lords, and
freedom of conscience and equality to
be guaranteed before the law.

The Putney Debates first articulated
many of the ideals enshrined in the
American Constitution over 100 years
later, and Putney's historic legacy is
immense, but if you go there looking
for some monument to the freedoms
first mooted here you will be disappointed. The only memorial is a small
plaque placed in St Mary's Church by
the Cromwell Association.

Oliver Cromwell's ancestor THOMAS
CROMWELL, Chancellor of England and
Henry VIII's agent for the Dissolution
of the Monasteries, was born in Putney
in 1485.

Wandsworth

Moving east, Putney blends into
WANDSWORTH, LONDON'S OLDEST
INDUSTRIAL AREA, which grew up
around the mouth of the RIVER
WANDLE, the largest tributary of
the Thames in London. Only 11
miles (18 km) long, the Wandle rises
near Croydon and drops 100 ft (30
m) during its course, providing plenty
of hydro power for breweries and
water-wheels at Wandsworth. The RAM
BREWERY, now being converted into
high-rise flats, was operating in
Wandsworth as far back as 1581, and
until it closed in 2006 was THE OLDEST
CONTINUOUSLY WORKING BREWERY IN
BRITAIN.

Hurlingham

Across the river from Wandsworth, its chimneys just visible through the trees behind a high bank, is HURLINGHAM HOUSE, a neo-classical mansion that was originally a country cottage built in 1760 by Dr William Cadogan. In 1869 the HURLINGHAM CLUB was founded to hold pigeon shooting competitions in the grounds, which explains the pigeon on the club's crest. Hurlingham is where POLO was introduced into England in 1874 and the governing body of the sport is known as the Hurlingham Polo Association, even though polo is no longer played there.

The Thames now flows under WANDSWORTH BRIDGE, opened in 1940 as the second on the site and probably the least interesting bridge in London. On the south bank is the village of Battersea.

St Mary's Church
Battersea

ST MARY'S, BATTERSEA, sits right on the river, a rare thing of dignity amongst the towering blocks of flats, old and modern. There has been a church here

since Saxon times, but the present building was designed by local architect Joseph Dixon in 1777. The 17th-century east window of painted glass encased in stonework of 1379 survives from the previous church.

BENEDICT ARNOLD (1741–1801) and his family are buried in the crypt of St Mary's. Patriot or traitor depending on your point of view, Arnold fought courageously for the Continental Army during the War of Independence but became disillusioned, particularly when the Americans formed an alliance with the French, and devised a plan to help the British capture the fort at West Point on the Hudson River.

In 1782 the poet and artist WILLIAM BLAKE, who wrote the words to the hymn 'Jerusalem', married Catherine Boucher, the daughter of a Battersea market gardener, at St Mary's. She signed the register with an 'x', which suggests that she was not well educated, but she provided love and support for the eccentric Blake for 45 years until his death in 1827, and his last words to her were 'You have ever been an angel to me!'

J.M.W. TURNER used to enjoy rowing over to St Mary's from his house in Cheyne Walk. He would sit in a tall chair by the bay window of the vestry, sketching the Thames and Battersea Bridge. The chair is still there.

Chelsea Harbour

Across from Battersea and just downstream of Battersea Railway Bridge, Chelsea Creek marks the point at which Fulham becomes Chelsea. CHELSEA HARBOUR is on the Fulham side of the creek, so should really be called Fulham Harbour. It was all built on behalf of P & O in the 1980s and has become a favourite haunt of pop stars and footballers – Sir Elton John and Robbie Williams have both owned apartments in the 21-storey Belvedere Tower, which is 250 feet (76 m) high and is crowned by a golden 'tide ball' which moves up and down with the tide.

Lots Road

On the north bank of Chelsea Creek, which comes in from the west, is LOTS ROAD POWER STATION, opened in 1905 to provide electric power for the District Line, which was previously steam powered. At the time Lots Road was THE LARGEST POWER STATION EVER BUILT and eventually ended up providing power for almost all of London's underground. In 2002 the power station was decommissioned and began to

undergo conversion into flats, but not before achieving status as THE WORLD'S LONGEST SERVING POWER STATION.

Cheyne Walk – Nos. 119–92

Despite the ever busy road that separates CHEYNE WALK from the river, its mix of glorious Queen Anne houses and artistic heritage has lured numerous artists, writers and musicians to this Chelsea street.

Set back a little from the bustle of the houseboats near Battersea Bridge is No. 119 Cheyne Walk, where J.M.W. TURNER lived out his final years from 1846 to 1852. He lived anonymously as Mr Booth and built himself a roof gallery from where he could watch the sunsets. Ian Fleming's mother EVE came to live here in the 1920s, while Ian was still at Eton, and had a passionate affair with the painter AUGUSTUS JOHN who lived next door. They had a child together in 1925.

LINDSEY HOUSE, built in 1639 and

THE OLDEST HOUSE IN CHELSEA, was divided into four separate dwellings in 1775 and now forms 96–100 Cheyne Walk. Engineer MARC BRUNEL lived at No. 98 from 1808 to 1826 and his son ISAMBARD KINGDOM BRUNEL grew up there. From 1866 to 1878 JAMES MCNEILL WHISTLER lived at No. 96, and it was there that he painted the immortal picture of his mother that hangs in the Louvre – she was staying with him to avoid the American Civil War. In 1972 Northern Ireland Secretary Willie Whitelaw secretly met here with the IRA's Martin McGuinness and Gerry Adams, while publicly insisting that ministers 'would never talk to terrorists'. The house belonged to Tory MP PAUL CHANNON at the time. It is now owned by the National Trust, and members can sometimes visit the small garden at the back, which was designed by Gertrude Jekyll.

No. 93 Cheyne Walk is a pretty house with a balcony where Elizabeth Stevenson, the future author MRS GASKELL, was born in 1810. Her sickly mother died a few weeks later and Elizabeth was sent to live with her aunt in Knutsford, Cheshire.

At No. 92, New Labour cheerleaders thriller writer KEN FOLLETT and his wife BARBARA threw their famous political soirées in the late 1990s, before they became disillusioned.

Battersea Bridge

The present BATTERSEA BRIDGE was built of cast iron by Sir Joseph Bazalgette in 1890. At just 40 ft (12 m) wide it is LONDON'S NARROWEST ROAD BRIDGE. From here the Thames starts to flow between 19th-century embankments – also the work of Sir Joseph and constructed largely to contain his new sewers – as far as the City.

Crosby Hall

The 15th-century CROSBY HALL is all that survives of Crosby Place, Sir Thomas More's house in Bishopsgate in the City. When Crosby Place was threatened with demolition in 1908, the Great Hall was taken down stone by stone and rebuilt on the site of More's garden in Chelsea. More recently the Hall has been incorporated into a neo-Tudor mansion as part of a private residence.

Chelsea Old Church

The present CHELSEA OLD CHURCH is a good restoration of the original, which was founded in Norman times, added to over the centuries and badly damaged in the Blitz. In the More Chapel there is an impressive monument to SIR THOMAS MORE, Henry VIII's Lord Chancellor. He was beheaded in 1535 and, while his head was sent to Canterbury, some believe that his body was secretly brought back to Chelsea and laid to rest here by his daughter Margaret Roper.

His statue sits in the garden outside the church, looking out over the Thames.

It was Sir Thomas More who made the quiet country village of CHELSEA fashionable when he moved here in 1520 and built BEAUFORT HOUSE on the river front, near where Beaufort Street is today. Henry VIII, who visited often, so liked the place that he decided to acquire nearby CHELSEA MANOR, which he subsequently enlarged. The site of Chelsea Manor is now occupied by Nos. 19–26 Cheyne Walk.

In CARLYLE MANSIONS, nicknamed 'Writers' Block', the poet T.S. ELIOT lived with a bare light bulb and a crucifix over the bed, American writer HENRY JAMES lodged from 1912 until his lonely

death in 1916, and IAN FLEMING began writing his first James Bond novel *Casino Royale*.

Carlyle Mansions was named after the 'Sage of Chelsea', THOMAS CARLYLE, who lived a No. 24 (then No. 5) in CHEYNE ROW. Carlyle and his wife moved to unfashionable Chelsea from Scotland in 1834, and within a few years their house had become a meeting place for writers such as Tennyson, Dickens and Browning. Dickens said of him, 'I would go at all times farther to see Carlyle than any man alive.' Carlyle had a room on the top floor soundproofed and here he wrote perhaps his most famous work, *The French Revolution: A History*. He died in the first-floor drawing-room in 1881, and in 1895 the house was bought by public subscription to be administered by a memorial trust as LONDON'S FIRST LITERARY SHRINE. The National Trust took it over in 1936.

A splendid bronze of Thomas Carlyle by Sir Edgar Boehm can be seen in a small garden by Albert Bridge.

Albert Bridge

Opened in 1873 and described by Sir John Betjeman as 'one of the beauties of the London river', ALBERT BRIDGE was designed as half cantilever and half suspension bridge by Rowland Ordish, who built the rooves of the Albert Hall and St Pancras Station. When the bridge opened, the large number of people stepping along it in unison caused the bridge to sway, a phenomenon that was to reoccur when the 'wobbly' Millen-

nium Bridge opened downstream in 2001. There is a sign on the Albert Bridge stating, 'All troops must break step when marching over this bridge' – advice that the designers of the Wobbly Bridge would have done well to heed.

Chelsea Manor

Nos. 19–26 Cheyne Walk sit where Henry VIII's CHELSEA MANOR once stood. The manor became something of a depository for queens. The day after Anne Boleyn was executed in 1536, Henry secretly married JANE SEYMOUR at Chelsea, and in 1543 he gave the house to his last wife CATHERINE PARR as a wedding gift. Amongst her retinue was the Nine Day Queen LADY JANE GREY. The future Queen ELIZABETH I stayed at Chelsea as a 14-year-old after her father died, and ANNE OF CLEVES died in the house in 1557.

A plaque records that SIR HANS SLOANE (1660–1753) moved into Chelsea Manor in 1712. After he died he was buried in the churchyard of Chelsea Old Church and the manor was demolished. Sloane's art collection became the nucleus of the newly founded British Museum, while his name was inherited by a square, a street and a type of upper-class girl.

Cheyne Walk – Nos. 16 to 3

In 1862 Pre-Raphaelite artist DANTE GABRIEL ROSETTI introduced a menagerie of zebras, kangaroos, wombats, wallabies and a racoon to the garden at No. 16, but the neighbours only started to complain when he indulged in some peacocks.

Novelist GEORGE ELIOT moved into No. 4 in 1880 and died there a few weeks later. No. 3 Cheyne Walk was home to Rolling Stone guitarist KEITH RICHARDS from 1969 to 1978. He was joined here, from time to time, by ANITA PALLENBERG, and their bed was used for the love scenes involving Mick Jagger and Anita in the 1970 film *Performance*.

Physic Garden

CHELSEA PHYSIC GARDEN, THE SECOND OLDEST BOTANIC GARDEN IN ENGLAND, was planted in 1673 as a nursery for trainee apothecaries. In the middle stands a statue of Sir Hans Sloane, who donated the land to the Society of Apothecaries on condition that every year they sent seeds or dried plants to the Royal Society. In 1732 cotton seed from the garden was sent to James Oglethorpe in America, who used it to establish in Georgia the American cotton industry. ENGLAND'S

EARLIEST ROCK GARDEN is here, made with old building stone from the Tower of London and Icelandic lava given by Sir Joseph Banks. THE FIRST CEDAR TREES IN ENGLAND were grown here, and in 1681 ENGLAND'S FIRST GREENHOUSE AND STOVE were built here. Another feature is a 30 ft (9 m) high olive tree, THE BIGGEST OLIVE TREE IN BRITAIN.

Royal Hospital

Withdrawn from the river, Sir Christopher Wren's glorious CHELSEA ROYAL HOSPITAL is often overlooked and yet is one of the finest buildings on the Thames. It was founded in 1682 for the 'succour and relief of veterans broken by age and war', by Charles II, encouraged by his mistress Nell Gwyn, whose own father had been made destitute in the Civil War.

Ranelagh Gardens

In a corner of the Hospital grounds are RANELAGH GARDENS, once the private grounds of the Earl of Ranelagh. In the summer of 1717, HANDEL'S WATER MUSIC WAS PLAYED IN PUBLIC FOR THE FIRST TIME while George I picnicked in the grounds with Lady Ranelagh.

In 1742 the grounds were opened as the RANELAGH PLEASURE GARDENS, and they quickly became the place to be seen. As Horace Walpole wrote in 1744, 'You can't set your foot without treading on a Prince or a Duke of Cumberland.' At the heart of the gardens was a huge wooden Rotunda, 185 ft (56 m) across, with galleries and booths where people could sup tea and coffee or drink wine. There was a massive fireplace in the middle, 'large enough to roast half a score of people at once', and after dark, the whole place was lit by candlelight. An orchestra serenaded the quality as they paraded themselves about, and in 1761 a concert was given by 'the celebrated and astonishing Master Mozart, a child of seven years of age'. The gardens suddenly fell from favour after the Napoleonic Wars, the Rotunda having been demolished in 1805, and the grounds reverted back to the hospital.

Battersea Park

Across the river from Chelsea is BATTERSEA PARK, its 200 acres (80 ha) laid out in 1858 on an area of isolated fertile marshland called Battersea Fields. THE FIRST ASPARAGUS IN BRITAIN WAS GROWN here, known as a Battersea bundle. In the early 19th century the rumbustious Red House Tavern nearby attracted the rougher element and the area became notorious for hooliganism and brawling – and even duelling. On Battersea Fields in 1829 the Prime Minister of the day, the Duke of Wellington, squared up to the Earl of Winchilsea, who had accused him of 'treacherously plotting the destruction of the Protestant constitution' with his Catholic Emancipation Act. Wellington deliberately fired wide, while Winchilsea fired into the air and later apologised. Wellington thus became THE LAST BRITISH PRIME MINISTER TO FIGHT A DUEL.

On 9 January 1864, THE FIRST FOOTBALL MATCH EVER PLAYED UNDER FOOTBALL ASSOCIATION RULES took place in Battersea Park.

In 1985 Buddhist monks from Japan donated a PEACE PAGODA to Battersea Park to commemorate the 40th anniversary of the Hiroshima bomb.

Battersea Power Station

The gaunt outline of BATTERSEA POWER STATION, designed by Sir Giles Gilbert Scott, is one of the great iconic landmarks of London. It was built between 1929 and 1939 and the four fluted chimneys soar to a height of 337 ft (103 m). Originally there were just two chimneys, but the station was later doubled in size to become THE BIGGEST BRICK BUILDING IN EUROPE. On 20 April 1964 there was a fire at Battersea which caused blackouts all over London, notably at the BBC Television Centre where they were intending, that very evening, to launch the new BBC2 channel. The launch had to be put back until the following day and a rather patchy news bulletin was broadcast from Alexandra Palace instead. The power station closed in 1983 and has since been the subject of numerous planning applications which have so far come to nought.

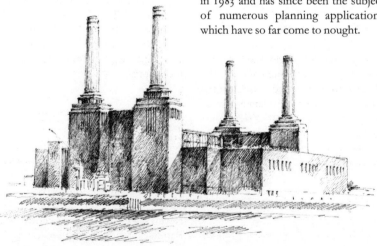

Well, I never **knew this**
about
THE RIVER THAMES

CHELSEA OLD CHURCH IS THE ONLY CHURCH IN LONDON TO HAVE ITS OWN CHAINED BOOKS, donated by Sir Hans Sloane, who is buried there.

CHELSEA has given its name to a bun, a porcelain, an ankle-height elastic-sided boot, and a large four-wheel-drive vehicle used for the school run, the Chelsea Tractor.

MICK JAGGER was living with Marianne Faithfull at No. 48 CHEYNE WALK when he was busted for drugs in 1969 – he claimed he was framed by the police.

BRITAIN'S FIRST TELEVISED CHURCH SERVICE was broadcast from the ROYAL HOSPITAL CHAPEL in 1949.

The Royal Horticultural Society's CHELSEA FLOWER SHOW has been held in the Royal Hospital grounds annually in May since 1913.

The present CHELSEA BRIDGE was opened in 1937 and is the second bridge on the site. It was THE FIRST SELF-ANCHORED SUSPENSION BRIDGE IN BRITAIN. The WESTBOURNE RIVER joins the Thames by Chelsea Bridge.

The GROSVENOR BRIDGE near Battersea Power Station was THE FIRST RAILWAY BRIDGE ACROSS THE THAMES. It opened in 1860 and was rebuilt in 1967.

PIMLICO TO WESTMINSTER

Tate Britain – built on the profits from sugar cubes

Pimlico

PIMLICO, between Chelsea and West-minster, was built on marshland stabilised by rubble from the building of St Katharine's Dock by Tower Bridge.

DOLPHIN SQUARE WAS THE LARGEST BLOCK OF FLATS IN EUROPE when it was completed in 1937. It comprises 1,250 luxury apartments and covers 8 acres (3.2 ha). Along with the neigh-bouring Churchill Gardens Estate it was heated by hot Thames water from Battersea Power Station across the river.

ST GEORGE'S SQUARE IS THE ONLY LONDON SQUARE BUILT TO FACE THE RIVER. BRAM STOKER (1847–1912), the author of *Dracula*, died at No. 26, and an innocent young LADY DIANA SPENCER was photographed holding a child and wearing a see-through dress while work-ing in St George's Square at the Young England Kindergarten.

The RIVER TYBURN, which gave its name to the Tyburn gallows near Marble Arch, runs into the Thames, just upstream of Vauxhall Bridge.

Vauxhall Bridge

Vauxhall is the site of LONDON'S OLDEST BRIDGE. A little way upstream of the present VAUXHALL BRIDGE, oak post stumps, remnants of a Bronze Age wooden bridge dating from around 1500 BC, have been uncovered. The river would have been much shallower then, flowing through several channels between gravel islands, which may have been linked by a series of bridges.

The first Vauxhall Bridge of modern times, built by James Walker and opened in 1816, was THE FIRST IRON BRIDGE OVER THE THAMES IN LONDON. This was replaced in 1906 with the present bridge, designed by Sir Alexander Binnie and THE FIRST BRIDGE ACROSS THE THAMES TO CARRY TRAMS.

Vauxhall

VAUXHALL, a village on the south bank, is where the RIVER EFFRA runs into the River Thames, and takes its name from one of King John's knights, FALKES DE BREAUTÉ. He built a house here called Falkes Hall, which over time became Faukeshall, then Foxhall and finally Vauxhall.

Perhaps the most striking building associated with Vauxhall today is the understated, top-secret headquarters of MI6 known officially as 85 VAUXHALL CROSS, unofficially as Legoland, the Aztec Temple, Ceaucescu Towers or Babylon on Thames. Designed by Terry Farrell, it opened in 1995 and stars in the opening sequence of the 1999 James Bond film *The World is Not Enough*, when Bond's boat explodes out of the side of the building and lands in the river. Bullet-proof and bomb-proof, the building was left unscathed by a rocket attack by the Real IRA, in 2000.

Vauxhall Gardens

SPRING GARDENS, across the road from the MI6 headquarters, are all that is left of the celebrated VAUXHALL PLEASURE GARDENS which opened in 1661 and boasted illuminated fountains, lamp-lit walks, sculpture galleries, firework displays, music and pageants.

Vauxhall Gardens inspired the Tivoli Gardens in Copenhagen and such was their fame that Vauxhall ('Vokzal') became the Russian word for a railway station. Russia's first railway went from St Petersburg to the pleasure gardens at Pavlovsk, which were named Vokzal in homage to the London gardens. Hence, going to Vokzal became associated with the first railway station and eventually Vokzal entered into the Russian language as the generic word for any railway station.

Vauxhall Pleasure Gardens finally closed in 1859 after gaining a reputation as a haunt for prostitutes and footpads.

Millbank

Across the river from Vauxhall is MILL-BANK on the site of the Westminster Abbey water-mills, the last of which was demolished in the early 18th century. The CHELSEA COLLEGE OF ART & DESIGN now occupies the former Royal Army Medical College where THE VACCINE FOR TYPHOID WAS DEVELOPED.

This was the site, in the 19th century, of BRITAIN'S FIRST MODERN PRISON, and THE LARGEST PRISON IN BRITAIN, the infamous MILLBANK PENITEN-TIARY, opened in 1816. It was built in the shape of a star with six wings radi-ating out from a central block guard tower, all designed to 'induce in the inmate a state of conscious and perma-nent visibility that assures the automatic functioning of power'. Although based on enlightened princi-ples the prison, which held convicts awaiting transportation to Australia, gained a reputation for harsh treatment and was closed down in 1897. The underground tunnels through which the prisoners were loaded on to river barges are reputed to be still there.

Tate Britain

The TATE GALLERY was built in 1897, funded largely by SIR HENRY TATE (1819–99), on the profits from sugar cubes, as a place to show off the finest of British Art. Sir Henry donated his own collection of British paintings to form a nucleus for the early displays. Since May 2000 and the opening of the

Tate Modern on Bankside this gallery has become the Tate Britain.

The 32-storey steel and glass MILL-BANK TOWER was built in 1963 as the Vickers Tower, headquarters of the Vick-ers Group, and had a Spitfire displayed on the forecourt. From 1995 until 2002 New Labour had its headquarters here, which gave rise to the term 'Millbank Tendency', referring to those who practise the art of political spin-doctoring.

THAMES HOUSE, with its massive metal doors, is the headquarters of the domestic security service MI5.

Lambeth Bridge

LAMBETH BRIDGE was built in 1932, replacing a suspension bridge of 1862, which in turn replaced the only ferry in London allowed to carry a horse and carriage. This ferry, which is commem-orated on the west bank by Horseferry Road, was operated by the Archbishops of Canterbury whose London home, Lambeth Palace, lies at the eastern end of the bridge. The horse ferry regularly either got stuck in the mud or sank; it went under in 1633 with all of Arch-bishop Laud's possessions on board and again in 1656 with Oliver Cromwell as a passenger. In 1688, when James II was deposed by the Glorious Revolution, his Catholic wife Mary of Modena, disguised as a washerwoman, took the ferry to escape across the river during a storm, with her baby son James, who would grow up to become the Old Pretender. She then sheltered in the corner between the tower of St Mary's and the gatehouse of Lambeth Palace, while waiting for a carriage to take her to Gravesend and into exile in France.

The pillars at the end of the bridge are topped with pineapples, which were introduced into England from Barbados by the royal gardener John Tradescant the Younger, who is buried in St Mary's churchyard.

St Mary-at-Lambeth

The tall 14th-century tower of ST MARY-AT-LAMBETH stands hard up against the gatehouse of Lambeth Palace. St Mary's used to be the parish church of Lambeth but was deconsecrated in the 1970s, and in 1977 it became THE WORLD'S FIRST MUSEUM OF GARDEN HISTORY, a tribute to the royal gardeners the Tradescants, father and son, both called John, who are buried in the churchyard. Nearby is the big chest tomb of CAPTAIN WILLIAM BLIGH OF THE BOUNTY (1754–1817).

Lambeth Palace

LAMBETH PALACE has been the London seat of the Archbishops of Canterbury since the end of the 12th century, but the present eclectic string of mismatched buildings dates from almost every age. The most recognisable part of the palace is the 15th-century gatehouse known as MORTON'S TOWER, regarded as THE FINEST EARLY TUDOR BRICK GATEHOUSE IN ENGLAND.

Beneath the chapel in Lambeth Palace is an exquisite crypt of 1220 where ARCHBISHOP CRANMER forced ANNE BOLEYN

to confess to adultery three days before she was beheaded. He later compiled the 1552 *Book of Common Prayer* in his study in the Tudor Cranmer Tower above the east end of the chapel.

Above the west end of the chapel, where ARCHBISHOP MATTHEW PARKER, the original 'nosey' Parker, is buried, is LOLLARD'S TOWER, so named because in the 14th century a number of Lollards, or followers of John Wycliffe, the first man to translate the Bible into English, were imprisoned in a small room at the top. The prison's wood panelling, carved with the names of inmates, survives along with the metal rings to which they were chained. In 1649 during the Civil War the Royalist poet RICHARD LOVELACE was detained here, and wrote of the experience, 'Stone walls do not a prison make . . .'

The great glory of Lambeth Palace is

the 17th-century Great Hall, begun by Archbishop Juxon, which houses one of the earliest free public libraries in England. Growing against the wall outside is THE OLDEST FIG TREE IN BRITAIN, planted in the 16th century by CARDINAL POLE, ENGLAND'S LAST ROMAN CATHOLIC ARCHBISHOP.

Westminster

Facing Lambeth Palace across the river in Westminster are VICTORIA TOWER GARDENS, the setting for a sculpture of *The Burghers of Calais* by Rodin and frequently for open-air political interviews. Behind, at No. 4 Millbank, are the MILLBANK STUDIOS, where politicians give interviews for television 'live from our Westminster Studios'.

Houses of Parliament

All that remains of the medieval Palace of Westminster is WESTMINSTER HALL, built for William II in 1097 and THE OLDEST CEREMONIAL HALL IN BRITAIN.

In 1834, officials burning documents in the basement caused a fire that destroyed the rest of the old palace. Burning documents in the basement, the present Houses of Parliament designed by SIR CHARLES BARRY (1795–1860) were opened in 1867. The Duke of Wellington stipulated that the new building should back on to the river, so that it could not be surrounded by the rebellious mob. Likewise, the stretch of river in front of the Houses of Parliament is THE ONLY RESTRICTED AREA ON THE NAVIGABLE THAMES. River traffic must keep to the St Thomas's side, to prevent anyone lobbing a bomb on to the terraces where MPs and Lords gather beneath red and green striped awnings to make merry and thrash out affairs of state.

The river frontage is 940 ft (287 m) long, with a terrace of 700 ft (213 m), and the palace covers 8 acres (3.2 ha), has 11 courtyards, 100 staircases, 2 miles (3.2 km) of passageways and over 1,100 rooms.

At the south corner stands the VICTORIA TOWER, 75 ft (23 m) square and 336 ft (101 m) high. When it was built it was THE BIGGEST AND THE HIGHEST TOWER IN THE WORLD. The flagpole is over 50 ft (15 m) tall, and when the flag flies to show that Parliament is sitting it flies higher than the Cross on the dome of St Paul's. Inside are kept records of every law passed in England since the 11th century – over three million of them, so far.

At the north corner stands the Clock Tower, 320 ft (98 m) high, and home

Works when the bell was hung, or from the popular prize fight champion of the time Benjamin Caunt, whose nickname was Big Ben.

The four clock faces, designed by Augustus Pugin, are 180 ft (55 m) above the ground. Each face is 23 ft (7 m) across, each minute hand is 14 ft (4.2 m) long, and the Great Clock of Westminster is THE LARGEST FOUR-FACED CHIMING CLOCK IN THE WORLD. Big Ben rang out across London for the first time on 31 May 1859.

Westminster Bridge

The view of London from WESTMINSTER BRIDGE in the early morning inspired William Wordsworth in 1802 to declare that 'earth has not anything to show more fair'. The present bridge, designed in a style to complement the Houses of Parliament, was opened in 1862.

to the clock known the world over as BIG BEN. In fact the name Big Ben refers only to the hour bell of THE GREAT CLOCK OF WESTMINSTER, and it was taken either from Sir Benjamin Hall, who was Chief Commissioner of

Well, I never knew this about
THE RIVER THAMES

VAUXHALL CARS were founded in VAUX- HALL in 1857, and the company's Griffin emblem is derived from Falkes de Breauté's coat of arms.

The big yellow amphibious bus of LONDON DUCK TOURS enters the River Thames via a slipway beside the MI6 building at VAUXHALL.

In deference to the traditions of Parliament, LAMBETH BRIDGE is painted red to match the red leather of the benches in the House of Lords, while

WESTMINSTER BRIDGE is painted green to match the green leather of the benches in the Commons.

The garden at LAMBETH PALACE IS THE SECOND LARGEST PRIVATE GARDEN IN LONDON.

ST THOMAS' HOSPITAL, founded in the early 12th century in Southwark, moved to its present site opposite the Houses of Parliament in 1871. FLORENCE NIGHTINGALE established her School of Nursing here, and to this day nurses of St Thomas' are known as 'Nightingales'.

The flamboyant statue of BOADICEA, Queen of the Iceni, and her daughters in their chariot, which stands at the western end of WESTMINSTER BRIDGE, was made by Thomas Thornycroft in 1856 and unveiled in 1902.

WESTMINSTER TO LONDON BRIDGE

St Paul's Cathedral – Britain's only domed Anglican cathedral

Victoria Embankment

Bronze-clad PORTCULLIS HOUSE, completed at a cost of £235 million in 2001, IS THE MOST EXPENSIVE OFFICE BLOCK EVER BUILT IN BRITAIN. Providing conference facilities and offices for 200 MPs, the interior boasts tinkling fountains and water features, fig trees, cafés, a stunning glass-topped atrium and, just in case, padded lifts.

The former NEW SCOTLAND YARD buildings are now used by MPs, but from 1890 until 1967 this red and white baroque structure designed by Norman Shaw was the headquarters of the Metropolitan Police. When the 'Met' was founded by Sir Robert Peel in 1829 their headquarters was a row of houses occupying the area of Whitehall Palace where Scottish kings were lodged when visiting London, and called in their honour Scotland Yard.

By the riverside just down from Westminster Bridge is the moving BATTLE OF BRITAIN LONDON MONUMENT showing battle scenes and names in bronze relief. It was unveiled by the Prince of Wales in 2005, in front of 70 surviving Battle of Britain pilots.

The MINISTRY OF DEFENCE BUILDING,

a fine example of Edwardian grandeur, occupies the site of Whitehall Palace, and Henry VIII's wine cellar survives in the basement. A flight of steps built by Christopher Wren for Mary II, which can be seen up against the east wall, marks the edge of the river before the Embankment was constructed in 1869.

The French Renaissance extravaganza that is WHITEHALL COURT was built in 1887 by Alfred Waterhouse. Though largely occupied by a hotel and private apartments, it is best known as the home of the NATIONAL LIBERAL CLUB. William Gladstone was the first president of the club, whose members must refrain from uttering anti-liberal views. The interior of the club is sumptuous and ornate, particularly the bathrooms which are so splendid that Lord Birkenhead, a Conservative, used to make a point of using them for his ablutions, even though he was not a member. When challenged he is reported to have said, 'Good heavens! I had no idea it was a club as well as a lavatory!'

Hungerford Bridge

HUNGERFORD BRIDGE takes its name from the old Hungerford market, demolished to make way for Charing Cross Station on the north bank. The pedestrian bridges running along both sides were opened in 2002, and thankfully hide the ugly railway bridge of 1864.

The platforms of Charing Cross Station are now covered by EMBANKMENT PLACE, a modern office complex designed by Terry Farrell, which contains the headquarters of accountants PRICEWATERHOUSECOOPERS.

EMBANKMENT STATION at the bottom of Villiers Street was the site of the black boot polish factory where CHARLES DICKENS worked as a 12-year-old, which he later recreated in *David Copperfield* as Murdstone and Grinby.

Cleopatra's Needle

CLEOPATRA'S NEEDLE IS THE SECOND OLDEST OUTSIDE ARTEFACT IN LONDON. The pink granite column, 60 feet (18 m) high and carved with dedications to various gods and Pharaohs, comes from the quarries of Aswan in Egypt and was erected at Heliopolis in 1475 BC. It was moved by the Roman Emperor Augustus to Alexandria where, after several hundred years, it eventually toppled over into the sand. The obelisk was presented to the British in 1819 by the Turkish Viceroy of Egypt, Mohammed Ali, and towed back to Britain on a specially constructed pontoon. During a storm in the Bay of Biscay it was nearly lost – six men died in saving it – but it was eventually brought into a Spanish port and from there made it safely to London, where it was raised on the Embankment in 1878. In 1917, during the First World War, Cleopatra's Needle became THE FIRST MONUMENT IN LONDON TO BE HIT DURING AN AIR RAID.

The Adelphi

The ADELPHI is a characterless 1930s block that stands on the site of Robert and James Adam's huge Adelphi project, begun in 1768, a grand terrace of houses raised on arches above the riverbank. The Adams brothers lived here (Adelphi is the Greek word for brothers), as did the actor DAVID GARRICK.

Shell Mex

SHELL MEX HOUSE was built in the 1930s on the site of the 800-bedroom HOTEL CECIL which, when it was put up in the 1880s, was THE BIGGEST HOTEL IN THE WORLD. Shell Mex House was the original London headquarters of Shell Petroleum, and the Art Deco clock face, THE BIGGEST CLOCK FACE IN LONDON, was nick-named 'BIG BENZINE'.

Savoy

The name SAVOY derives from the Count of Savoy, an uncle-in-law of Henry III. He owned land here that became the site of a 'mansion without equal' built for himself by the 1st Duke of Lancaster and later inherited by John of Gaunt.

The SAVOY HOTEL, built in 1889 by RICHARD D'OYLY CARTE, was THE FIRST HOTEL IN BRITAIN TO HAVE ELECTRIC LIGHTS AND LIFTS. It was designed as somewhere to stay for patrons of the SAVOY THEATRE next door, which had been built in 1881 as a venue for D'Oyly Carte Opera productions of Gilbert and Sullivan, and was itself THE FIRST PUBLIC BUILDING IN LONDON TO BE LIT BY ELECTRICITY.

SAVOY CHAPEL, a restored 16th-century church lost in the shadows of the Edwardian edifices that dominate Savoy Place, in 1890 became THE FIRST CHURCH IN BRITAIN TO BE LIT WITH ELECTRICITY. Five hundred years before that, in 1366, Geoffrey Chaucer started a tradition by marrying Phillipa Roet in John of Gaunt's original Savoy Chapel, and by the end of the 19th century Savoy had become the most fashionable place in London to be married. In 1936 the Savoy Chapel became the chapel of the Royal Victorian Order and is now a private chapel of the Queen, although it is open to the public at certain times.

In 1878 the VICTORIA EMBANKMENT here became THE FIRST SECTION OF STREET IN BRITAIN TO BE LIT WITH ELECTRICITY, using THE FIRST UNDERGROUND ELECTRIC CABLES IN THE COUNTRY.

Somerset House

The original SOMERSET HOUSE, built in 1550 for the Lord Protector Somerset, was THE FIRST RENAISSANCE PALACE IN ENGLAND. INIGO JONES died in his apartment there in 1652, and in 1658

OLIVER CROMWELL lay in state there, provoking rioters who threw mud over the gates. In 1676 Somerset House was advertised as THE FIRST BUILDING IN ENGLAND TO HAVE PARQUET FLOORING.

The palace was demolished in 1775 and replaced with a new, Palladian-style building designed by Sir William Chambers. Allocated for government use, it was THE FIRST LARGE, PURPOSE-BUILT OFFICE BLOCK EVER BUILT. Over the next 200 years Somerset House played host to a number of government bodies, most famously the Register of Births, Marriages and Deaths, where the public could go and examine interesting wills, or pick up a copy of their birth certificate. Today Somerset House is home to the COURTAULD INSTITUTE OF ART, and in the winter months an ice rink is set up in the courtyard.

King's Reach

Down by the river, the western boundary of the City is marked by two silver dragons and a relief of Queen Victoria,

at the spot where she received the City sword in 1900.

On the river front is the KING'S REACH WATERGATE, built as part of Sir Joseph Bazalgette's VICTORIA EMBANKMENT, which was the fulfilment of a much-needed scheme to bank up the Thames for several miles through central London. For hundreds of years the Thames had been an open sewer, receiving the accumulated detritus and untreated sewage of hundreds of thousands of people from countless drains and tributaries. In 1858 the 'Great Stink' occurred, when a heatwave caused the festering river to reek

worse than ever, and it became impossible for Parliament to go about its business except behind closed curtains doused in disinfectant. By 1874 SIR JOSEPH BAZALGETTE had built several miles of the VICTORIA EMBANKMENT on the north side of the river, and of the ALBERT EMBANKMENT on the south side, linked to a system of sewers that carried waste off to treatment stations and outfalls further down the Thames estuary at BECKTON and CROSSNESS. The embankments had the effect of narrowing and deepening the river, causing it to flow faster, which also helped to keep it clean. At various stages along the river, gardens were laid out on the reclaimed land, ornate cast-iron lamp-posts were erected along the top of the granite parapets, and mooring rings set into the river walls. This stretch of the Thames was named KING'S REACH in 1935 in honour of King George V.

Temple

MIDDLE TEMPLE and INNER TEMPLE, where, according to Wordsworth, lawyers 'look out on waters, walks and gardens green', are two of the four Inns of Court. The name comes from the Knights Templar, a group of nobles who formed a brotherhood to protect pilgrims travelling to the Holy Land and who established their English headquarters here in the 12th century. When the Templars were disbanded in 1312, their properties were leased as 'inns', or hostels, to groups of lawyers needing somewhere to set up their practices.

The lawyers were eventually granted the estate in perpetuity by James I.

The TEMPLE CHURCH, begun in 1185 and one of only four round churches in England, contains the effigies of a number of Crusader knights, and the church has become a place of pilgrimage for fans of Dan Brown's novel *The Da Vinci Code*, in which it features as a possible hiding-place for Templar treasures. Scenes from the film of the book were shot there.

Blackfriars Bridge

When BLACKFRIARS BRIDGE opened in 1769 it was named William Pitt Bridge, after William Pitt the Elder, but the name never caught on and it has always been referred to as Blackfriars Bridge. The present structure was built in 1869 with the piers built to resemble pulpits, reflecting the monastic origins of the area. A slightly less salubrious religious connection dates from June 1982 when the body of ROBERTO CALVI, former chairman of Italy's largest private bank, the Banco Ambrosiano, was found hanging beneath the bridge with five bricks and $14,000 in his pocket. Calvi, known as 'God's Banker' because the Vatican Bank had shares in Banco Ambrosiano, was on the run from Italy accused of embezzling funds, probably in order to pay off the Mafia, to whom he was in some way indebted. After an initial verdict of suicide, a second inquest decided that Calvi had been murdered by the Mafia, and in 2005 five suspected members of the Mafia were put on trial in Rome but acquitted as a result of insufficient evidence.

South Bank

Posing proudly on the Waterloo end of Westminster Bridge is the SOUTH BANK LION, one of the last known examples of COADE STONE, a virtually indestructable material made from a long-lost secret recipe by ELEANOR COADE, at her factory close to where County Hall now stands, in the 18th century. The lion was originally painted red and stood over the entrance to the Red Lion Brewery on the south bank. When the brewery was demolished to make way for the Festival Hall in 1951, the lion was rescued on the orders of George VI and moved to its present location in 1966.

The imposing COUNTY HALL was designed by Ralph Knott as a home for London's government and served as such from 1922 until 1986. The magnificent central debating chamber survives as a spectacular venue for talks and exhibitions. The rest of the huge complex is filled with a mix of conference rooms, a hotel, a Japanese restaurant, galleries and the London Aquarium.

London Eye

Outside County Hall stands the LONDON EYE, THE TALLEST OBSERVATION WHEEL IN THE WESTERN HEMISPHERE, 443 ft (135 m) high and one of the tallest structure in London. The circumference of the wheel is 1,392 ft (424 m), almost twice the height of Canary Wharf Tower. Opened in March 2000, the London Eye is THE ONLY CANTILEVERED STRUCTURE OF ITS KIND IN THE WORLD and THE LARGEST STRUCTURE EVER HOISTED INTO A VERTICAL POSITION IN ONE OPERATION.

Since the Festival of Britain in 1951 the SOUTH BANK has developed into BRITAIN'S LARGEST ARTS CENTRE and includes the NATIONAL FILM THEATRE, opened in 1957, the QUEEN ELIZABETH HALL and PURCELL ROOM (1967), the HAYWARD GALLERY (1968) and the NATIONAL THEATRE (1976).

THE FESTIVAL HALL is the only remnant from the Festival and was THE FIRST POST-WAR BUILDING IN ENGLAND TO BE GRADE 1 LISTED.

Waterloo Bridge

The first WATERLOO BRIDGE was designed by John Rennie in 1817 and was described by the Italian sculptor Antonio Canova as 'the noblest bridge in the world'. Constable and Monet both painted it, and people who came 'from the remotest corners of the earth' to see it were not disappointed.

The present, supremely elegant bridge was designed by Sir Giles Gilbert Scott and opened in 1945. It is sometimes referred to as the 'Ladies Bridge' because it was constructed during the war years mostly by women, the men being away fighting. Also it is faced with Portland stone which cleans itself in the rain, the sort of practical detail only a woman would have thought of.

Because of its position at a bend of the river, the views from *Waterloo Bridge* are considered the finest from any bridge in London and inspired the song 'Waterloo Sunset', written in 1967 by RAY DAVIES of the Kinks. Two films called *Waterloo Bridge* have been made, in 1931 and 1940, the latter starring Vivien Leigh as the heroine who throws herself off the bridge at the film's climax.

Oxo Tower

THE OXO BUILDING, originally part of a power station, was bought in the 1920s by the Liebig Extract of Meat Company as a home for THE WORLD'S LARGEST MEAT PACKING AND STORAGE CENTRE. Advertising restrictions meant they could not erect signs to publicise their product, but they got around this by adding a 220 ft (67 m) tower with OXO spelled out in glazing bars on the windows of all four sides. Since it was then the second highest commercial building in London, this proved very effective, and it still draws attention to the product even today. The OXO tower now houses apartments, small craft shops and a smart restaurant.

Back on the north bank, and rising proudly above the drab office blocks that line the river here at Blackfriars, is Sir Christopher Wren's ST PAUL'S CATHEDRAL, THE ONLY DOMED CATHEDRAL IN ENGLAND.

St Paul's Cathedral

The tip of the golden cross over the dome stands 365 ft (111 m) above the city streets, and there are majestic views from the golden gallery beneath, reached by a climb of 627 steps. The dome itself, with a span of 122 ft (37 m), is THE THIRD LARGEST CHURCH DOME IN THE WORLD, after Santa Maria del Fiore in Florence and St Peter's in Rome, and is an iconic symbol of London, most memorably when seen rising above the

ners also own some of them, along with the Dyers. A representative of the Vintners observes the annual 'swan-upping' in July, when all the swans on the river are counted and marked – cygnets belonging to the Vintners are marked with two nicks on the beak. Swans are no longer served at the Vintners' traditional 'Swan Feast', turkey being the preferred substitute.

smoke during the Blitz in a famous black-and-white photograph of the period. St Paul's survived the bombing thanks to the heroics of the St Paul's Watch, a band of men and women who stood by night after night to douse fires and ward off or defuse any incendiaries that came close.

Doggett's Coat and Badge

Vintners' Hall

The VINTNERS' HALL sits on a site the Vintners have occupied since 1446. Despite the myth that the Queen owns all the swans on the Thames, the Vint-

The classical FISHMONGERS' HALL on the north bank beside London Bridge

The Marchioness

In August 1989, the worst ever disaster on the Thames in central London occurred on the stretch of river between Southwark Bridge and the Cannon Street Rail Bridge, at 1.50 in the morning. The pleasure boat *MARCHIONESS*, carrying 132 birthday revellers, was struck by the dredger *BOWBELLE*, rolled over and sank with the loss of 51 lives. As a result of the incident THE FIRST THAMES LIFEBOAT SERVICE was set up, with stations at Gravesend, Tower Pier, Chiswick Pier and Teddington.

was built in 1831. From here the Company of Fishmongers administer the DOGGETT'S COAT AND BADGE race, THE OLDEST ANNUALLY CONTESTED SPORTING EVENT IN BRITAIN and THE OLDEST AND LONGEST ROWING RACE IN THE WORLD. Run over nearly 5 miles (8 km) from London Bridge to Chelsea, it was established in 1715 by THOMAS DOGGETT, an Irish actor and manager of the Drury Lane Theatre, to mark the accession of George I and as an incentive for apprentice watermen. The contestants are drawn from the Watermen and Lightermen's Company and the prize is a scarlet coat, a silver badge and a special lunch held at the Fishmongers' Hall in the winner's honour.

Well, I never knew this about
THE RIVER THAMES

Moored just upstream of Blackfriars Bridge is HMS *PRESIDENT*, THE ONLY SURVIVING 'Q' SHIP FROM THE FIRST WORLD WAR. 'Q' ships were armed vessels constructed by the Royal Navy to look like merchant ships and so lure German U-boats to the surface. The 'Q' ship would then throw back the covers to reveal its guns and hopefully sink the U-boat before it could dive. HMS *President* is now used as a venue for events and entertainment.

Set back from the Jubilee Gardens on the South Bank is the 351 ft (107 m) high SHELL CENTRE. Built in 1961 as the headquarters of the Shell oil company, it was THE FIRST SKYSCRAPER IN LONDON TO EXCEED THE HEIGHT OF THE VICTORIA TOWER at the Houses of Parliament. At the time of its construction the Shell Centre, including the downstream block on the other side of the railway lines, was THE BIGGEST OFFICE BLOCK IN EUROPE.

At 1,250 ft (381m), WATERLOO BRIDGE is THE LONGEST BRIDGE IN CENTRAL LONDON.

In 1978 Bulgarian dissident GEORGI MARKOV was stabbed in the thigh with a poisoned umbrella while waiting for a bus on WATERLOO BRIDGE.

The LONDON STUDIOS, which occupy the white tower block next door to the National Theatre, are home to such popular televisions shows as *Have I Got News for You*, *GMTV* and, before it was ended, *The South Bank Show*.

Just downstream of Blackfriars Bridge on the north bank is PUDDLE DOCK, where GEOFFREY CHAUCER was born in 1343. Today it is home to THE MERMAID THEATRE, established in a dilapidated Victorian warehouse in 1959 by actor BERNARD MILES, and now used as a BBC concert hall and recording studio.

CANNON STREET STATION was opened in 1866 on the site of the Roman Governor's palace. Covering the platforms was a huge single-span arch, 680 ft (207 m) long and 103 ft (31 m) high, which was destroyed in the Blitz. The station was remodelled in the 1960s, and all that is left of the original are the two brick towers on the river front, which contain water tanks to power the hydraulic lifts in the station.

LONDON BRIDGE
TO TOWER BRIDGE

Old London Bridge, where driving on the left became compulsory

London Bridge

The first LONDON BRIDGE was built around AD 52 by the invading Roman army of the Emperor Claudius, somewhere near the site of the present bridge. There followed a succession of temporary wooden affairs until the middle of the 9th century, when another more lasting wooden bridge was constructed. In 1014 the Danes held London, and the Saxon King Ethelred the Unready sailed up the Thames, tied his boats to the bridge supports and rowed away, pulling the bridge down behind him and giving rise to the song 'London Bridge is falling down...'

The first stone bridge was begun in 1176, in the reign of Henry II. It was paid for by a tax on wool and took 33 years to complete. When it was finished in 1209 it was 20 ft (6 m) wide, 600 ft (183 m) long and had 20 arches. There was a gatehouse at each end, a drawbridge near the Southwark end that could be raised to allow ships to pass, and a chapel in the middle dedicated to St Thomas à Becket. King John decreed that houses and shops should be built on the bridge to provide rents for its upkeep, and London Bridge became one of the wonders of the world, lasting for over 600 years.

By the 15th century, buildings lined the whole length of the bridge, some of them seven or eight storeys high and touching at the top, making the bridge into a tunnel.

In the 16th, 17th and 18th centuries, prior to the building of the Victorian embankments, the river was shallower and the narrow arches of the bridge slowed the flow of water upstream so that the river froze, allowing Frost Fairs to be held on the Thames, most famously in 1683–4 when Charles II attended.

London Bridge escaped the Great Fire of London thanks to a gap at the northern end, caused by a previous fire in 1633, that acted as a firebreak.

In 1831 a new London Bridge, designed by John Rennie and built by his son, also John, was opened by William IV and Queen Adelaide, 180 ft (55 m) to the west of the old bridge.

The present London Bridge was opened by the Queen in 1973. It was made from concrete and was designed with hollow caissons suitable for carrying essential services across the river, making it THE ONLY HOLLOW BRIDGE OVER THE THAMES. The pavements are heated during cold spells to prevent icing.

St Magnus the Martyr

ST MAGNUS THE MARTYR, THE SECOND CHURCH TO BE CONSUMED BY THE GREAT FIRE, was rebuilt by Sir Christo-pher Wren in 1671–6. One of his finest steeples, 185 ft (56 m) high, was added in 1705. The approach to the old London Bridge ran by St Magnus, and when the bridge was widened in the 18th century the aisles of the church were shortened so that the pavement could pass directly underneath the tower, which then strad-dled the walkway. Some stones from Old London Bridge can be seen just inside the gates of the churchyard. Tucked in beside one of the tower's pillars is a wooden post from the Roman wharf of the 1st century, found on Fish Hill and as solid today as it was nearly 2,000 years ago.

Billingsgate

The building that once housed BILLINGSGATE FISH MARKET dates from 1877. It was converted into offices by Richard Rogers after the market moved to the Isle of Dogs in 1982, but still proclaims its heritage with a fish on top of the weather-vanes at each end. This was the site of the Roman wharf and original port of London, and was a landing place and market for all kinds of goods until 1699, when it was made a free market for fish. Passengers also used to pass through Billingsgate, heading for Gravesend, where they would transfer on to ocean-going vessels, no doubt stopping their ears against the foul language for which Billingsgate was a byword. The writer GEORGE ORWELL worked at Billingsgate in the 1930s, as did the KRAY TWINS, RONNIE AND REGGIE, in the 1950s.

Custom House

In 1275 the first CUSTOM HOUSE was built beside Billingsgate market to process the duties imposed on exports of wool, leather and hides by Edward I, a practice which laid the foundations of our modern customs system. Between 1379 and 1385, Geoffrey Chaucer worked here as Comptroller of Petty Customs for the Port of London. The imposing 1,190 ft (363 m) long façade of the present Custom House, designed in 1825 by Robert Smirke, architect of

the British Museum, is best viewed from the river. As a young man, the poet and hymn writer WILLIAM COWPER (1731–1800) came to Custom House Quay to drown himself, while suffering from a severe bout of depression. However, the water was too low and he survived to write his inspirational poetry.

Tower of London

Another palace seen at its best from the river, THE TOWER OF LONDON stands sentinel just outside the City of London. Begun by William the Conqueror in 1078, the central keep, 90 ft (27 m) high, was THE TALLEST BUILDING IN LONDON at the time and is now THE OLDEST COMPLETE BUILDING IN LONDON. It was renamed the White Tower after being whitewashed in 1240.

It is interesting to note that the White Tower has three square towers and one round – the round tower contains the only staircase in the keep, which established the custom of building staircases

that spiralled in a clockwise direction to give the defender the advantage, as long as he held his sword in his right hand. The White Tower was also THE FIRST BUILDING IN ENGLAND TO HAVE LATRINES – it had two garderobes, complete with seats and chutes, on each of the top three floors.

Prisoners brought to the tower by river would enter by TRAITORS' GATE, built by Edward I in 1280. Those who passed through the gate never to return include Sir Thomas More, Thomas Cromwell, Anne Boleyn, Catherine Howard, Lady Jane Grey and the Duke of Monmouth.

Southwark

SOUTHWARK, across the river from the City of London, was, in the 18th century, the site of William Blake's 'dark, satanic mills', specifically the ALBION MILLS, which stood at the southern end of Blackfriars Bridge, not far from Blake's Lambeth home. Albion Mills, set up by Boulton and Watt, was LONDON'S FIRST FACTORY, and one of the first steam-powered mills in Britain, and it belched forth smoke and noise 24 hours a day. It finally burned down in 1791 and remained as a blackened shell for years. Today the site is occupied by the *Daily Express*.

Tate Modern

BANKSIDE POWER STATION was Sir Giles Gilbert Scott's second brick power station on the Thames in London. It is made up of some four and a half million bricks and covers an area of 8½ acres (3.4 ha), with a river frontage 650 ft (198 m) long. The chimney was deliberately capped at 325 ft (99 m) high, so as to be lower than the dome of St Paul's opposite it, which reaches 375 ft (114 m). It was completed in 1963 and closed less than 20 years later in 1981.

Unlike Battersea Power Station, Bankside has been successfully converted, into Europe's finest new modern art gallery, TATE MODERN, which opened in May 2000. The architects were the little-known Swiss practice of Herzog and de Meuron, and their masterstroke was to leave the monumental brick shell of the building alone while utilising the grand space inside. The Turbine Hall, 500 ft (152 m) long and 115 ft (35 m) high, makes a truly spectacular entrance and exhibition space.

Millennium Bridge

Linking Tate Modern with St Paul's is the MILLENNIUM BRIDGE, designed by Norman Foster and THE FIRST NEW BRIDGE PUT OVER THE THAMES IN LONDON FOR OVER 100 YEARS, since Tower Bridge in 1894. Known almost from the start as the WOBBLY BRIDGE, it had to be closed within days of opening in 2001 because it wobbled sickeningly when too many people were walking across it at the same time. It turned out that a small initial sway caused pedestrians to step down in unison, thus aggravating the wobble, a process known as 'excitation'. They should have taken the advice of the builders of the Albert Bridge, who had already discovered the phenomenon in 1873 (see Albert Bridge, p. 182).

Globe Theatre

The modern reconstruction of Shakespeare's GLOBE THEATRE includes THE FIRST THATCHED ROOF SEEN IN THE CENTRE OF LONDON SINCE THE GREAT FIRE of 1666. The builders of the replica Globe used the same materials,

construction techniques and layout as their Elizabethan counterparts, and Shakespeare's plays are now staged in authentic surroundings during the summer months. Theatregoers can choose to stand and mingle with the actors in the open-air auditorium, or sit and heckle from the encircling galleries.

A rare survivor of old Southwark can be found in a row of crooked 17th-century houses, complete with tiny back gardens and stretch of cobbled street called CARDINAL CAP ALLEY. No. 49 exhibits a sporty red door and is supposed to be where Christopher Wren lived while St Paul's was being built across the river.

The Clink

Most of Southwark, known as the LIBERTY OF THE CLINK, was owned by the Bishops of Winchester. The Bishop used to profit mightily from the various enterprises that went on locally and had his own palace here from the 12th century. The brothels were particularly lucrative, and the women who worked in them became known as 'Winchester geese'. Crime was rife, and prisons were needed in which to incarcerate those who overstepped the mark. The most notorious of these, on Clink Street, was known simply as the CLINK, and to be 'in the clink' became a general term meaning to be in gaol. The original Clink was burned down in the Gordon Riots in 1780, and a museum celebrating the history of prisons now occupies the site.

Southwark Cathedral

The Cathedral Church of St Saviour and St Mary Overie became SOUTHWARK CATHEDRAL in 1905. A nunnery was founded here in the 7th century, on the site of a Roman villa, by a ferryman made wealthy during the years when there was no bridge. He named it in honour of his daughter Mary, hence 'Mary of the ferry', or possibly 'Mary over the water'. Parts of the pavement from the Roman villa can be seen inside the church.

Being close to the theatres of Bankside, including the Rose and the Globe, St Mary Overie established a lot of theatrical connections, and many of the actors who appear on the front of Shakespeare's First Folio also appear on the church register. William Shakespeare's younger brother EDMUND SHAKESPEARE (1580–1607), who followed William to London and became an actor at the Globe, is buried in the cathedral in an unmarked grave. There is also a memorial to William Shakespeare himself, and a service is held in the cathedral every year to mark the Bard's birthday.

Off the North Transept is the HARVARD MEMORIAL CHAPEL named in memory of Southwark's most celebrated emigrant JOHN HARVARD, founder of America's Harvard University. Harvard was born in Southwark in 1607 and baptised in the cathedral. When he was 28 he inherited from his parents the Queen's Head, one of Southwark's many coaching inns, along with the extensive family library. With his parents and all his brothers and sisters gone, John decided to emigrate with his wife to Boston in America. He died of consumption the following year, aged just 30, leaving half his estate and his library to the new college he was helping to establish in Boston, which was subsequently named Harvard after its main benefactor.

Well, I never knew this
about
THE RIVER THAMES

OLD LONDON BRIDGE grew so narrow and congested that it became necessary to create some rules to keep the traffic flowing smoothly. In 1722 the Lord Mayor ordered that bridge traffic should keep to the left, THE FIRST TIME THAT DRIVING ON THE LEFT WAS MADE COMPULSORY IN BRITAIN.

When ADELAIDE HOUSE was built at the north end of London Bridge in 1925 it was, at 148 ft (45 m) high, THE TALLEST OFFICE BLOCK IN LONDON. Named in honour of William IV's wife, who opened Rennie's London Bridge in 1831, Adelaide House was THE FIRST BUILDING IN THE CITY TO EMPLOY THE STEEL FRAME TECHNIQUE, later widely used for the skyscrapers of New York and Chicago. The discreet art deco design of Adelaide House includes Egyptian influences, popular at the time after the recent discovery of Tutankhamen's tomb. Adelaide House was also THE FIRST OFFICE BLOCK IN BRITAIN TO HAVE CENTRAL VENTILATION and TELEPHONE AND ELECTRIC CONNECTIONS ON EVERY FLOOR. There was once a golf course on the flat roof.

THE MONUMENT is THE TALLEST ISOLATED STONE COLUMN IN THE WORLD, 202 ft (61.5 m) high and standing 202 ft away from where the Great

Fire of London started, in a baker's shop in Pudding Lane, on 2 September 1666. The fire raged for five days and destroyed four-fifths of the City, including St Paul's Cathedral and 87 churches.

Hard by Tower Pier there is a small round brick building that marks the entrance to THE WORLD'S FIRST UNDERGROUND TUBE RAILWAY, the TOWER SUBWAY. It was built in 1869, using the new tunnelling shield designed by James Henry Greathead, and was THE FIRST TUNNEL EVER TO BE LINED WITH CAST-IRON, NOT BRICK. At first, cable-hauled trams carried 12 passengers at a time through the tunnel, but this proved financially unviable, and it was converted into a foot tunnel with steam lifts at either end. This closed in 1896 after Tower Bridge opened and people could cross the river for free.

The first SOUTHWARK BRIDGE was built from cast iron by John Rennie in 1817–19. With a central span of 240 ft (73 m), it was THE LARGEST CAST-IRON BRIDGE EVER MADE. The present bridge opened in 1921.

THE ANCHOR INN is an 18th-century pub built on the site of an earlier tavern that was patronised by Shakespeare when he was performing at the nearby Globe. A bar in the present building is dedicated to DR JOHNSON, who used to drink here when the landlord was his friend Henry Thrale, owner of the nearby ANCHOR BREWERY, at that time THE LARGEST BREWERY IN THE WORLD.

BOROUGH MARKET is LONDON'S OLDEST FRUIT AND VEGETABLE MARKET and has been trading on and around Borough High Street for over 1,000 years. At one time it even spread on to London Bridge, but in the 18th century it was finally confined within the boundaries it now occupies. Today, particularly at the weekend, Borough is the chosen market of 'foodies' and TV chefs, providing

just about any kind of speciality produce from anywhere in the world.

HMS *BELFAST*, moored above Tower Bridge as a museum of naval warfare, is THE LARGEST CRUISER EVER BUILT FOR THE ROYAL NAVY. She was launched in Belfast in 1938, spent much of the Second World War protecting the Atlantic convoys, took part in the sinking of the *Scharnhorst* in 1943 and was the first Allied ship to open fire on the German positions during the Normandy landings on 'Gold' and 'Juno' beaches in 1945.

Beside Tower Bridge is CITY HALL, designed by Norman Foster and opened in 2002 as the new home for the Mayor of London and the London Assembly.

TOWER BRIDGE TO GREENWICH

Tower Bridge – last of the Victorian Bridges across the Thames in London

Tower Bridge

TOWER BRIDGE, as the most recognisable of all London's bridges, is often mistaken for London Bridge. Opened in 1894, it was the last of the Victorian bridges across the Thames and is THE ONLY ONE THAT OPENS. It was designed by Horace Jones and built by SIR JOHN WOLFE BARRY, the son of Sir Charles Barry who built the Houses of Parliament. Its total length is 800 ft (244 m)

and it has a central span of 200 ft (61 m), with each of the lifting bascules weighing 1,000 tons. In 1952 a crowded double-decker bus was caught on the bridge as it started to open and the driver had no choice but to accelerate and jump the gap.

The towers are 213 ft (65 m) high and are linked by twin walkways 142 ft (43 m) above the water. These were closed in 1910, having become a haunt for prostitutes and pickpockets, but have recently reopened.

Wapping

WAPPING HIGH STREET now runs along the north bank for a couple of miles.

Close by WAPPING OLD STAIRS is the TOWN OF RAMSGATE pub, where CAPTAIN BLIGH and FLETCHER CHRISTIAN met for a drink in 1787 before setting off for the Pacific – and the mutiny on the Bounty. JUDGE JEFFREYS was caught here in 1688 while trying to flee from retribution for sentencing over 300 men to death after the Monmouth Rebellion.

Further on, and conspicuous in white amongst the grey warehouses, is the striking modern headquarters of the THAMES RIVER POLICE, THE OLDEST ORGANISED POLICE FORCE IN THE WORLD, founded as the Marine Police in 1798 to deal with thieving from ships moored in the river.

Wapping underground station stands at the western end of THE VERY FIRST UNDERWATER THOROUGHFARE IN THE WORLD, the most significant tunnel ever built, the THAMES TUNNEL. Constructed over 18 years by MARC BRUNEL, using a specially designed tunnelling shield, this remarkable engineering feat was opened in 1843 and taught the world how to tunnel underwater. The Thames Tunnel consists of two identical shafts, 1,200 ft (366 m) long and lined with brick. It was intended for vehicular traffic, but funds were not available for the carriageway entrances at either end and so it was used as a foot tunnel. For a while it was London's favourite day out, but eventually the tunnel became a magnet for thieves and prostitutes who would lurk in the arches, and it was sold to the East London Railway Company in 1865. Today London underground trains run through the tunnel between Wapping and Rotherhithe.

The PROSPECT OF WHITBY on Wapping Wall claims the title of London's oldest riverside pub – there has been a tavern here since at least as far back as 1520, so it is certainly a contender.

Bermondsey

The BERMONDSEY bank south of the Thames downstream from Tower Bridge is dominated by vast warehouses and wharves that are being rapidly regenerated into eye-wateringly expensive apartments, restaurants and shopping outlets. Nearest to the bridge is the old ANCHOR BREWHOUSE, rebuilt in the late 19th century as an attractive jumble of brick and white clapboard topped with a cupola and weather-vane.

Next door BUTLER'S WHARF, completed in 1873, was THE LARGEST WAREHOUSE COMPLEX ON THE THAMES. At the eastern end is Terence Conran's DESIGN MUSEUM, THE FIRST MUSEUM IN THE WORLD DEDICATED TO THE DESIGN OF EVERYDAY OBJECTS, housed in a converted 1950s warehouse. On the inland side of the warehouses is the iconic and much photographed SHAD THAMES, a narrow street criss-crossed with latticed iron walkways linking the two sides at first-floor level. It was here that John Cleese was hung out of a window by Kevin Kline in the comedy film *A Fish Called Wanda*.

CHERRY GARDEN PIER is where boats used to sound their horns if they wanted Tower Bridge to open, and is named after the pleasure gardens where Samuel Pepys would go to buy cherries for his wife. The gardens are long gone, but new cherry trees have recently been replanted in the area. It was from here, in 1838, that J.M.W. Turner painted the *FIGHTING TEMERAIRE* as it came up the Thames to the breaker's yard at Rotherhithe.

On the waterfront at Cherry Gardens, by the scant remains of a moated 14th-century manor-house belonging to Edward III, is the ANGEL, a delightful old pub built by the monks of Bermondsey Abbey. Part of the building rests on piles over the river and there are trapdoors in the floor, no doubt of interest to smugglers. There is also a shady balcony from where Judge Jeffreys would sit and watch the hangings at Execution Dock across the river. Samuel Pepys and Captain Cook drank here; and Turner and Whistler drew the Thames from here. Bermondsey now becomes . . .

Rotherhithe

ST MARY'S, ROTHERHITHE, dates from 1715, but there has been a church on the site since Saxon days. Buried here, in an unmarked grave, is CHRISTOPHER JONES, CAPTAIN OF THE *MAYFLOWER*, the ship that carried the Pilgrim Fathers across the Atlantic in 1620 to begin the New World.

Like its captain, the *Mayflower* finished its days in Rotherhithe, allowed to rot on the river beside the Shippe Tavern. The shippe was rebuilt, possibly using timbers from the *Mayflower*, and renamed the *Mayflower*, at a later date. It is THE ONLY PUB IN BRITAIN LICENSED TO SELL BRITISH (AND AMERICAN) POSTAGE STAMPS. The pub is quite small but has a wooden terrace on the river, from which there are fine views of the stretch of river from where the *Mayflower* set sail at the start of its momentous voyage.

The ROTHERHITHE TUNNEL, opened in 1904, runs under the Thames here at a depth of up to 75 ft (23 m). At the northern end of the Rotherhithe Tunnel is ...

Limehouse

LIMEHOUSE takes its name from the many lime kilns that were located here from the 14th century onwards, burning chalk brought up the river from Kent, and producing lime for London's building industry. It was the location of LONDON'S FIRST CHINATOWN, when Chinese sailors arriving on ships bringing tea from China settled in the area during the late 19th and early 20th centuries.

The spine of Limehouse is NARROW STREET, which runs for almost a mile along the waterfront. Off Narrow Street is LIMEHOUSE BASIN, created in the early 19th century as a dock where river boats could unload their cargo on to canal boats, for onward passage along the Regent's Canal and the national canal network. Limehouse Basin also lies at the southern end of LONDON'S OLDEST CANAL, the LIMEHOUSE CUT, begun in 1766. Originally linked directly to the Thames, the Cut provides a short cut from Limehouse Reach to the River Lea, avoiding the long haul round the Isle of Dogs and the tortuous Bow Creek.

Former Labour Foreign Secretary DR DAVID OWEN lives at No. 78 Narrow Street. On Sunday 25 January 1981, he and three other former Labour ministers, Shirley Williams, William Rodgers and Roy Jenkins, met here to issue the LIMEHOUSE DECLARATION which led to the formation of the short-lived Social Democratic Party or SDP.

No. 138 is DUNBAR WHARF, from where the first emigrants going of their own free will to Australia departed – convicts were boarded from Wapping Old Stairs.

No. 148 is LIMEKILN WHARF where a number of old warehouses, converted within but untouched on the outside, back on to and surround a muddy inlet – the atmosphere is redolent of how Limehouse must have been. One of these warehouses was the home of

LIMEHOUSE POTTERY, established in 1740 AS THE FIRST SOFT-PASTE PORCE-LAIN FACTORY IN ENGLAND.

DAVID LEAN, director of such films as *Lawrence of Arabia* and *The Bridge on the River Kwai*, lived at Sun Wharf on Narrow Street, Limehouse. Other showbusiness residents of Limehouse are actors SIR IAN MCKELLAN and STEVEN BERKOFF.

The Thames now makes a great loop around the . . .

Isle of Dogs

Originally known as Stepney Marshes, the peninsula known as the ISLE OF DOGS was where the Tudor monarchs of Greenwich Palace kept their hunting dogs. Once 800 acres (320 ha) of lush pastureland, the area became a real island in 1802 when cut off by the building of the WEST INDIA DOCKS, London's FIRST PURPOSE-BUILT CARGO DOCKS, and THE LARGEST STRUCTURE OF THEIR KIND IN THE WORLD. Heavy bombing during the Blitz and competition from the container docks at Tilbury brought about the closure of the docks in the 1980s.

Canary Wharf

CANARY WHARF, originally constructed in 1937 for handling cargoes of fruit from the Canary Islands, is now the most highly visible sign of the immense regeneration happening in London's docklands, which began in the mid 1980s and is still spreading eastwards, despite a few financial hiccups along the way. The original developers, the Canadian firm Olympia and York, went bankrupt during the recession of the early 1990s, and for many years the huge new office blocks remained half empty.

Canary Wharf appears in the *Guinness Book of Records* as THE LARGEST COMMERCIAL DEVELOPMENT IN THE WORLD and now features the three tallest buildings in Britain. ONE CANADA SQUARE, known as Canary Wharf, is 771 ft (235 m) high, and (as of 2010) THE TALLEST BUILDING IN BRITAIN.

Millwall

As you travel south from Canary Wharf the pace and calibre of the new developments begin to peter out. The offices and houses around Millwall Dock are laid out like a village, a pleasant relief from the Manhattan effect to the north. MILLWALL is named after a series of windmills that used to line the western embankment of the Isle of Dogs.

Tucked away beneath the river wall

are the remains of the massive timber slipway of JOHN SCOTT RUSSELL's shipyard, from where ISAMBARD KINGDOM BRUNEL's *Leviathan* was launched in 1858. Later renamed the *GREAT EASTERN*, this enormous ship was over 700 ft (213 m) long, with room for 4,000 passengers, and for the next 40 years remained THE BIGGEST SHIP IN THE WORLD. Because it was so large the ship could not be launched stern first in case the stern dug into the river bed, or the ship's momentum took it across the Thames and into the opposite bank. So Brunel built it to be launched sideways.

The famous picture of Isambard Kingdom Brunel in a tall hat, standing in front of some great iron chain links and smoking a cigar, was taken at John Scott Russell's yard, during construction of the *Great Eastern*.

Deptford

Across the river from Millwall is DEPTFORD, the 'deep ford' at the mouth of the Ravensbourne. The FIRST ROYAL DOCKYARD was established at Deptford

in 1513 for Henry VIII, and within 20 years it had become the most important dockyard in England. It is where the Trinity House lighthouse authority, founded by Henry VIII in 1514, had its first headquarters, and over the next 250 years many of the most famous voyages of discovery set sail from there.

In 1577 FRANCIS DRAKE departed from Deptford to become the FIRST ENGLISHMAN TO SAIL AROUND THE WORLD, and on his return he entertained Elizabeth I to dinner on board the *Golden Hind* at Deptford, after which he was knighted. Elizabeth ordered that the *Golden Hind* should be preserved for ever at Deptford, and for 100 years it was, but eventually the timbers rotted and the ship was broken up and made into furniture.

A few years later, in 1588, LORD HOWARD OF EFFINGHAM left from his home at Deptford Green to deal with the Spanish Armada.

In 1661 THE FIRST YACHT EVER TO BE BUILT IN BRITAIN was constructed in the yards at Deptford, for Charles II. It was launched in March and named 'Katherine' after the Queen. Later that year Charles raced *Katherine* against his brother James's yacht *Anne*, from Greenwich to Gravesend, in THE FIRST YACHT RACE THE WORLD HAD EVER WITNESSED.

In 1768 CAPTAIN COOK left from Deptford in the *Endeavour* to become THE FIRST EUROPEAN TO CHART AUSTRALIA. A few years later he said goodbye to England at Deptford once more, this time aboard the *Resolution*, never to return.

Well, I never knew this
about
THE RIVER THAMES

ST KATHARINES DOCKS, westernmost of London's wet docks, was opened in 1827 on the site of St Katharine's Hospital, ENGLAND'S OLDEST ROYAL CHARITY, founded by Empress Matilda in 1148. During the building of the dock, 11,000 people were forcibly removed from their homes, most without compensation, and the excavated soil was removed upriver and spread on to the marshes to provide level foundations for what became Pimlico. The dock was badly bombed during the Blitz and was the first of London's docks to undergo redevelopment.

ST ANNE'S CHURCH, at Limehouse, was built in the 1720s by Nicholas Hawksmoor. Its magnificent tower has been a prominent landmark for sailors on the river since it was raised, and boasts

THE HIGHEST CHURCH CLOCK IN LONDON – actually the second highest on any London building after Big Ben.

An intriguing structure nestling amongst the paper shops and council terraces on the east side of Westferry Road is ST PAUL'S PRESBYTERIAN CHURCH, built in 1859 in the style of a small-scale Pisa Cathedral. It is now a performing arts centre known as THE SPACE. The foundation stone was laid by JOHN SCOTT RUSSELL, whose shipyard just down the road built Isambard Kingdom Brunel's mighty *Leviathan*.

The band DIRE STRAITS were formed in DEPTFORD in 1977.

DEPTFORD has LONDON'S LARGEST BUDDHIST COMMUNITY.

In 1836 LONDON'S FIRST RAILWAY, the LONDON TO GREENWICH RAILWAY, was built through DEPTFORD on a viaduct of 878 arches, 3 miles (4.8 km) long, that was one of the wonders of the world at the time. The London to Greenwich Railway was THE FIRST RAILWAY COMPANY TO ISSUE SEASON TICKETS, in 1843.

In 1843 THE WORLD'S FIRST ARTIFICIAL FERTILISER was manufactured at DEPTFORD CREEK by JOHN BENNET LAWES, who would go on to pioneer chemical farming at his Rothamsted estate in Hertfordshire.

In 1889 the electrical engineer SEBAST-IAN DE FERRANTI (1864–1930) designed and built what was then THE WORLD'S LARGEST POWER STATION and THE FIRST TO GENERATE ELECTRICITY AT HIGH TENSION, at DEPTFORD.

GREENWICH
TO DARTFORD

Greenwich – Sir Christopher Wren's favourite view

Greenwich

GREENWICH, seen from across the River Thames, was said to be Sir Christopher Wren's favourite view. According to the widely travelled Daniel Defoe, Greenwich in 1720 possessed 'fine buildings . . . the most beautiful river in Europe, the best air, best prospect and the best conversation in Europe'. Today it is a worthy World Heritage Site.

The ROYAL NAVAL COLLEGE stands on the site of the medieval Palace of Placentia where HENRY VIII was born in 1491. In 1516 his first daughter Mary was born there, with Cardinal Wolsey as godfather. In 1533 Anne Boleyn gave birth to ELIZABETH I there, and the sickly young EDWARD VI died at Greenwich in 1553.

Elizabeth I made Greenwich her favoured summer residence, and it was there that SIR WALTER RALEIGH placed his cape over a puddle so that she wouldn't get her feet wet. And it was at Greenwich in 1587 that Elizabeth signed the death warrant of Mary Queen of Scots.

JAMES I gave Greenwich to his wife ANNE OF DENMARK and commissioned INIGO JONES to build a house for her at Greenwich. Jones came up with THE FIRST PALLADIAN BUILDING IN BRITAIN, the Queen's House, now incorporated into the NATIONAL MARITIME MUSEUM.

CHARLES II set about having the palace rebuilt but ran out of money with only one part completed. QUEEN MARY II then ordered that Greenwich should be completed as a seamen's hospital, the naval equivalent of the Royal Chelsea Hospital. Her one request was that the view of the Queen's House should not be obstructed, and so Christopher Wren and his assistant Nicholas Hawksmoor designed pairs of separate buildings with the Queen's House at the centre of the vista. The result is acknowledged as one of the great architectural panoramas of Britain.

THE PAINTED HALL has a marvellous roof painting by Sir James Thornhill which is THE LARGEST PAINTING IN BRITAIN. It took Thornhill 20 years to finish, which he finally did in 1727. LORD NELSON lay in state in the Painted Hall in 1805.

The Painted Hall is balanced across the courtyard by the ornate QUEEN'S CHAPEL, redesigned after a fire by James 'Athenian' Stuart. The chapel was used as the setting for one of the weddings in the film *Four Weddings and a Funeral*.

The Royal Naval Hospital at Greenwich closed in 1869, and in 1873 the Royal Naval College took over. Today the complex is part of the University of Greenwich.

Royal Observatory

Overlooking Greenwich from the summit of the park, with one of the great views of London, is the ROYAL OBSERVATORY, THE FIRST OBSERVATORY IN ENGLAND. It was designed by Christopher Wren and built in 1675.

In 1833 a time ball, THE FIRST VISUAL TIME SIGNAL IN THE WORLD, was placed on top of the observatory, and ever since that day the time ball has been raised at 12.55 and dropped precisely at 13.00, so that ships on the river can set their clocks accurately.

In 1884 a conference in Washington voted that Greenwich should be the location of the PRIME MERIDIAN, or 0 degrees longitude, for two reasons. First, the observatory's work had been instrumental in calculating new methods of navigation and time-keeping; and second, a large proportion of the world's shipping at that time passed through the Port of London. Hence EAST MEETS WEST AT GREENWICH and THE WORLD SET ITS CLOCKS BY GREENWICH MEAN TIME.

Running through the courtyard of the observatory is a line marking the Prime Meridian, and at night a laser light shines out from the observatory along the line of the Prime Meridian which crosses the river near Blackwall.

FLAMSTEED HOUSE, Sir Christopher Wren's original observatory building, which was named after John Flamsteed, the first Astronomer Royal, contains LONDON'S ONLY PUBLIC CAMERA OBSCURA.

Millennium Dome

THE MILLENNIUM DOME, built on the Prime Meridian to celebrate the new millennium, was completed just in time, in June 1999. It is THE LARGEST DOME IN THE WORLD and also THE LARGEST SINGLE-ROOFED STRUCTURE IN THE WORLD. The Dome featured in the pre-title sequence of the 1999 James Bond film *The World Is Not Enough*.

Blackwall

BLACKWALL, across the river from the Dome, is named after the river wall along the eastern side of the Isle of Dogs which was painted black.

The BLACKWALL TUNNEL, built by Sir Alexander Binnie, was THE LONGEST UNDERWATER TUNNEL IN THE WORLD when it opened in 1897. A second bore was opened in 1967.

The sinister-looking black glass cube at Blackwall is the new headquarters of REUTERS, THE WORLD'S LARGEST INTERNATIONAL NEWS AGENCY, which moved here from Fleet Street in 2005.

First Settlers' Monument

Standing on the waterfront above the tunnel, in front of a new apartment complex called Virginia Quay, is the FIRST SETTLERS' MONUMENT, commemorating the cold December day in 1606 when three ships sponsored by the Virginia Company, the *Susan Constant*, the *Godspeed* and the *Discovery*, slipped away from Blackwall Stairs taking 105 adventurers to start a new life and found a new world. They landed on Cape Henry, at the mouth of Chesapeake Bay, on 26 April 1607, and sailed on up the wide James River until, on 13 May 1607, they settled on a protected site at a bend in the river which they named JAMESTOWN after their King, James I of England. Here, under the strong leadership of CAPTAIN JOHN SMITH, they founded THE FIRST PERMANENT ENGLISH COLONY IN AMERICA. They were the forebears of the Founding Fathers of America, and it is largely thanks to them that English became the first language of America.

John Smith was captured by a tribe of local Indians after a skirmish but wrote that his life was saved by the intervention of the Indian chief's daughter,

POCAHONTAS. In 1614 she married the man who had created Virginia's first tobacco plantation, CAPTAIN JOHN ROLFE, and they returned to England with their son and settled in Blackwall, where Pocahontas unexpectedly bumped into John Smith, whom she had thought dead. Pocahontas herself died of an illness on a trip down the Thames and is buried in Gravesend.

Royal Docks

The ROYAL DOCKS are comprised of the ROYAL VICTORIA, the ROYAL ALBERT and the KING GEORGE V docks. They were closed in the early 1980s and are now experiencing the regeneration spreading eastwards from Canary Wharf. When the King George V dock was completed in 1921, the Royal Docks made up THE BIGGEST AREA OF ENCLOSED DOCKS IN THE WORLD.

The ROYAL VICTORIA DOCK, when it opened in 1855, was the most technologically advanced dock in the world, THE FIRST TO BE BUILT SPECIFICALLY FOR STEAMSHIPS, THE FIRST TO BE INTEGRATED DIRECTLY INTO THE RAILWAY SYSTEM and ONE OF THE FIRST TO MAKE USE OF THE NEW HYDRAULIC POWERED ENGINES to operate the gates and cranes.

Today, most of the North Quayside is taken up with LONDON'S LARGEST SINGLE-SITE EXHIBITION CENTRE, EXCEL, which opened in 2000. Looming massively over the fragile-looking modern glass apartments on the South Quayside is a derelict survivor from the 1930s, the huge, spooky, magnificent

MILLENNIUM MILL, patiently awaiting conversion into flats.

The ROYAL ALBERT DOCK opened in 1880. With a length of 1¾ miles (2.8 km) and covering 87 acres (35 ha), it was THE LARGEST PURPOSE-BUILT DOCK IN THE WORLD and also THE FIRST DOCK TO BE LIT BY ELECTRICITY.

Situated on the quay between the Royal Albert and King George V docks is the LONDON CITY AIRPORT, opened in 1987 and now handling some two million passengers a year. In 1995 the airport introduced THE FIRST TICKETLESS AIR TRAVEL IN THE UK.

The KING GEORGE V DOCK, which opened in 1921, was entered via a triple lock system, THE LARGEST IN LONDON, designed to allow access by ocean liners. The biggest ship to use the dock was the 35,000-ton *Mauretania* in 1939. The King George V Dock also possessed THE LARGEST DRY DOCK IN LONDON. One of the last ships to use it was HMS *Belfast*, now moored above Tower Bridge.

Thames Barrier

The THAMES BARRIER is 1,716 feet (523 m) across and is THE WORLD'S SECOND LARGEST MOVABLE FLOOD BARRIER. It became operational in 1982 and doommongers say it will be obsolete by 2030, when sea levels will have risen to such

an extent that it will no longer be possible to protect London. The barrier consists of ten separate movable gates positioned end-to-end across the river, two drop gates at either end and six central gates that pivot between concrete piers housing the operating equipment. The four largest central navigation channels are 200 ft (61 m) wide to allow access for large ships. The rising gates, when not in use, lie in curved recessed concrete sills in the river bed. The Thames Barrier is just the largest component in the Thames flood defences which include smaller barriers at several locations along the river, such as Barking Creek and Dartford.

Woolwich

WOOLWICH was second only to Deptford as a Royal Dockyard. Its first commission was for Henry VIII's flagship THE *GREAT HARRY*, which remained THE LARGEST SHIP EVER BUILT for more than 200 years. Woolwich's other claim to fame is as the home of WOOLWICH ARSENAL, established in 1695 as England's major weapons storehouse up until 1967, when the Royal Ordnance factory closed.

In 1886 workers at the arsenal formed a football team called Dial Square, which became the Woolwich Reds after they were gifted some red shirts, and then the Woolwich Arsenal. In 1913 the team relocated to North London as the ARSENAL Football Club.

The ROYAL ARTILLERY BAND, formed at the Woolwich barracks in 1762, is BRITAIN'S OLDEST ORCHESTRA.

The WOOLWICH FREE FERRY has been operating since 1889, although there has been some sort of ferry here since the 14th century. Today it provides a useful link between the North and South Circular roads.

Beckton

BECKTON was the site of THE WORLD'S BIGGEST GASWORKS, erected on flat marshy ground at the southern fringe of East Ham by the Gas, Light and Coke Company in 1870. Along with housing for its workers, the gasworks covered over 400 acres (162 ha) and the whole area was named after the Governor of the company, SAMUEL ADAM BECK. It was closed in 1969 when the discovery of natural gas in the North Sea made the production of artificial gas unprofitable. The only remains of it today are a couple of empty gas tanks, lost amongst the huge warehouses of the GALLIONS REACH RETAIL PARK, THE FIRST NEW, PURPOSE-BUILT RETAIL PARK TO BE BUILT WITHIN THE M25.

Before the area was cleaned up and rebuilt, the broken remains of the disused gasworks created a wonderfully apocalyptic landscape much sought after by film-makers. Scenes from the 1975 crime thriller *Brannigan*, starring

JOHN WAYNE, were filmed here. In 1981 James Bond, in the guise of ROGER MOORE, dropped a wheelchair-bound Ernst Stavro Blofeld down the old gasworks chimney, in the pre-title sequence of *For Your Eyes Only*. In 1987 Steven Spielberg turned Beckton into a Japanese detention centre in *Empire of the Sun*, while Stanley Kubrick created Vietnam here in *Full Metal Jacket*.

When the breeze is from the east it is just possible to get a whiff of Beckton's other superlative, the BECKTON SEWAGE WORKS, which lies just beyond the site of the old gasworks. Sewage from most of the London boroughs north of the river ends up here, pumped from the Abbey Mills pumping station along the Northern Outfall sewer as part of Sir Joseph Bazalgette's plans for cleaning up London. When the outfall first arrived in 1864, raw sewage was emptied straight into the Thames, a practice that continued until the *Princess Alice* disaster forced the water board to build a treatment works, which has since grown into THE BIGGEST SEWAGE TREATMENT WORKS IN EUROPE.

Princess Alice

On the evening of 3 September 1878, the paddle steamer SS PRINCESS ALICE, laden with passengers returning from a day trip to the Rosherville Pleasure Gardens at Gravesend, was approaching North Woolwich along Gallions Reach when it collided with a collier, the *Bywell Castle*. Over 700 people were pitched into the grimy water, of whom only 100 were rescued. The river was toxic with sewage just released from the recently opened Northern Outfall sewer, and many of the 600 or more who died were not drowned but poisoned by swallowing the contaminated water.

The disaster initiated several important safety regulations we now take for granted, including the rule that ships should always pass each other on the port side, already standard practice on the open sea but not on inland waterways; a limit to the number of passengers that could be carried; the compulsory provision of enough life-belts for everyone on board; and the installation of watertight bulkheads so that a ship would have a chance of staying afloat even if holed below the waterline. On shore, a treatment works was built to prevent raw sewage from being dumped into the river. The start of the gradual clean-up of the River Thames from one of the most polluted to one of the least polluted urban rivers in the world can be traced back to that awful September evening when the *Princess Alice* sank – with THE LARGEST LOSS OF LIFE EVER EXPERIENCED IN PEACETIME BRITAIN.

Barking Creek

A striking landmark across the mouth of the RIVER RODING at CREEKMOUTH is the 200 ft (61 m) high BARKING CREEK FLOOD BARRIER, with a huge gate held high above the water – ready, at the first signs of a high tide, to drop down and seal off the Roding estuary. It was completed in 1982 as part of the same flood prevention scheme that gave us the Thames Barrier. In the early 1800s the River Roding here was home TO THE LARGEST FISHING FLEET IN THE WORLD, taking advantage of the easy access to Billingsgate fish market up the river in London.

Thamesmead

The marshland on the south side of the river from Woolwich all the way round to Erith has been steadily transformed since the late 1960s into Thamesmead, the 'Town of the 21st Century'. Early development was concentrated on Thamesmead South and favoured grey concrete tower blocks, the perfect setting in 1971 for Stanley Kubrick's film *A Clockwork Orange*. Latterly the developers seem to have made more of an effort to create a nicer environment with red-brick terraces and town houses.

The controversial BELMARSH prison, home at one time or another to Great Train Robber RONNIE BIGGS, author JEFFREY ARCHER and politician JONATHAN AITKEN, looms over Thamesmead South West. Dubbed 'Britain's own Guantanamo Bay' by civil rights campaigners, this is where 21st-century terrorist suspects are held without trial.

Crossness

CROSSNESS PUMPING STATION was opened in 1865 as part of Sir Joseph Bazalgette's vast London sewerage system. The interior of the Beam Engine House, monumental in scale and Romanesque in style, is filled with spectacular Victorian ironwork and THE FOUR LARGEST SURVIVING ROTATING BEAM ENGINES IN THE WORLD. The pumping station was abandoned in 1953 but has been restored as a museum, with one of the beam engines brought back to working order and run on open days.

Next door is the modern metallic sludge incinerator which now takes care of the odorous business – hundreds of sprays positioned around the site are used to alleviate the reek on hot days.

Dagenham

Spreading itself along the Essex bank is the massive DAGENHAM FORD FACTORY, supported on 22,000 concrete piles driven into the marshy clay. It was opened in 1931 and was the only factory in the south of England to have its own blast furnace and electricity generating station. At its peak this was THE LARGEST CAR PLANT IN EUROPE, covering over 500 acres (202 ha) and producing 60,000 vehicles a year – in its 71-year production life it produced almost 11 million vehicles. Car production ended in 2002, but the factory now builds diesel engines for Ford. Dagenham-born singer SANDIE SHAW (b.1947), famous for performing in bare feet and THE FIRST UK ACT TO WIN THE EUROVISION SONG CONTEST (with 'Puppet on a String' in 1967), worked at the factory as a 17-year-old.

Rotating intermittently atop their tall shafts next to the factory are the wind turbines of DAGENHAM WIND FARM, THE FIRST WIND FARM IN LONDON, erected in 2004.

Behind the factory is the attractive little enclave of OLD DAGENHAM, which in the 1920s was still a small rural village. Today it is almost overwhelmed by the 27,000 homes of THE LARGEST COUNCIL ESTATE IN THE WORLD, THE BECONTREE ESTATE, begun in 1921 and spread over 4 square miles (1,036 ha), with a population of over 100,000.

Dagenham is the birthplace of two England football managers, SIR ALF RAMSEY (1920–99), whose England team won the World Cup in 1966, and TERRY VENABLES (b.1943), England manager from 1994 to 1996. Also born in Dagenham was comedian and film star DUDLEY MOORE (1935–2002).

Rainham

A row of factories conceals RAINHAM CREEK, where the RIVER INGREBOURNE enters the Thames. At the top of Rainham Creek, beyond the A13 and the high-speed rail link, is the old centre of Rainham, gathered around a lovely Norman church of 1178, complete with massive pillars and highly carved chancel arch. Nearby is perhaps the finest house on the Thames estuary, the handsome RAINHAM HALL, built in 1720 by John Harle, the owner of Rainham Wharf. The hall belongs to the National Trust and is awaiting restoration but can be visited on Saturday afternoons.

Back on the river, at the end of the row of factories, is the warehouse of TILDA RICE, THE COMPANY WHO INTRODUCED BASMATI RICE TO THE WESTERN WORLD in the 1970s. They moved here in the 1980s.

Rainham Marshes

Formerly the site of an army firing range, the 850 acres (344 ha) of Rainham's Thames-side marshland was acquired in 2000 by the Royal Society for the Protection of Birds (RSPB) and now makes up THE ONLY RSPB NATURE

The Diver

Standing in the mud just beyond the Tilda warehouse and beside a desolate collection of derelict, barnacle-encrusted Thames barges is THE DIVER, THE ONLY SCULPTURE LOCATED ACTUALLY IN THE THAMES and often completely submerged by the tide. Standing 15 ft (4.6 m) high and made out of galvanised steel, the Diver was erected in August 2000 by self-taught sculptor JOHN KAUFMAN (1941–2002) as a tribute to his grandfather, who worked as a diver in the London Docks.

RESERVE IN GREATER LONDON. The RSPB's futuristic visitor centre sits by the river at the eastern end of the marshes near Purfleet.

Erith

ERITH, on the Kentish side of the river, is announced by the huge silos of the former British Oil and Cake Mills, now owned by Pura Foods, manufacturers of edible oils and fats. Holding its own amongst the giant factories and terraced houses a little further on is St John the Baptist Church, with Saxon arches, Norman walls and a shapely spire, easily the oldest building in town. Erith was an important part of Henry VIII's royal dockyard and it was here that the world's biggest ship, the *Great Harry*, was kitted out to take Henry across the Channel to meet the King of France on the Field of the Cloth of Gold in 1520.

WILLIAM CORY PROMENADE on the waterfront recalls Cory Brothers coal merchants, who established Coryton oil refinery downstream and had a large coal depot here in Erith. In the 1880s, on the private roads of the Corys' property in Erith, EDWARD BUTLER tried out his BUTLER PETRO CYCLE, regarded as THE VERY FIRST BRITISH-BUILT CAR – he also ran alongside while his wife drove, making her THE VERY FIRST BRITISH LADY DRIVER.

In the first half of the 20th century Erith was the worldwide centre for high-quality cable production, and Erith-based Callendars Cables laid a pipeline across the English Channel through which fuel was supplied to the Allied armies on D-Day.

Erith still has THE LONGEST PIER ON THE THAMES IN LONDON, despite the fact that it is only half as long as when it opened in 1957. In 1999 the pier was restored for public use by Morrison's as part of a deal allowing them to build a supermarket on the site.

DENIS 'DEAR BILL' THATCHER was managing director of his grandfather's Atlas Preservative Company, based in Erith, and it was in Erith in 1950 that he met his future wife MARGARET, who was campaigning there.

Comedian LINDA SMITH (1958–2006) was born in Erith. She commented that while her home town wasn't twinned with anywhere, it did 'have a suicide pact with Dagenham'.

Just east of Erith a tall flood barrier, similar to that at Barking Creek, marks where the RIVER DARENT joins the Thames across 2 miles (3.2 km) of salt marshes from Dartford. The Darent also marks the point where the Thames leaves Greater London and enters Kent.

used to be stored in Purfleet in the 18th century, when the ROYAL GUNPOWDER MAGAZINES were transferred here from Woolwich Arsenal after an explosion in 1760. Most of the site is now housing, but Magazine Number 5 has been preserved and converted into a Heritage Museum.

In 1916 gunners guarding the magazines at Purfleet won a prize from the Lord Mayor of London for being THE FIRST TO SHOOT DOWN A ZEPPELIN.

Purfleet features in Bram Stoker's *Dracula* as the location of Carfax House, purchased by Count Dracula as a base for his blood-sucking activities: 'At Purfleet, on a byroad, I came across just such a place as seemed to be required.'

Purfleet

PURFLEET is on the north bank, where Greater London ends and Essex begins. From here it is factories pretty much all the way to Tilbury, and Purfleet can boast of THE BIGGEST MARGARINE FACTORY IN THE WORLD, owned by Unilever and producing such delights as Stork, Flora, Bertolli and 'I Can't Believe It's Not Butter!'

Margarine is far healthier than what

Littlebrook

The chimney of the LITTLEBROOK power station, just upstream of the Queen Elizabeth II Bridge in Kent (see p. 231), is 705 feet (215 m) high and is THE TALLEST CHIMNEY ON THE THAMES and THE THIRD TALLEST CHIMNEY IN ENGLAND. It was erected in 1981. The chimney of the Isle of Grain power station, just beyond the mouth of the Thames, is taller at 801 ft (244 m).

Well, I never knew this about
THE RIVER THAMES

GREENWICH PARK, laid out in 1433, is THE OLDEST PARK IN LONDON and is the starting point for the London Marathon.

In 1957 THE FIRST SON ET LUMIÈRE PERFORMANCE SEEN IN BRITAIN was held at the Royal Naval College, Greenwich.

TRINITY BUOY WHARF in Blackwall is the home of LONDON'S ONLY LIGHTHOUSE.

BOW CREEK at the mouth of the RIVER LEA was the site of the great Thames Ironworks where HMS *WARRIOR*, the WORLD'S FIRST IRON-HULLED, ARMOUR-PLATED FRIGATE, was launched in 1860 – then THE LONGEST AND LARGEST WARSHIP EVER BUILT.

The TATE & LYLE sugar refinery in SILVERTOWN is THE LARGEST SUGAR CANE REFINERY IN THE WORLD.

In 1975 the FIRST McDONALDS HAMBURGER RESTAURANT IN BRITAIN opened in WOOLWICH.

THE WOOLWICH, BRITAIN'S FIRST PERMANENT BUILDING SOCIETY, was formed in the upstairs room of a Woolwich pub around 1844, and first registered in 1847.

In the late 19th century the ROYAL HOTEL at PURFLEET was a favourite destination of the Prince of Wales (later Edward VII), who would travel here incognito to enjoy the whitebait suppers for which the hotel was renowned.

DARTFORD TO
THE CROW STONE

Queen Elizabeth II Bridge, linking Essex and Kent

Dartford Crossing

Traffic goes both under and over the river at the DARTFORD CROSSING, the last road crossing on the Thames. The first tunnel at Dartford, almost 1 mile (1.6 km) long, opened in 1963 and a second bore was completed in 1980. The slender and spectacular QUEEN ELIZABETH II BRIDGE, only THE SECOND BRIDGE EVER BUILT OVER THE THAMES DOWNSTREAM FROM LONDON BRIDGE, was opened in 1991 and carries M25 traffic southbound from Essex into Kent. THE LARGEST CABLE-SUPPORTED BRIDGE IN EUROPE WHEN IT WAS BUILT, the QE II Bridge has a total length of 9,423 feet (2,872 m) and a central span of 1,476 ft (450 m) with a clearance of 189 ft (57.6 m) and floats across the drab industrial landscape as a thing of beauty.

Stone

After passing under the QE II Bridge, the Thames runs by the forgotten 13th-century church of ST MARY AT STONE.

Set up on a chalk bluff, it was once known as the Lantern of Kent for the beacon that used to burn in its tower to guide sailors along the river – in the 19th century, when London was the biggest port in the world, over half of all the merchant ships in existence would at one time or another sail past this little church, at the point where the estuary becomes a river. The uninteresting exterior of the church conceals a rich and startling interior which was created by the same mason who built the Lady Chapel of Westminster Abbey and is almost comparable in beauty, particularly the chancel – the stonework is amongst the finest of any church in England. Surrounded by ugliness, this church is another of the Thames's hidden treasures.

Greenhithe

Overlooked by the old church at Stone, GREENHITHE maintains a pleasant 18th-century village centre with, to the east, a smart new housing development in grounds laid out by Capability Brown for the big house, INGRESS ABBEY. The original 14th-century Ingress Abbey was demolished in the 1830s and a new house built, using stone from the old London Bridge. This now forms the centrepiece of the estate and looks down a long avenue of trees to the river where HMS *Worcester* of the Thames Nautical Training College was moored until the 1970s. *Cutty Sark* was also moored here from 1938 until 1954 before moving to Greenwich.

Further Crossings

Just downstream from the QE II Bridge the high-speed Channel Tunnel rail link runs under the Thames, while above the river a power cable passes overhead supported by THE TWO TALLEST ELECTRICITY PYLONS IN BRITAIN, 623 feet (190 m) high. They were built in 1965 and are set 1,500 yards (1,372 m) apart, one on the West Thurrock marshes, on the north bank, and one on the Greenhithe marshes, on the south. The line sags in the middle to a minimum height above the water of 250 feet (76 m).

St Clement's

Just visible from the river, peeking through the industrial smoke of West Thurrock, is the nautical weathervane perched on top of the 15th-century tower of ancient ST CLEMENT'S. This bizarre occupies perhaps the most unlikely location of any church in Britain, completely enveloped in an apocalyptic landscape of steel cylinders and belching chimneys, its flint-banded tower hard up against the bright red factory wall of its saviour Proctor & Gamble, who restored the church in 1987 and made the churchyard into a nature reserve. St Clement's sits on the site of a Saxon church and its nave was once the chancel of a round Norman church – very rare. It is a surreal place and was chosen as a location for the funeral in the hugely successful 1994 film *Four Weddings and a Funeral*, with the QE II Bridge forming a memorable backdrop.

Swanscombe

The river now does a tight loop around the Swanscombe peninsula, where the skull of a palaeolithic woman, cunningly dubbed the Swanscombe Man, was uncovered in the 1930s, and then swoops down between Tilbury and Northfleet docks to Gravesend.

Tilbury Docks

Tilbury Docks opened in 1886. At first the location in the Essex marshes was too isolated, but as ships got bigger and the railway reached Tilbury, the new docks took over from those further upstream. Before the Second World War the combined docks along the Thames made London the biggest port in the world. In 1969 Europe's largest bulk grain terminal opened at Tilbury, and in 1970 a container service was established at Tilbury which developed into Britain's largest container port (now at Felixstowe). Since the 1930s and the building of

what is now the London Cruise Terminal, Tilbury has been London's main berth for ocean-going passenger vessels, and in 1948 the *Empire Windrush*, carrying the first 1,000 West Indian immigrant families, docked here.

Tilbury Docks now cover both sides of the river and Tilbury is Britain's main port for the import of paper and newsprint.

Tilbury Fort

Downstream from the docks is Tilbury Fort, one of the best surviving examples of this unusual type of star-shaped bastioned fort in Britain. It was built in the 1670s for Charles II on the site of an earlier fort as a defence against the Dutch, who had already caused mayhem in 1667 by sailing up the river and destroying part of the church at East Tilbury.

Local people remember sailing on the complex of moats that guard the fort – criss-crossed by a series of tantalising wooden drawbridges that illustrate the ingenuity of the defences – but, alas, the joyless Health and Safety commissars no longer trust us near water and so there is little point in visiting the fort today, and it remains bleak and wasted. Architectural connoisseurs may appreciate the splendid baroque gatehouse of 1682, and of interest to historians is a memorial plaque to those imprisoned here after being captured at the Battle of Culloden in 1746.

Henry VIII built the first fortification at Tilbury in 1539, and in 1588 his daughter Elizabeth I came here to deliver perhaps the most famous inspirational speech of any English monarch to her troops, who were encamped at West Tilbury on the hill above the fort, as they awaited the arrival of the Spanish Armada.

'I know I have the body of a weak and feeble woman, but I have the heart of a king, and a King of England, too, and think foul scorn that any Prince of Europe should dare to invade the borders of my realm.'

Gravesend

The North Downs come tumbling down to the river at GRAVESEND, the first accessible high ground from which

to observe ships sailing up the Thames. Windmill Hill behind the town has long been a popular viewing point, and in Victorian times there was a Camera Obscura at the top.

The Thames narrows at this point, and a foot ferry still operates between Gravesend and Tilbury, as it has for hundreds of years. Before the Dartford Crossing was built there was also a vehicle ferry here.

From the 14th century the bargemen of Gravesend had the exclusive right to ferry passengers the final 26 miles (42 km) up the Thames into London. When the steamers were introduced Gravesend became a day trip destination for Londoners, and a huge pleasure garden called ROSHERVILLE was opened next door in a disused chalk pit at Northfleet.

Seen from the river, Gravesend is a jumble of Georgian and Victorian houses and shops, dominated by a tall Victorian clock tower designed to look like the clock tower at Westminster. The Georgian spire of ST GEORGE'S CHURCH indicates where the American Indian princess POCAHONTAS is buried – she died here of consumption in 1617 on the eve of sailing home to Virginia (see p. 223).

The timber-frame THREE DAWS pub on the waterfront at Gravesend dates from the 15th century and is said to be THE OLDEST PUB IN KENT.

The TOWN PIER at Gravesend was built in 1834 using THE FIRST KNOWN IRON CYLINDERS for its foundations and

is THE WORLD'S OLDEST SURVIVING
CAST-IRON PIER.

Cliffe Fort

CLIFFE FORT in Kent lies directly across
the river from its almost identical twin
on the Essex shore, Coalhouse Fort.
What Cliffe has that Coalhouse doesn't
is a BRENNAN TORPEDO STATION that
was added in 1890. LOUIS BRENNAN,
born in County Mayo in 1852, invented
THE WORLD'S FIRST GUIDED MISSILE
SYSTEM, consisting of a torpedo with
two propellers, each connected to a
separate reel of wire. The torpedo was
launched from a runway on land and
then steered via the wires by an engineer
on shore, who could follow the
torpedo's progress by watching a small
mast fixed to the weapon that
protruded from the water. The launch
rails at Cliffe can be seen at low tide.

Coalhouse Fort

Opposite Cliffe Fort, just where the river
turns north, there are the stark, rusting
remains of what is still marked on many
maps as a water tower, but was in fact a
secret early radar tower operated during
WWII from COALHOUSE FORT, which
squats low, massive and solid, a little
further on behind a crescent lake. Coalhouse is considered to be THE BEST
EXAMPLE OF AN ARMOURED CASEMENT
FORT LEFT IN BRITAIN and was one of a
series of forts built in the 1860s by
General Gordon of Khartoum as part
of the Coastal Defence network. Inde-

structable but decaying, Coalhouse is
being slowly restored by volunteers.

Watching over Coalhouse Fort from
on top of a nearby hill, where St Cedd
founded a minster in the 7th century, is a
little Norman church that lost its tower
to the Dutch in 1667.

Coryton

The river soon turns back east to sweep
past the nightmare landscape of pipes
and tanks and flaming chimneys that is
CORYTON, THE LAST OF THE THREE
MAJOR OIL REFINERIES ON THE THAMES
STILL OPERATING. The complex began
life in 1897 as an explosives factory,
which was taken over and renamed by
the Cory Brothers coal merchants (see
Erith, p. 228) in 1919 to be an oil storage
depot. Today the refinery is run by
PETROPLUS, EUROPE'S LARGEST INDE-
PENDENT OIL REFINER.

Standing on a hill behind the refinery
is the enchanting Saxon church at
CORRINGHAM with its sturdy Norman
tower that has gazed out across this
watery scenery to Kent for over a thousand years.

Hoo Peninsula

The Thames now snakes around the Hoo Peninsula, an area of marshland and chalk hills on the south bank in Kent that separates the Thames from the Medway. The atmospheric marshland features in Charles Dickens's *Great Expectations* and stood in for the paddy fields of Vietnam in Stanley Kubrick's 1987 film *Full Metal Jacket.*

A number of interesting villages stand back from the marshes on the hills beyond.

Cliffe

In the Middle Ages CLIFFE was a considerable port, as indicated by the size of the 13th-century church, one of the largest parish churches in Kent, and the only one dedicated to St Helen. There are some vivid wall paintings inside, depicting the martyrdom of St Edmund, as well as a Jacobean pulpit and some fine stone carvings.

Cooling

COOLING is a magical place, a tiny, isolated hamlet on a misty hilltop consisting of a castle, a church and a farm cottage or two. The castle was built in the 14th century to defend the port at Cliffe, and the two round bastions of the gatehouse are an impressive survival – most of the rest is in ruins, with a newer residence constructed inside. COOLING CASTLE, once the home of SIR JOHN OLDCASTLE, Lord Cobham,

on whom Shakespeare based his Falstaff, is today the home of musician Jools Holland.

The desolate churchyard contains a long row of unnamed children's graves which inspired Charles Dickens to set the beginning of *Great Expectations* here – the villainous Magwitch jumps out on Pip from 'among the graves by the side of the church porch'. The marshes and villages of Hoo are virtually unchanged since Dickens tramped the area in the 1860s.

Canvey Island

Back on the Essex side, the popular resort of CANVEY ISLAND is separated from the mainland by a series of creeks, and much of it was reclaimed from the Thames by Dutch engineers in the 17th century. Two tiny octagonal cottages remain from that time, and one of them, the 'DUTCH COTTAGE', houses the island's museum. Once the Dutch had left, the sea defences deteriorated and in 1953 the whole island was flooded with the loss of 58 lives. A new sea wall was constructed afterwards and strengthened in the 1980s.

On the extreme southwestern tip there is a delightful weather-boarded pub called the LOBSTER SMACK, which also dates from the 17th century and gets a mention in *Great Expectations*. The pub once enjoyed magnificent views of the Thames, but now the huge sea wall stands in the way – even so the sea breezes and atmosphere of this ancient place are magical.

Further east, standing on top of the sea wall is the modernist LABWORTH CAFÉ, built in 1933 by Ove Arup, the design engineer of the Sydney Opera House, to look like the bridge of the Queen Mary – it is THE ONLY BUILDING OVE ARUP EVER DESIGNED PURELY BY HIMSELF.

Hadleigh Castle

The dramatic ruins of HADLEIGH CASTLE, standing prominently on the brow of the high hill behind Canvey Island, create a noble backdrop. The view across the Thames estuary from the castle is one of England's most glorious spectacles and was supremely captured in oil by John Constable in 1829. The castle was begun in 1230 during the reign of Henry III, and the

towers still standing date from that of Edward III in the 14th century.

In 1890 WILLIAM BOOTH, founder of the Salvation Army, bought Hadleigh Farm and 800 acres (324 ha) of land around it to create a centre where poor men from London could be trained to become farmers. The farm is still owned by the Salvation Army today and helps adults with special needs to learn about agriculture and the countryside.

Leigh-on-Sea

The lovely old fishing village of LEIGH-ON-SEA, the prettiest village on the Thames east of London, is mentioned in the Domesday Book of 1086, and for 700 years after that it remained isolated on the edge of the Essex marshes. Then in the 18th century the Essex coast was suddenly discovered and was built over with villas and hotels stretching east all the way along the shoreline to Shoeburyness, some 7 miles (11 km) distant. While the newer resort of Leigh climbs the steep hill behind with red brick and bungalows, Old Leigh has somehow managed to keep its character of narrow cobbled streets, rows of timber buildings and old pubs, and fishing boats drawn up on the muddy beach. The village is noted for its shellfish and cockles, which are still delivered fresh every day to the local pubs.

Allhallows

Across the water is Allhallows-on-Sea, the northernmost village in Kent and the easternmost village on the Thames. It was once lined up to be the leading holiday resort in Europe, but the plans did not survive the Second World War, and now just rows of caravans, and a tiny Saxon church, gaze across the estuary towards the twinkling neon lights of Southend.

London Stone

One mile (1.6 km) east of Allhallows, at the mouth of the Yantlet Creek, which separates Hoo from the Isle of Grain, is the LONDON STONE, which marks, on the south bank, the end of the River Thames. Directly opposite on the north bank is the Crow Stone.

The Crow Stone

About a mile east of Leigh-on-Sea, our journey draws to a close, for here, standing on a platform that juts out into the water, is the CROW STONE, marking the end, on the north bank, of the River Thames. We have reached the sea.

Well, I never knew this about
THE RIVER THAMES

GREENHITHE was the last place explorer SIR JOHN FRANKLIN set foot in England. On the morning of 19 May 1845, he set sail from Greenhithe at the start of his last fateful expedition to seek out the North West Passage, from which he never returned.

The boat chase scene from *Indiana Jones and the Last Crusade* was filmed at TILBURY DOCKS, as were several scenes from *Batman Begins*.

RADIO CAROLINE occasionally broadcasts from the ship *ROSS REVENGE*, which has been moored by the London Cruise Terminal at TILBURY DOCKS since 2005.

Three miles (4.8 km) on from Gravesend, derelict and isolated on the edge of the marshes, is the stark ruin of SHORNMEAD FORT, constructed by General Gordon in the 1850s to stop any ship that managed to evade the crossfire of the Coalhouse and Cliffe forts downstream. Gordon built Shornmead so well that it has defied all attempts to demolish it.

Seen across the fields from COALHOUSE FORT is the slightly more modern community of 'BATA-VILLE', built for the workers of the big shoe factory established here in the 1930s by the Czech Bata shoe company. The factory closed in the 1980s, and the scruffy, half-empty building stares out across the windswept landscape from rows of sightless windows, creating a rather desolate and sinister atmosphere.

In 1959 CANVEY ISLAND received THE WORLD'S FIRST DELIVERY BY CONTAINER SHIP OF LIQUEFIED NATURAL GAS.

The pub rock band DR FEELGOOD were formed on CANVEY ISLAND in 1971.

HADLEIGH FARM by Hadleigh Castle was selected as the site of the mountain biking competition in the 2012 Olympic Games.

The tennis-playing LLOYD BROTHERS, DAVID (b.1948) and JOHN (b.1954), were born in LEIGH-ON-SEA, as was John FOWLES (1926–2005), author of *The French Lieutenant's Woman*.

One mile (1.6 km) beyond the Crow Stone, reaching out from the Essex shore as if to stop the Thames leaving, is SOUTHEND PIER, at 1.3 miles (2.1 km) in length THE LONGEST PLEASURE PIER IN THE WORLD.

Gazetteer

Interesting places and locations that can be accessed by the public.

NT = National Trust (www.nationaltrust.org.uk)
EH = English Heritage (www.english-heritage.org.uk)
Map grid references are from Ordnance Survey Landranger Series.

CRICKLADE TO LECHLADE

St John the Baptist, Inglesham, Wilts
  Map 163 ref SU 204984

LECHLADE TO RADCOT

Buscot Park NT
  Faringdon, Oxon SN7 8BU
  Tel: 01367 240932 or 01367 240786
  www.buscot-park.com

Kelmscott Manor
  Kelmscott, Lechlade
  Glos GL7 3HJ
  Tel: 01367 252486
  www.kelmscottmanor.org.uk

RADCOT TO OXFORD

Shifford Chapel
  Shifford, Oxon
  Map 164 ref SP 373019

OXFORD

Christ Church Cathedral
  Opening Times: Mon to Sat: 9am –
  5pm,
  and Sun: 2pm – 5pm
  www.chch.ox.ac.uk
  Tel: 01865 276492

The University of Oxford Botanic
Garden
  Rose Lane, Oxford OX1 4AZ
  Tel: 01865 286690
  www.botanic-garden.ox.ac.uk

IFFLEY TO CLIFTON HAMPDEN

St Mary the Virgin, Iffley
  Map 164 ref SP 526034

CLIFTON HAMPDEN TO WALLINGFORD

Dorchester Abbey
  Open 8am – 6pm every day
  www.dorchester-abbey.org.uk

GORING TO WHITCHURCH

Basildon Park NT
  Lower Basildon, Reading,
  Berkshire RG8 9NR
  Tel: 01189 843040
  www.nationaltrust.org.uk

Childe Beale Wildlife Park
  Lower Basildon, Reading,
  Berkshire RG8 9NH
  Tel: 08448 261761
  www.bealepark.co.uk

WHITCHURCH TO SONNING

Mapledurham House and Mill
    Reading RG4 7TR
    Tel: 01189 723350
    www.mapledurham.co.uk

MARLOW TO MAIDENHEAD

Stanley Spencer Gallery
    High Street, Cookham
    SL6 9SJ
    Tel: 01628 471885
    www.kwantes.com

Cliveden NT
    Taplow, Maidenhead,
    Buckinghamshire SL6 0JA
    Tel: 01494 755562
    www.nationaltrust.org.uk

MAIDENHEAD TO WINDSOR

St Mary's Church
    Boveney, near Windsor
    Map 175 ref SU 940766

WINDSOR TO STAINES

Windsor Castle
    Information Office Tel: 02077
    667304
    www.royalcollection.org.uk

Runnymede NT
    Runnymede Estate Office, North
    Lodge,
    Windsor Road, Old Windsor,
    Berkshire SL4 2JL
    Tel: 01784 432891

STAINES TO HAMPTON COURT

Garrick's Temple
    Enquiries to The Curator,
    Orleans House Gallery, Riverside,
    Twickenham TW1 3DJ

Tel: 02088 316000
www.garrickstemple.org.uk

HAMPTON COURT TO TEDDINGTON

Hampton Court Palace
    Surrey KT8 9AU
    Tel: 08444 827777
    www.hrp.org.uk/hamptoncourt-
    palace

TEDDINGTON TO RICHMOND

Strawberry Hill House,
    Twickenham TW1 4SX
    Tel: 02087 443124
    www.friendsofstrawberryhill.org

Orleans House Gallery
    Riverside, Twickenham
    TW1 3DJ
    Tel: 02088 316000
    www.richmond.gov.uk/orleans_hou
    se_gallery

Marble Hill House EH
    Richmond, Surrey TW1 2NL
    Tel: 02088 925115
    www.english-heritage.org.uk

Ham House NT
    Ham Street, Ham,
    Richmond-upon-Thames,
    Surrey TW10 7RS
    Tel: 02089 401950
    www.nationaltrust.org.uk

RICHMOND TO HAMMERSMITH

Syon Park
    Brentford, Middlesex
    TW8 8JF
    Tel: 02085 600882
    www.syonpark.co.uk

Kew Gardens
  Kew, Richmond,
  Surrey TW9 3AB
  Tel: 02083 325655
  www.kew.org

Kew Palace and the Royal Botanic
Gardens
  Kew, Richmond,
  Surrey TW9 3AB
  Tel: 08444 827777
  www.hrp.org.uk/kewpalace

National Archives
  Kew, Richmond,
  Surrey TW9 4DU
  Tel: 02088 763444
  www.nationalarchives.gov.uk

Chiswick House EH
  Chiswick W4 2RP
  Tel: 02089 950508
  www.chgt.org.uk

Musical Museum
  399 High Street, Brentford
  Middlesex TW8 0DU
  Tel: 02085 608108
  ww.musicalmuseum.co.uk

Kew Bridge Steam Museum
  Green Dragon Lane, Brentford
  Middlesex TW8 0EN
  Tel: 02085 684757
  www.kbsm.org

Kelmscott House Museum
  26 Upper Mall, Hammersmith
  London W6 9TA
  Tel: 02087 423735
  www.morrissociety.org

HAMMERSMITH BRIDGE TO PIMLICO

London Wetland Centre
  Queen Elizabeth's Walk,
  Barnes, London SW13 9WT
  Tel: 02084 094400
  ww.wwt.org.uk

Fulham Palace
  Bishops Park, London
  SW6 6EA
  Tel: 020 7736 8140
  www.fulhampalace.org

Chelsea Physic Garden
  66 Royal Hospital Road,
  Chelsea, London
  SW3 4HS
  Tel: 02073 525646
  www.chelseaphysicgarden.co.uk

Royal Hospital
  Royal Hospital Road
  Chelsea, London
  SW3 4SR
  Tel: 02078 815200
  www.chelsea-pensioners.co.uk

PIMLICO TO WESTMINSTER

Tate Britain
  Millbank, London
  SW1P 4RG
  Tel: 02078 878888
  www.tate.org.uk

Museum of Garden History
  St Mary-at-Lambeth
  Lambeth Palace Road,
  London SE1 7JU
  Tel: 02074 018865
  www.museumgardenhistory.org

Lambeth Palace Library
  London SE1 7JU
  Tel: 02078 981263
  www.lambethpalacelibrary.org

WESTMINSTER TO LONDON BRIDGE

London Eye
  County Hall, Westminster Bridge
  Road
  London SE1 7PB
  Tel: 08717 813000
  www.londoneye.com

St Paul's Cathedral
  St Paul's Church Yard
  London EC4M 8AD
  Tel: 02072 364128
  www.stpauls.co.uk

LONDON BRIDGE
TO TOWER BRIDGE

Tower of London
  London EC3N 4AB
  Tel: 08444 827777
  www.hrp.org.uk/TowerOfLondon

Tate Modern
  Bankside, London
  SE1 9TG
  Tel: 02078 878888
  www.tate.org.uk/modern

Globe Theatre
  21 New Globe Walk, Bankside,
  London SE1 9DT
  Tel: 02079 021400
  www.shakespeares-globe.org

The Clink Prison Museum
  1 Clink Street, London
  SE1 9DG
  Tel: 02074 030900
  www.clink.co.uk

Southwark Cathedral
  London Bridge, London
  SE1 9DA
  Tel: 02073 676700
  www.cathedral.southwark.anglican.org

The Monument,
  Monument St and Fish Street Hill,
  London, EC3
  Tel: 02076 262717
  www.themonument.info

HMS Belfast
  Tooley St, London
  SE1 2JH
  Tel: 02074 036246
  www.hmsbelfast.iwm.org.uk

TOWER BRIDGE TO GREENWICH

Tower Bridge
  London SE14
  Tel: 02074 033761
  www.towerbridge.org.uk

Design Museum
  Shad Thames,
  London SE1 2YD
  Tel: 08709 099009
  www.designmuseum.org

GREENWICH TO DARTFORD

The Painted Hall
  Old Royal Naval College
  Park Row, Greenwich,
  London SE10 9NW
  Tel: 02082 694747
  www.oldroyalnavalcollege.org

National Maritime Museum
  Romney Road,
  Greenwich, London
  SE10 9NF
  Tel: 02083 126565
  www.nmm.ac.uk

Royal Observatory
  Blackheath Avenue,
  Greenwich, London
  SE10 8XJ
  Tel: 02083 126565
  www.nmm.ac.uk/places/royal-obser-
  vatory

The O2 (the Millenium Dome)
  Drawdock Road, London
  SE10 0BB
  Tel: 02084 632000
  www.theo2.co.uk
  wwp.millennium-dome.com

Thames Barrier Exhibition Centre
  Unity Way, Woolwich
  London SE18 5NJ
  Tel: 02083 054188
  www.environment-agency.gov.uk/
  homeandleisure/floods/38353.aspx

Crossness Pumping Station
  Belvedere Road,
  Abbey Wood,
  London SE2 9AQ
  Tel: 02083 113711
  www.crossness.org.uk

Rainham Hall NT
  The Broadway, Rainham,
  London RM13 9YN
  Tel: 02077 994552
  www.nationaltrust.org.uk

Royal Gunpowder Magazine.
  Purfleet
  Map 177 ref TQ 548 784

DARTFORD TO THE CROW STONE

St Clement's
  London Road, Grays
  RM20 4AR
  Tel: 01708 891007
  Map 177 ref TQ 593773

Tilbury Fort EH
  Thurrock RM18 7NR
  Tel: 01375 858489
  www.english-heritage.org.uk

Cliffe Fort
  Kent
  Map 178 Ref TQ 706766

Coalhouse Fort
  Princess Margaret Road,
  East Tilbury, Essex RM18 8PB
  Tel: 01375 844203
  coalhousefort-gallery.com

Hadleigh Castle
  Castle Lane,
  Essex SS7 2PP
  Tel: 01760 755161
  www.english-heritage.org.uk

Southend Pier
  Western Esplanade,
  Southend-on-Sea SS1 2EL
  www.southendpier.com

Index of People

Index of Places

Acknowledgements

My thanks to the home team at Ebury – Carey Smith, Imogen Fortes and Samantha Smith – for their patience, advice and inspiration, and to Steve Dobell for his sympathetic editing.

Thanks as always to Ros for her support and wisdom.

Mai and I would like to thank Caversham Boat Services for trusting us with the *Baron* and providing such a professional and friendly service. It was a magical two weeks.

And thank you to Mai. Your mastery of locks and knots and a life afloat is as astounding as your artwork is inspiring.